AF378349

Healing and Wholeness

Reflections on the Healing Ministry

ROBERT J. HILLMAN

with

Coral Chamberlain and Linda Harding

regnum

Copyright © 2002 The Bob Hillman Foundation and Coral Chamberlain

First published 2002 by
Regnum Books International
in association with Paternoster Press, PO Box 300, Carlisle, CA3 0QS, UK
and PO Box 1047, Waynesboro, GA 30830-2047, USA

Regnum Books International

PO Box 70, Oxford, OX2 6HB, UK

55 Fair Drive, Costa Mesa, CA 92626, USA

José Marmol 1734, 1602 Florida, Buenos Aires, Argentina

PO Box 76, Akropong-Akuapem, Ghana

Post Bag number 21, Vasant Kunj, New Delhi 110057, India

c/o Glad Sound SDN, BHD, PO Box 1019,
Jalan Semangat, 46970 Petaling Jaya, Malaysia

08 07 06 05 04 03 02   7 6 5 4 3 2 1

The right of Robert Hillman, Coral Chamberlain and Linda Harding to be identified as
the Authors of this Work has been asserted by them in accordance with the Copyright,
Designs and Patents Act 1988.

*All rights reserved. No part of this publication may be reproduced, stored in a retrieval system, or
transmitted in any form or by any means, electric, mechanical, photocopying, recording or otherwise, without the prior permission of the publisher or a licence permitting restricted copying. In
the UK such licences are issued by the Copyright Licensing Agency, 90 Tottenham Court Road,
London, W1P 9HE.*

British Library Cataloguing in Publication Data

A catalogue record for this book is available from the British Library.

ISBN 1-870345-35-5

Unless otherwise indicated, biblical quotations are taken from the *Holy Bible, New International Version*, Copyright © 1973, 1978, 1984 International Bible Society, used by permission of Zondervan Publishing Corp. All rights reserved. 'NIV' is a registered
trademark of the International Bible Society: UK trademark number 1448790.

Typeset by Reesprint,
Radley, Oxfordshire, OX14 3AJ, UK

Printed and bound in Great Britain by Bell & Bain Ltd, Glasgow

Dedication

To the glory of God and

for the healing of the Church

'Our postmodern world is hungry for teaching about spiritual healing, but Christians are often afraid to deal with this issue. This book will help answer their questions and overcome their reservations.'

Tony Campolo
Professor of Sociology, Eastern College, St Davids PA

'I wholeheartedly recommend this book to all who seek a deeper understanding of Christ's call to heal and how to hold that truth alongside the reality of our mortality. Dr Hillman's insights, gained while facing his own mortality, will be invaluable to all Christians alongside people who are desperately ill.'

Dr Gareth Tuckwell
Director for London, Anglia & SE England
Macmillan Cancer Relief

'Robert Hillman was a man of integrity and learning, blessed with a wonderful pastoral heart. This book on healing is timely: we've needed an exposition of this complex biblical idea free from what St Paul calls 'party spirit'. Every pastor/leader/elder in every church should read, study and discuss this excellent book.'

Rowland Croucher
Director, John Mark Ministries, Melbourne, Australia

'If there is one area of Christian ministry which requires wise pastoral judgement coupled with theological integrity, it is the place of healing in today's church. In this introductory overview, Robert Hillman makes a wise and compassionate contribution that will help churches of all shades make progress in their care for one another.'

Jonathan Lamb, Regional Secretary for Europe and the CIS
International Fellowship of Evangelical Students

'Balanced and thorough. Chamberlain and Harding have done us a great service in completing Robert Hillman's excellent book on healing. It could become a standard text on the subject.'

Michael Frost
Director, Centre for Evangelism and Global Mission
Morling College, Sydney, Australia

Contents

Appendices

List of Contributors

Robert J. Hillman, BA BD PhD was a minister of the Word in the Methodist and Uniting Churches of Australia for many years. A gifted teacher, he conducted conferences and seminars throughout Australia, presenting the essence of biblical teaching on healing and spiritual gifts in simple, down-to-earth terms. He completed his doctorate in Systematic Theology at Fuller Theological Seminary, California, USA, in 1978. The diagnosis of lymphoma four years later meant ongoing drastic medical treatment and eventually, in 1988, early retirement from parish ministry. He continued in pastoral ministry, mainly caring for people who were seriously ill, until shortly before he died in April 1992. He is the author of three other books, *The Church: Growing Up and Growing Out* (Sydney: Unichurch, 1981); *27 Spiritual Gifts* (Melbourne: JBCE, 1986) and *There is Hope: For Those Who are Ill and Those Who Care for Them* (Sydney: ANZEA, 1992).

Coral G. Chamberlain, MSc PhD is a senior academic involved in biomedical research. Since completing her doctorate in 1974, she has published many scientific papers and reviews in international journals. She met Robert Hillman shortly before he retired, when he took up a brief appointment at her church, and has worked with him on various writing projects, including the book *There is Hope*. Her link with co-writer Linda Harding was established through their mutual interest in music and youth ministry.

Linda A. Harding, BA Dip Ed is a writer, speaker and trainer for Youth for Christ Australia and also a singer–song writer. A former high school and college teacher with experience in special education, she has been involved full-time in youth ministry since 1981 with her husband Chris. She met Robert Hillman in 1988 when she was invited to sing at his church.

Peter A.R. Ralphs, BD MTh ThD Dip D&M, who contributed Appendix II, is a minister of the Word in the Uniting Church in Australia. He has served in several parishes in New South Wales and Victoria, including six years of team ministry with Robert Hillman, and as Lecturer in New Testament at Sydney Missionary and Bible College. He is currently Lecturer in New Testament and Theology at the Bible College of Queensland.

Preface

It is my conviction that a sound understanding of biblical teaching about healing is the only safe starting point for a ministry of healing. An inadequate understanding of such teaching seems to be the major factor limiting the effectiveness and widespread acceptance of the healing ministry today. In this book, drawing on many different sources, I seek to present a concise biblical theology of healing: a solid foundation on which a variety of ways of exercising a comprehensive, practical, God-glorifying healing ministry may be built. While a broad range of issues is covered, particular attention has been given to points at which weak theology may lead to undermining, misunderstanding or mistrust of the healing ministry.

I have been thrust into a special awareness of the healing ministry by my own struggle with serious illness for over twenty years. I write in the midst of struggle, as one who, having been cured of major illness on two previous occasions, does not know the outcome of this present illness – a cancer of the lymph glands. For many years God has called on me to minister in weakness, to be a 'wounded' healer. I do not offer false hope or simplistic solutions. I offer only the truth of God's Word, as I have come to understand it, and the testimony of his grace and healing in my own life and the lives of others.

The strategies for promoting health and healing I present are well tested. Through God's grace, they have, I believe, helped prolong my life far beyond medical expectation. Although 'terminally' ill, I have experienced a remarkable quality of life, which has allowed me to undertake the writing of this book. I am truly grateful to God for this.

As someone who has sought to centre his life, thinking and teaching on the biblical gospel of Jesus Christ over the past forty years, I have come to realise that healing means more than physical healing. It involves the whole person. It means integration that is wholeness realised in Christ. Naturally, I hope that this book will encourage those who are ill to seek all the physical healing God has for them from every legitimate source. But, more than this, I long for people to know the grace and peace of God, whether he chooses to heal them physically or not.

In my travels as a teacher and preacher and in my years of pastoring those who are ill, I have met many who have been hurt by well-intentioned but inappropriate healing ministries. When physical healing is overemphasised, continuing illness can easily seem like failure. I am deeply concerned that some healing ministries, because they lack an adequate theology, are inadvertently wounding churches as well as individuals. Indeed, it seems that unresolved issues arising out of the contemporary healing movement may be standing in the way of the unity and true renewal we should all be experiencing.

I want to affirm that the healing ministry is a valid expression of the Holy Spirit's work among us. I believe that every church should be offering ministry, in appropriate ways, to those who are ill. These ministries should be comprehensive, addressing the needs of the whole person and drawing on the vast array of healing resources God provides. Most importantly, while rejoicing with those who receive healing, they should be providing ongoing support for those who are not healed. We need to explore different ways of conducting our ministries of healing. We need to be open to new ideas, but we also need to test them against Scripture. In this book, I discuss the strengths and weaknesses of existing approaches and offer some alternatives.

I should make it clear, however, that this is not a 'how to conduct a healing ministry' manual. While I do offer some practical guidelines, I have tried to present issues in conceptual rather than prescriptive terms. My real hope is that each church, with God's help, will develop its own unique ministry – a ministry that, while remaining consistent with biblical teaching, is always open to the dynamic inspiration of the Spirit.

Although largely about theology, this book is not intended only for theologians. Topics are dealt with in a general way in the main text. More detailed notes are included at the end of each chapter for those who may wish to delve more deeply. I do not expect every reader to agree with everything I have written. For example, I write as one who believes that God on occasions does heal 'miraculously', knowing that this is not the view of all Christians. On the whole, however, my focus is more on the elements of our faith that unite us than the differences of opinion that divide us.

I have come to the conclusion that Christians are generally united in their longing to reach out in compassion to those who are ill. Sadly, however, they seem to have a great deal of difficulty reaching a consensus about how this should be done. In fact, strong reservations about existing approaches prevent many churches from offering a ministry of healing at all. I hope that this book, by presenting less radical options, will provide previously hesitant congregations and their leaders with a starting point and enable them to develop effective and appropriate healing ministries.

Whatever style of healing ministry we adopt, the gospel and the glory of God must be our priorities. This is the context in which the working of the Holy Spirit in healing and renewal must always be understood. In effective ministries, healing, gospel and Spirit will each receive their proper emphasis.

This book is addressed to all Christians – the Church universal, the whole body of Christ – regardless of denominational, doctrinal or theological preferences. While affirming all who honour Christ as Lord, I have tried to offer positive, biblical alternatives that bridge the gap between the extremes of theological opinion being expressed within the Christian community today. I believe that the latter positions are sometimes adopted by default because of the apparent lack of more suitable options. Perhaps among the teaching and comments gathered together in this book are some insights that may contribute to genuine reform of the Church, reform that is carried out in a spirit of unity.

Because of the unusual circumstances surrounding the writing of this book, I have needed, and have received, an extraordinary amount of assistance. Above all else, I want to testify to the providential grace of God: to express my deep-felt gratitude to the Father for his love, to his Son, who is the great Physician and our continuing healer, and to his Spirit for the way he has led and sustained me.

My wife, Jeanette, has walked with me through difficult times and expressed her love and loyalty in countless ways. I am especially grateful to her for her support throughout my years of illness: for being with me during the frequent visits to specialists and hospitals, for caring for me day after day in the home and during my studies overseas. Our three daughters, Roz, Jen and Chris, have also sustained me with their love and utmost support.

John Mallison, my weekly prayer partner and encourager for the past ten years, has also been a very significant person in my life and in the genesis of this book. I am deeply grateful to him for his friendship and his affirmation of my ministry and also to the members and supporters of The Bob Hillman Foundation, over which he presides. This Foundation sponsored and upheld me in my teaching ministry for many years and strongly encouraged me to write this book, which is based on material I developed during that time.

My special thanks go to my co-writers, Coral Chamberlain and Linda Harding. Their enthusiasm for this project and their commitment to it encouraged me to begin writing and have helped me to persevere. We seem to share a common vision. I have also been affirmed in this task by Peter Ralphs, my close friend and colleague, who has allowed me to include excellent material from his doctoral thesis in an appendix and elsewhere. In doing this he has not only enriched the book but also spared me considerable effort. I count it a great privilege to be associated with him in this project.

I gratefully acknowledge the contribution of members of the faculty of Fuller Theological College, Pasadena, California, who were my mentors during my four years of study there. Their input was crucial to my understanding of the comprehensive nature of God's healing.

I also value the prayerful, discerning support I have received from innumerable brothers and sisters in Christ over the years. Throughout my illness, I have been enabled to continue in ministry by the healing grace of Christ coming to me through the prayers of churches all over the world. In addition, the seminars and healing services that were part of my ministry brought me into contact with many people and gave me confirmation and guidance for the content of this book. In this respect, I am indebted to members of congregations in virtually every church I have visited.

My cancer specialist, a highly respected physician and a convinced Christian, is another who has played a key role in bringing this work to completion. Over the years he has always been available with the latest treatment and provided inestimable support and encouragement.

The views I present, formulated over a lifetime of study and reflection, have come from many different sources, far too many to mention individually even if I could recall them all. Where I have knowingly used the works of other authors I have given due acknowledgment, but my thinking has undoubtedly been influenced by many others. I sincerely thank all who have contributed to the development of the ideas and principles presented in this book.

Here and there, I express concerns about views presented by certain authors. They are not necessarily more deserving of such comment than others I could have cited. Nor should we assume that they still hold these views. Change is to be expected; authentic Christian living is dynamic. I have done my best to be objective and respectful in my discussions of differing viewpoints. If I have not always achieved this goal, I am sorry.

My fervent prayer is that this book will encourage and gently challenge individuals, congregations and the Church as a whole to review present attitudes and move closer to the ultimate goal of finding true wholeness and unity in the living Christ.

Robert J. Hillman

Robert Hillman suffered an overwhelming infection and died peacefully at 5 a.m. on 1 April 1992.

◆ ◆ ◆

Bob Hillman invited us to help him with the writing of this book at a very early stage of its development. He was seriously ill – terminally ill, according to his cancer specialist. Although to a certain extent writing was part of our everyday work, this was a new role for both of us and nothing in our backgrounds made us an obvious choice. We were simply there, and available, with hearts that shared Bob's hopes and longings for the Church and for this book.

For three years before he died, working in our spare time, we turned Bob's notes into drafts and sent them to him for assessment. His comments and suggestions, his gratitude and his enthusiasm were a continual source of encouragement to us. Bob became our dear friend and brother in Christ, a wise spiritual mentor and a fervent intercessor on our behalf. Our lives have been deeply touched by his ministry to us. We witnessed him, day by day, living the principles he teaches in this book.

When Bob died, it was left to us to finish this work. We had the assurance of knowing that he had given his approval to a complete outline and that we had his permission to do whatever was necessary to bring the book to publication without him. We had many pages of notes and a long list of relevant reference books. We also had the encouragement and the prayers of other Christians – Bob's family and friends, The Bob Hillman Foundation and its supporters, and our own churches, families and friends. In addition, we had a strong sense of calling to this task, as individuals and as part of a 'ministry team'. The team has included a group of people (listed below) who have assisted us by reading the manuscript during its preparation. This has been a reassuring hedge against our fallibility.

Gradually, over the years that have elapsed since Bob's death, this book has come together. It is as if he left a sketch of a stained-glass window and the pieces he had gathered towards its completion over his lifetime. Some were already perfectly shaped; these have been placed carefully in key positions. The rest we sorted and arranged around them, reshaping, polishing and supplementing as necessary, with frequent reference to the original design.

The task has taken much longer than we envisaged. Each of us has had to work around other major commitments and through personal difficulties that slowed us to snail's pace at times. Perhaps, in some ways, we too were being challenged to live what we were writing. Without a doubt the wise, biblical teaching we were receiving as we worked not only enriched us but also safeguarded us. We are very grateful to God for this.

With our friend's gentle voice sounding through the words before us, we wrote through tears at times. But we have been wonderfully sustained by God's grace and the prayers of his people. We have done our best to stay within agreed guidelines, while remaining open to the Spirit. We have also tried to maintain a style consistent with Bob's personality – affirming, gracious, non-polemical, respectful. Please forgive us if we have fallen short of these ideals at any point.

We have chosen to present this book as if completed in March 1992, the time of our last discussions with Bob, thus allowing him to tell his own story. Undoubtedly, in some respects, the Church has moved on since then. Bob's insights remain relevant, however, because they represent timeless biblical teaching and wisdom born of experience. Here and there we have added a reference to a book that has become available since 1992 or a more recent comment; to assist the reader; these asides are enclosed in square brackets. Any further 'updating' did not seem necessary or appropriate to us.

Despite the unusual circumstances of this book, our primary motivation for completing it has not been the need to fulfil a promise to a dying friend. In typically gracious fashion, in our last joint meeting with him, Bob released us from any sense of obligation to finish this work for his sake. It has truly been a labour of love, for the sake of the kingdom, and it has been a privilege to be involved.

There have been delightful opportunities to meet and exchange ideas with others who share Bob's vision for the Church. We want to express our deep gratitude to the Chairman of The Bob Hillman Foundation, Rev John Mallison, and other committee members. They consistently affirmed and encouraged us in our unusual and difficult role – even when it became clear that this project was going to take much longer than any of us had imagined.

Many others helped in various ways and we gratefully acknowledge their contributions and their support. The following assisted by reading drafts of the manuscript: Rev Dr Peter Ralphs and (in alphabetical order) Dr Robert Claxton, Deborah Coles, Bill Gilliver, Rev Colin Murdoch, Jill Robertson, Rev Brian Trowbridge, Andrew Wilson and Daniela Witschel. Their perceptive and informed comments were an invaluable guide to us. Alan McCartin typed early drafts, Bill Gilliver provided initial editorial advice, Anthea Cousins expertly edited the manuscript in its final stages, and Glenn Myers prepared the bibliography and index of authors.

We owe much to Jeremy Mudditt of Regnum Books International and our friend Andrew Wilson for taking care of the business of publication with skill, enthusiasm and grace, to David Bussau of Maranatha Trust for assisting and facilitating the publication process, and to Dr Robin Rees our typesetter.

From start to finish, the production of this book has been upheld by the prayers of many people that God will use it towards the healing of his Church and the enhancing of its witness to the world. That has been, and will continue to be, our heartfelt prayer as well.

Coral Chamberlain

Linda Harding

Chapter 1

Of Beginnings and Endings

In May 1989 my doctor made it clear that there was not much more that medical science could do for me. Barring a miracle of healing (a possibility I did not discount) my earthly life was drawing to an end. It was time to take stock: how could I best use whatever time was left? Prayerfully, I sought the advice of family and valued friends. The writing of this book, a project that had been at the back of my mind for a long time, emerged as a clear priority.

This book is born of my deep desire to see the Holy Spirit awaken the Church[1] to all the possibilities for healing that God provides and an even greater desire to see it experience a true spiritual revival that will make it a more effective witness to the world. For reasons that should become apparent, I believe there is a strong connection between the realisation of both these goals.

I can see now that, in many different ways, I have been gathering material for this book all my life. In this chapter, I describe some of the influences that have shaped my thinking and given me such a strong motivation for this task. These include my own experience of serious illness and many years of ministering[2] to those who are ill; the careful study of God's Word that has been a source of great joy and inspiration to me for virtually the whole of my life; and the many wonderful opportunities I have had to glean wisdom and insights from others.

MY OWN NEED FOR HEALING

I am not writing detached theology or mere theory. A major motivation for exploring healing has been my own urgent need for it over many years. In mid-1972, after a long period of undiagnosed ill-health, I underwent emergency surgery for the removal of a malignant tumour that had caused a blockage of my bowel. Peritonitis had set in and for some days my recovery was in doubt. Through God's grace and the prayers of the church I recovered.

About a year later I began experiencing severe back pain, the first indication of a chronic spinal problem that was to persist for several years. Soon afterwards, I went overseas to study for my PhD at Fuller Seminary in California. I did most of my work there either lying down or standing up, because I could sit for only a few minutes at a time. To function, even at this level, I needed to swim almost every day. Eventually I had major surgery, again with the strong prayer support of my church. The operation was a success, achieving about a ninety per cent cure.

After graduation I returned to Australia. Just four years later, in January 1982, I noticed a lump in the base of my neck. Extensive tests followed and I was shocked to discover that I had non-Hodgkin's lymphoma, a cancer of the lymph glands. It was already well advanced, classified as grade 3A on a scale that only went to four. A scan revealed dozens of malignant tumours, some as big as golf balls, scattered throughout my body. I was told that without radical chemotherapy I would probably die within twelve months, and even with treatment the prognosis was poor. That was ten years ago[3] – ten years in which I have been wonderfully sustained by God's grace as I have sought to open my life to all the healing he has for me from every authentic source.

I am deeply grateful to God for extending my life far beyond medical expectation. Furthermore, I have enjoyed a remarkable quality of life despite extensive chemotherapy, the continuing growth of the tumours and the spread of the cancer into my bone marrow and blood. Often I can still hike long distances and climb many flights of stairs without tiring.[3] The last ten years have been difficult, of course, but – within my physical limitations – they have also been very fulfilling. My ministry has gradually changed over this period. Intercessory prayer and writing now occupy a larger part of my time, but to a certain extent I am still able to be involved in the pastoral care of others with serious illness.

Learning to cope with life-threatening illness (and sharing with many others in similar situations) has been an invaluable preparation for the writing of this book.[4]

THE INSPIRATION OF GOD'S WORD

My journey of faith began with three threepenny Gospels given to me by a Sunday school teacher, who encouraged me to begin a lifelong habit of daily Bible reading. More than forty years later my lifestyle and my thinking are still being transformed by these same wonderful Scriptures – although no longer the threepenny versions! The living nature of the Word of God is an abiding source of wonder and joy to me, as is its revelation of God's grace epitomised in the gospel it proclaims.

Few people would choose to spend their twenty-first birthday on their own in a hotel room in a small country town. Perhaps fewer still would choose to curl up with a book on theology to celebrate but I quite happily did just that. I was working as a primary school teacher at the time and living at Mara in south western New South Wales. Theology was my passion and it still is: not speculative theology, but theology that centres on the gospel of the biblical, living Christ and relates to the issues people wrestle with in their own lives.

I left teaching to enter the ministry and completed a Bachelor of Arts degree at the University of Sydney, majoring in psychology. This specialised training was to prove invaluable in my subsequent exploration of healing, making me more aware of possible links between physical, emotional and spiritual wholeness.

Following that, while working towards my Bachelor of Divinity degree, I went into parish ministry with the Methodist Church (which later became part of the Uniting Church in Australia) and before long I began conducting teaching missions and seminars in various parishes throughout Australia. Although the theology I had been obliged to study during my training was rather liberal, my personal background and commitment had always been to evangelical theology.[5] When I felt the need for further mid-career study, it was therefore quite natural for me to select a well known Evangelical[5] college: Fuller Theological Seminary in Pasadena, California.

THE FULLER EXPERIENCE – A WATERSHED

In 1974, accompanied by my wife and our young family, I began a four year course at Fuller leading to a PhD in Systematic Theology. My delightful task was to produce a dissertation on the preaching of grace in Calvin and Wesley. This kept me contentedly immersed for some years in the study of two of the most significant periods of spiritual growth in the history of the Church. With its emphasis on the centrality of grace to the gospel and the importance of preaching, it was a topic close to my heart and pivotal to the development of the ideas presented in this book. It gave me the opportunity to study and live with two great historical movements of the Spirit that transformed the church by bringing renewal, revival and reform, and transformed many nations by bringing spiritual awakening.

The Faculty at Fuller had a profound influence on me. In my encounters with theological liberalism in the church in Australia I had always tried to be gracious, balanced and scholarly, but my response had been largely negative. My group of fellow Evangelicals seemed so outnumbered and disregarded that we became dispirited and defensive. Fuller was a breath of fresh air. There I found a strong commitment to biblical, evangelical faith and to academic excellence. I found great scholars with Evangelical convictions who, partly because they were not restricted by sectarian or denominational thinking, were making a positive contribution to the Church in America and in many other countries as well. I found a balanced emphasis on the gospel, Scripture, the Church, scholarly study, concern for social need, and deep spirituality. I accepted this gratefully as part of God's loving provision for me.

During my stay I came in contact with John Wimber, who later became widely known through his promotion of a particular style of healing ministry. Soon after my return to Australia, Wimber was invited to assist Peter Wagner in presenting a course at Fuller entitled *The Miraculous and Church Growth*. This course, which turned out to be highly controversial, led to an important debate on the whole subject of miraculous healing and the pastoral ministry.[6] I have followed this issue and its implications with great interest over the years (and often with great concern) and I will refer to these matters again in later chapters.

I came back to Australia inspired by the lives of great Christians of the past and the teaching of gifted present-day Christians. I was full of enthusiasm to explore new avenues for ministry. I began in my own parish and elsewhere, through teaching and writing, to share some of the insights I had gained during my visit to Fuller – especially my growing understanding of biblical teaching about spiritual gifts and their importance to the vitality and growth of individual churches.[7]

Following the diagnosis of lymphoma in 1982, I was released from parish ministry by the church so that I could give my whole attention to conducting teaching missions. Healing was a topic I was often asked to address.

THE ONGOING WORK OF THE HOLY SPIRIT

Quite early in my Christian life, as I began delving more deeply into theology and the Word, I became aware of the Holy Spirit as a personal indwelling presence and knew the importance of trying to live daily in his power. This was well before the emergence of a recognisable Charismatic movement.[5] I also had a great yearning to see a widespread Spirit-led awakening throughout my own nation. So for some forty years my prayers, ministry and study have centred on the fulfilment of this vision, a vision that has expanded in recent years to include all the nations of the world.

Some kind of spiritual awakening does seem to be happening in secular society at present, although not the kind I have been praying for. There is increasing interest in spirituality generally throughout the world – in the East and in the West. This seems to be a sign of our times. Regrettably, many of the ways in which the current interest in spirituality is being expressed are quite incompatible with Christian faith and indeed are used as substitutes for it.

There also seems to be a new movement towards spirituality in churches worldwide that goes far beyond the Pentecostal and Charismatic movements of this century, although these have no doubt been influential. For example, throughout Australia in churches that are neither Pentecostal nor Charismatic, I have found very little resistance to the suggestion that God may choose to heal miraculously. Most Christians seem to have a simple faith that God can do the impossible. As part of the present trend towards spirituality, we are perhaps more open to this possibility now than in previous generations.[8] What I earnestly desire, and want to encourage through this book, is a thoroughly biblical expression of spirituality and an openness to the Spirit that is biblically authentic.

I believe there is a longing in the hearts of Christians everywhere for faith to be revitalised, for their own and the Church's life and witness to be more authentic and effective. Some Christians place great emphasis on the healing ministry as a key component of the renewal of the Church. They regard miraculous healings and other 'signs and wonders' as expressions of the Holy Spirit at work among us in new ways. Others are wary. They have misgivings about this particular model for renewal, with its distinctive teaching and practices, which colour their attitude towards the healing ministry in general.

A recurring message of this book is that involvement in the healing ministry does not necessarily mean aligning yourself with a recognised healing movement and accepting all its teachings and practices. We need to acknowledge that the Holy Spirit has often been, and still is, at work within such movements, but we also need to acknowledge that he has been, and still is, at work outside them. Indeed, I will argue that there is every reason for all of us (Evangelical, Pentecostal, Charismatic or otherwise) to be open to a whole range of different ways of being involved in the healing ministry and of understanding and experiencing renewal. I will also argue that, if the Church is to experience any lasting Spirit-led renewal, its focus must be on the gospel and Christ himself – not on the healing ministry or associated 'signs and wonders'.

I long for the Spirit's power to come upon his Church, to sweep across traditional barriers like a mighty wave – cleansing, healing and reviving us. I fear, however, that such a wave might come to nothing if we are not careful. It could leave us behind in confusion because we lack a sound theology and a balanced understanding of the Holy Spirit and miraculous healing. Unfortunately, I have already seen many people who thought they were riding the crest of a wave dumped for this very reason. On the other hand, the awesome force of such a wave could be dissipated: it could run up against an unyielding breakwater of conservatism, leaving those who shelter behind it apparently safe yet spiritually impoverished.

THE CHURCH IN NEED OF HEALING

Within the Church, people's attitudes to the Holy Spirit and to the healing ministry are often closely linked. Those who do not believe that the Holy Spirit is active in the Church today are also likely to question the validity of the healing ministry. Thus, ironically, the ministry of healing can be divisive – especially when its major focus is miraculous healing.[6] I began discovering this as I travelled throughout Australia visiting congregations of various denominations. While I found many people who were open to the healing ministry – open to God's Spirit and to balanced scriptural teaching about miraculous healing – I also found others who were strongly opposed to it. Many of the latter group had been deeply hurt, or knew of someone who had been hurt, through previous experiences with the healing movement. I weep for people who have suffered in this way. Bad theology always comes home to roost somewhere. If we have an inadequate theology of healing and an inadequate understanding of God, sooner or later people will get hurt.

I am also deeply saddened when I find individuals and churches divided over the issue of spiritual gifts, particularly gifts of healing. It should not be. We can and must do better than this. We need to be alive to the gifts of the Spirit and dead to our propensity towards divisiveness and straying from biblical truth. A healing ministry and the gifts given by the Spirit should strengthen the Church, and they will do so if our theology and practice are firmly grounded in God's Word. There is a great need for the healing ministry to embody, both in theology and practice, the biblical truth that the Spirit who empowers is also the Spirit of unity.

It seems that the Church itself is in need of healing: healing of individuals and the institutions they comprise, and of relationships between individuals and institutions. Without this healing we have no hope of authentic witness to the world. When Christ prays for all believers, his prayer is that they will be one as he and the Father are one (Jn. 17:20–26). He says the love we show will prove we are his disciples and our unity will prove that he is indeed who he claimed to be. Our oneness is to be the sign of Christ's reality to those around us who are lost. Yet sometimes it seems that we are the ones who are lost. We are confused and divided on many issues and it is, ironically, in our attitudes to healing that our disordered state often manifests itself.

These attitudes seem to fall into one of several categories: unbounded enthusiasm, cautious acceptance, bewildered uncertainty or outright rejection. Because those who are for the healing ministry are so strongly opposed by those who are against it, our progress as a body is hindered. How I long to see the Spirit bring unity to the wonderfully diverse body of Christ over this issue. By unity I do not mean dreary uniformity or even theological conformity, but a collective willingness to recognise and accept with gratitude the healing God so graciously provides – miraculously and otherwise.

Thus there is a need for healing within the Church itself. And it is only as we receive healing that we will become more effective in ministering to those who are ill and in spreading God's message of ultimate healing to the world around us. This healing of the Church is the renewing work of the Spirit we should be seeking – renewal that goes far beyond 'signs and wonders'. These may be part of renewal, but they are not in themselves evidence that renewal (or revival) has come. We will consider these important issues in greater depth in the last chapter.

THE TRUTH ABOUT THE TRUTH

No one individual, denomination or doctrinal school has the whole truth. Our common humanness means that our ideas will always be imperfect and incomplete. While generalising has its limitations, we may say that Evangelicals correctly emphasise the crucial importance of Scripture as a source of revelation but are not always open enough to the ongoing work of the Spirit. Charismatics correctly emphasise the importance of being open to the Spirit but need to beware of relying more on personal revelation than scriptural truth and of neglecting reason in favour of emotion. Liberals, while correctly acknowledging the importance of reason, can easily fall into the error of trying to reduce God to fit within the boundaries of human understanding.[9]

I am certainly not suggesting that this book has somehow escaped the imperfection that is common to all human endeavour. But I do warmly invite Christians of all persuasions to read it with an open mind and objectively consider its claims in the light of the plain truths of Scripture.[10] It is as important now as in days gone by that . . .

> We limit not the truth of God
> to our poor reach of mind,
> by notions of our day and sect,
> crude, partial and confined . . .[11]

It is time for each of us to stop defending the sometimes theologically shaky walls we have built around ourselves and our own particular clique of like-minded Christians. When these are threatened our natural instinct is to cling to cherished beliefs or self-righteous attitudes about our grasp of the truth, but our growth and witness as a body depend upon our being willing to let such attitudes go. Perhaps if we can focus more on the unity of purpose in Christ that underlies our differences we will find it easier to listen to each other with respect. We *all* need to open our lives to the power of the Holy Spirit. We all need to search the Scriptures, share our insights and in humility learn from God and one another. Our unity, our corporate healing, our witness to the world of the gospel's transforming power hinge on this godly teachability. We must be willing to let the Spirit of the living Christ change us.

Notes

1. Here and elsewhere, 'Church' (capitalised) means the Church universal, the entire body of Christ, as distinct from an individual (local) church. I have adopted this convention to emphasise that I am writing for the encouragement of the Church as a whole, not for the promotion of any particular denominational or theological viewpoint.
2. Throughout this book I use the term 'minister' in a general sense. A Christian does not have to be ordained in order to minister to others or to be in ministry. Indeed, all Christians are called to ministry and should be encouraged to find their own unique role in the overall ministry of the church. Where I need specifically to indicate that a person is a member of the clergy, I use the term 'minister of the Word'.
3. This was the author's situation shortly before he died in April 1992.
4. Another book has grown out of these experiences; see Robert J. Hillman with Coral Chamberlain, *There is Hope: For Those Who are Ill and Those Who Care for Them* (Sydney: ANZEA, 1992). It is much simpler in scope and style and suitable for both Christian and non-Christian readers.
5. While allowing for personal inspiration, Evangelicals place a great deal of emphasis on the final authority of Scripture over all other forms of inspiration and are very reluctant to see this compromised, for example, by direct personal revelation taking precedence over careful exegesis of Scripture. Liberal theology has a different approach to the Bible, seeing it as containing generalised truth and useful analogy rather than specific truth inspired by God and accurate and true to this day. These general comments do not represent comprehensive definitions. Labels such as these applied to various groupings of people within the Church usually have many shades of meaning; see, for example, Rowland Croucher, *Recent Trends Among Evangelicals: Biblical Agendas, Justice and Spirituality* (Sydney: Albatross; Bromley: MARC Europe, 1986). Thus, if used unwisely, they can contribute to misunderstandings between one group or individual and another.

    I prefer to spell 'evangelical' without an initial capital when I am using it in a general sense to indicate all Christians who are seeking to centre their lives, thinking and teaching on the biblical gospel of Jesus Christ. I capitalise it only when referring to a specific theological tradition or wing of the Church. Similarly, I use the term 'charismatic' in a general sense to indicate all Christians who are open to the working of the Holy Spirit in their lives and to his gifts. They may or may not be members of 'Charismatic' churches or part of the 'Charismatic' movement.

6.   The faculty at Fuller documented its experience of this. See Lewis B. Smedes (Ed.), *Ministry and the Miraculous: A Case Study at Fuller Theological Seminary* (Pasadena: Fuller, 1987). Copies of this excellent book, which summarises the deliberations of the faculty on this issue, should be available from the Fuller Book Store, Fuller Theological Seminary, Pasadena, CA 91182, USA. I was privileged to be graduate assistant to Lewis Smedes, Professor of Ethics and Theology, during most of my stay at Fuller Seminary.

7.   See Robert J. Hillman, *The Church: Growing Up and Growing Out* (Sydney: Unichurch, 1981); *27 Spiritual Gifts* (Melbourne: JBCE, 1986).

8.   A new openness to the miraculous working of the Spirit is often linked with involvement in the Pentecostal or Charismatic movements, probably because they appear to provide a ready form of expression through their established practices; however, it is important for Christians of all denominations to acknowledge that such involvement is not mandatory and that the activity of the Spirit is not confined to these movements.

9.   Acknowledging the latter tendency, Francis Schaeffer writes: 'I would suggest that it is perfectly possible for a Christian to be so infiltrated by twentieth-century thinking, that he lives most of his life as though the supernatural were not there. Indeed, I would suggest that all of us do this to some extent. The supernatural does not touch the Christian only at the new birth and then at his death, or at the second coming of Christ, leaving the believer on his own in a naturalistic world during all the time in between . . . Being a biblical Christian means living in the supernatural now, not only theoretically but in practice. If a man . . . denies the existence of the supernatural portion of the world, we say he is an unbeliever. What shall we call ourselves when . . . we live as though the supernatural were not there? . . . It is Christianity that has become a dialectic, or simply a "good philosophy" '; from *True Spirituality* by Francis A. Schaeffer, p. 64; copyright © 1971 by Tyndale House Publishers, Inc., Wheaton, Illinois. Used by permission; all rights reserved.

10. See Appendix I.

11. From a hymn written by George Rawson (1807–1889); see *The Australian Hymn Book* (Sydney: Collins, 1977), p. 420.

Chapter 2

A Basic Theology of Healing

I firmly believe that the healing ministry must be built on the foundation of a strong and balanced biblical theology. Only then will it reach its full potential for healing without harming and become more widely accepted throughout the Church. In this chapter, I attempt to present the essence of biblical teaching on a range of issues that are particularly relevant to the healing ministry, although much of it also applies to ministry in general. Important topics raised briefly here will be dealt with in greater depth in later chapters.

I am aware that some Christians feel uneasy about the notion of balance in relation to the healing ministry. Those who regard miraculous healing as an important, ongoing manifestation of the Holy Spirit's activity may be concerned that I am suggesting we should have a limited expectation of what he may do. But that is not my intention. I am not promoting the kind of theology that perceives God as acting only in ways that the human mind can understand. Nor am I advocating a theology that regards the open expression of human emotion (or belief in the miraculous) as a sign of a deranged or feeble mind. Such theology is completely out of tune with the biblical emphasis on loving God with all one's heart, soul, mind and strength.

To be truly balanced in our theology and in our healing ministry we need to acknowledge human ability, yet humbly admit its limitations; to respect God's sovereignty, yet recognise human responsibility for taking action; to uphold the 'plain truths' of Scripture,[1] yet be open to the promptings of the Holy Spirit and to the various ways in which he manifests his power today. Only then will we be fully effective.

Scripture contains numerous accounts of specific healings (see Appendix II). In this chapter we consider the general teaching of Scripture about healing. We find that it points us to a healing ministry that is comprehensive: a ministry that concerns itself with the needs of the whole person not just the need for physical healing. It also points us to a ministry that is kingdom-based, cross-centred and God-glorifying, bringing reconciliation at every level. We see that, above all, the healing ministry is not meant to be an end in itself; it must flow naturally from the principal ministry of the Church, the proclamation of the gospel of Jesus Christ.

HEALING AND THE WHOLE PERSON

A basic ingredient in our ministry is an understanding of the important biblical truth that healing really means wholeness. This wholeness has many facets, but it always includes relationship with others and it is always centred in Jesus Christ. He is the one true human, the one fully whole human, and it is only as we are in *him* that we can be completely whole. The cross of Jesus Christ, which is clearly cosmic in its impact, is of specific importance for the wholeness of the individual. Christ's death and resurrection bring healing that is comprehensive: embracing spirit, emotions, body, decisions, purpose and relationships.

In his book *Man: The Image of God*,[2] the theologian G.C. Berkouwer notes that the many different writers of the Bible never point to man in himself. Scripture 'deals fully with the actuality of humanness, but it is an actuality before God . . . Man never appears as an isolated self-contained entity.'[3] Thus mankind is presented primarily in relation to God. Relationships with the cosmos and other people are also of interest; however, they are of secondary significance. Again and again, the Bible makes it clear that our 'relation to God is of decisive and all-inclusive character in these other relationships'.[4] This is a profoundly important point; every aspect of our humanness is dependent on God and we cannot find our true humanness apart from him. Without him humanness is an abstraction, a phantom without true form or meaning. Some 1600 years ago, Augustine was referring to the same truth when he wrote, 'You made us for yourself and our hearts find no peace until they rest in you.'[5]

The totality of 'humanness'

Berkouwer[2] points out that Scripture encourages us to think of each individual in totality and unity, not as a loose conglomeration of functions. Admittedly, when describing the human condition, the Bible does use various descriptive terms like soul, body, spirit, heart, mind, flesh, innermost parts and conscience. But it does not depict one part as independent of the others. In fact, these terms are often used interchangeably or in a context that makes it clear that they are really being used to bring the whole human person into focus. In particular, the Bible does not teach that human beings have a special part that is more spiritual or 'God-like', although throughout history many people, including theologians, have tended to think of the 'soul' in this way.

Dividing the human person into parts like this – especially when an underlying conflict between the parts is suggested – is more consistent with ancient Greek thinking than with scriptural truth. People are not immortal souls imprisoned in inferior, fleshly, mortal bodies as the Gnostics taught. The Bible 'does not say that man *has* a soul, but that man is a soul'.[6] In this context I find it significant that when God created the world and the men and women who inhabit it he looked at them – as whole persons within his creation – and saw them as very good (Gen. 1:31). Our ministry, therefore, needs to be 'holistic' in a biblical sense;[7] we need to think in terms of the totality and unity of the person, just as the Bible does. Both sin and sickness affect the whole person.

Berkouwer[2] emphasises that Christ was concerned for the whole person in his many miracles of healing. He also notes that in the Bible human 'bodiliness' is treated not as something secondary to spirit or soul, but as God's creative work, which will come to its climax in the resurrection of the body (1 Cor. 15). In the life to come we will not be disembodied spirits or souls; we will be fully human with resurrected bodies. When the resurrection comes at the end of the age it will be the resurrection of our total being. We know that 'we will be changed' (1 Cor. 15:51–53) but there is continuity as well as change. The Gospel writers are at pains to show that the resurrection body of Jesus was the body that had died on the cross. It was, however, different in that it could appear and disappear and move through closed doors. So it is for the resurrection body of the Christian. The body that dies is raised but it is changed, perfected and glorified: 'The body that is sown is perishable, it is raised imperishable; it is sown in dishonour, it is raised in glory; it is sown in weakness, it is raised in power; it is sown a natural body, it is raised a spiritual body' (1 Cor. 15:42–44).

It seems to me that the incarnation itself is a remarkable expression of God's commitment to the totality of humanness. Jesus was totally human with a physical body just like ours. When he cut himself in the carpenter's shop his blood ran red. He is truly divine but he was and is truly human as well. When Christ died, he died on our behalf as the representative human being. He died our death for us. The Church rejoices in the incarnation – God becoming a human person. This dignifies our humanity and is the basis for our healing ministry. There is an even more remarkable truth, however. When the Son of God rose from the dead and ascended to the Father, he took back into the Godhead our humanity. The one 'who ever lives' is the human–divine Christ.

All this underscores the importance of the whole person. Accordingly, the Christian approach to healing must be holistic and comprehensive: it must take into account all the needs of the individual – spiritual, emotional and psychological, physical and medical – and its goal must be the integration of the whole person. It should also lead towards integration and wholeness for families and communities of individuals, including the body of Christ. When we think in these terms, we begin to see that the healing ministry really includes every Christian ministry that is biblically fulfilling these aims. We also see that right at the heart of every ministry of healing must be this truth: *human beings cannot find wholeness apart from Jesus Christ*. Ultimately, the salvation he offers through his death and resurrection is the only way to wholeness.

HEALING AND THE KINGDOM

In Scripture there are close links between Christ's healing ministry, his saving work and the kingdom of God. If we are to have a balanced and biblical healing ministry, we need to understand the meaning of Christ's teaching about the kingdom.

The kingdom in perspective

Jesus' constant theme was the kingdom of God. He could announce, 'The kingdom of God is among you' because, as the king, he embodied the kingdom. Thus in his coming the kingdom was inaugurated; in his death and resurrection it came with power. In this sense it is clear that the kingdom has already come.[8]

The Bible also talks about a coming kingdom, a kingdom that arrives with the second coming of Christ – the parousia (lit. presence, a being alongside). The New Testament repeatedly refers to the future, imminent return of Christ and the consummation of the kingdom. Now is the time of betrothal; the wedding is yet to come (Rev. 19:7). While we are called to enter the kingdom now, through faith in Christ, entry into the kingdom in its fullest sense is in the future (Mt. 25:34).[9] Meanwhile, we are to live in the light of his coming kingdom, as the kingdom continues to grow through the operation of the Holy Spirit who applies the work of Christ.

If we imagine a time line joining the cross (Christ's first coming) and the parousia (his second coming), the present can be represented by marking a point somewhere in between. I believe we should place this mark very close to the parousia to remind us that we should live on the tiptoe of expectancy, eagerly awaiting the fulfilment of the kingdom. Clearly, in this 'time between the times', although the kingdom is already present, we still live in a fallen world and must continue to do so until Jesus comes again. These two things are present together in tension. To emphasise this, many theologians describe the present age as the 'now and not yet' time.[10] Although the glory and the power of the age to come have already dawned and we are living in its light and power *now*, it has *not yet* fully come in all its glory and completeness.

> [We] live, as it were, between two worlds. We are people of this sinful world: we are tempted and sin; we are weak and we fall; and the processes of degeneration and death are at work in us from the moment of our birth. But we are also people of the kingdom: though we sin, in God's sight we are sinless; we face death, but we have eternal life; we see a decaying world around us, but we also see the signs of a heavenly kingdom in the trans-formed lives of God's people.[11]

Because we are living in the 'now and not yet' time, those who pray for the sick in a ministry of healing may observe a whole range of responses. Some people will be healed instantaneously just as in New Testament times.[12] Some will be healed progressively, some partially, some temporarily, and some will not be healed physically at all. Whatever the degree of healing, whether healing occurs or not, we are more likely to be able to minister appropriately if we have a sound understanding of kingdom theology – if we understand that *the signs of the kingdom are with us but all has not yet been perfected*.

We also need to acknowledge that the way God governs in this in-between time is full of mystery. If we try to make everything transparent – if we aim to know, or claim to know, all there is to know about the way God heals – then we are reducing God and his revelation to human terms, to concepts small enough to be grasped by our finite minds. This kind of theological rationalism has led the church into all kinds of strife in the past. We must be careful to avoid it as we develop our basic theology of healing.

The nature of the kingdom

The kingdom is God's reign rather than his realm: his reign in Christ. It is not a geographical area over which Christ reigns as king but rather the exercise of his kingly sovereignty, not his domain but his dominion.[13] It is related to his reigning in our hearts, in society and over all.

> When Jesus says the kingdom of heaven is at hand, or has come near, he is really saying that heaven and the way it is ruled has now come within our reach and experience . . . This means turning from our sins, in other words from doing things our own way and not his, and then surrendering or believing in him . . . After such a surrender the agenda of Jesus becomes ours in the world around us.[14]

The kingdom has past, present and future aspects: *it has come* (Jesus embodied, inaugurated and announced it), it comes and is present in our lives through the power of the Spirit, *it will come* fully when Jesus comes again and everything alien to the kingdom is put under his feet.

Although it is difficult for finite minds to grasp the perfection and the overwhelming joy and beauty of the kingdom that is to come, Scripture does give us glimpses, especially in symbolic passages like Revelation 21 and 22.[15] In this new existence we will be completely at peace with ourselves, our Lord and each other. These are some of the features of the coming kingdom: no poor, no war, no oppressed people, no one demon-possessed, no one sick, no one lost.[16]

Signs that the kingdom has already come are described in Scripture. They include the following: proclaiming good news to the poor; liberating the oppressed; delivering the captives; healing the sick; restoring sight to the blind; healing the broken hearted; casting out demons; raising the dead (see Lk. 4:18,21; 7:21,22; 11:20). These present signs, however, should not be misinterpreted. They do not mean that the kingdom has already come *in all its fullness*. They are signs that the kingdom has been inaugurated and promises of what is yet to come.[17]

The priority of the kingdom

The Bible leaves us in no doubt about the importance of the kingdom. The Old Testament increasingly looks toward the coming of the kingdom of the Messiah for the ushering in of the day of salvation,[8] salvation that will be offered to 'everyone who believes' (Rom. 1:16) not only to members of the Jewish race. On his arrival, Jesus the Messiah (or Christ) announced that the kingdom had arrived. He and his followers proclaimed the gospel of the kingdom; his teaching is encompassed in the parables of the kingdom. Jesus' climaxing exhortation in the Sermon on the Mount was to seek first the kingdom of God (Mt. 6:33), in his model prayer he taught his followers to pray continuously, 'Your kingdom come' (Mt. 6:10), and he died on the cross with the sign over him, 'the King of the Jews'. There are many references to the kingdom throughout the New Testament. In fact, the distinguishing mark of the Christian is his or her acknowledgment of Jesus Christ as Lord – as 'King of kings and Lord of lords' (see, for example, 1 Cor. 8:6; Rev. 19:16).[18]

Our healing ministry, if it is to be balanced, must also emphasise the kingdom in these ways and recognise the 'now and not yet' perspective taught in Scripture. This will keep us in touch with reality and place the focus where it truly belongs. Theologically, the healing ministry must be based on the biblical teaching of the kingdom; spiritually, it must focus not on healing as an end in itself but on the kingdom and the King of kings.

HEALING AND THE CROSS

In Old Testament times there were miraculous healings and other evidences of the Spirit's presence (see Appendix II); however, the coming of the fullness of the Spirit, the overcoming of the evil one and the consequent multiplied signs of the kingdom (including many healings) depended on the arrival of the kingdom of the Messiah and especially on his redemptive death and resurrection.

The significance of the cross

It was by his death and resurrection that the sin-barrier to the working of the Spirit was overcome, that Satan's power was defeated and the Spirit's power released (Jn. 7:39; Acts 2:33). Accordingly, the healing ministry must not only be kingdom-based but also centred on the cross. Understanding this point may make a significant difference to the way we go about our ministry. I sense in some areas of the healing ministry a tendency, in both theology and practice, to shy away from the cross and its implications of submission, suffering and death.[19] Indeed, some who have overemphasised the ultimate victory of the kingdom have ended up with a triumphalist type of ministry. John Stott writes about this in terms of a tension between the 'already' and the 'not yet':

> Already we are God's sons and daughters, and no longer slaves; not yet have we entered 'the glorious freedom of the children of God'. . . An over-emphasis on the 'already' leads to triumphalism, the claim to perfection – either moral (sinlessness) or physical (complete health) – which belongs only to the consummated kingdom, the 'not yet'.[20]

In extreme cases this kind of thinking can lead, and has led, to healing ministries that are showy and pretentious and characterised by unrealistic expectations and extravagant promises of healing. For example, the impression may be given that everyone can be healed provided they have enough faith; all that has to be done is to claim or demand victory now in Jesus' name.

Triumphalism overlooks or under-emphasises the biblical truth of the 'now and not yet' struggle of the Christian pilgrimage in a still-fallen world. This rejection of sickness and suffering 'fits well into our age, with its denial of death and emphasis on positive thinking'.[21] The cross does represent Christ's absolute victory over death and sin but it also represents his costly sacrifice and his suffering. In the New Testament we are told that we as Christians will experience suffering too. The context usually suggests that this means standing up for Christ through one's lifestyle in the face of persecution, but it can also mean bearing up under the physical, mental and emotional pain of a fallen world. We need to remember that Jesus said: 'If anyone would come after me, he must deny himself and take up his cross daily and follow me' (Lk. 9:23). The following helpful comments on this issue are offered by the faculty at Fuller Seminary:

> When miraculous healing becomes the cutting edge of faith, people ask: 'Why should we suffer?' When discipleship becomes the cutting edge of faith, we ask: 'How can we turn our suffering to the service of our neighbour, to our own growth, and to the glory of God? . . . The apostle Paul

quite naturally wanted to be rid of his own thorn in the flesh. Instead he received grace sufficient to bear it. But he was not relieved of his desire to be free of it. Had he no desire to be rid of it, he would not have suffered from it – and would have needed no grace to bear it. His suffering was genuine and human. But grace enabled him to turn genuine human suffering into genuine Christian growth.[22]

Is healing in the atonement?

There has been much controversy about the role of the cross of Christ in healing.[23] Some claim that healing is in the atonement, that Christ died for our sicknesses as well as our sin. Isaiah 53:4–5 is usually cited in support:

> Surely he took up our infirmities and carried our sorrows, yet we considered him stricken by God, smitten by him, and afflicted. But he was pierced for our transgressions, he was crushed for our iniquities; the punishment that brought us peace was upon him, and by his wounds we are healed.

Because of this, they maintain, all Christians should expect healing here and now. John Stott disagrees with this point of view.[24] He argues that sickness is not in itself a sin that attracts a penalty; therefore, it does not make sense to say that Christ 'atoned for' our sickness. Drawing attention to two references to the Isaiah passage in the New Testament (Mt. 8:16–17; 1 Pet. 2:24), he notes that Matthew is commenting on Jesus' healing ministry, not the cross, and suggests that 'the contexts in both Isaiah and Peter make it clear the "healing" they have in mind is salvation from sin'.

I prefer to look at this issue another way. I am convinced that the teaching of Scripture is quite straightforward. As we have already discussed, the Bible treats the person not as parts but as a unity. This means that Christ died for the whole person, not just to save their 'soul' from sin. The cross is the source of our salvation – no Christian should want to deny this truth. He is going to save us as a whole and every aspect of our salvation has its origin in the cross. This salvation, achieved through the cross, includes the resurrection of the body. The death of Jesus has an impact on our bodily life now[25] and it will have an impact on our bodily resurrection hereafter.

Thus we can regard the atonement as the way to both forgiveness of sins and the wholeness we will experience in our resurrection bodies. If we look at it in this way, we must conclude that healing is in the atonement. There is, however, no justification for going on to conclude, as many do, that healing is available *now* to everyone who claims it in Jesus' name. In the past some have quite rightly resisted both the triumphalist style of ministry and inadequate teaching about healing and the atonement associated with it. It seems, however, that they may have been throwing the theological baby out with the bath water. There is, in fact, a clear link between healing and the atonement in Scripture; the atonement paves the way for some healing now and for ultimate healing in the age to come (see *Healing and reconciliation*, below).

Both experience and Scripture teach us that we do not receive all the benefits of Christ's atonement in this age. None of us lives a life of sinless perfection and none of us achieves perfect bodily health in this fallen world. Sometimes we may think we are in perfect health but that is only because we have never seen anyone in the perfect health of God's eternity. We are in the 'now and not yet' time: now entering into the benefits of Christ's death but not yet able to appropriate them fully. Complete healing, for all who are his, awaits the coming age.

A balanced healing ministry emphasises both cross and kingdom. It takes as its model the weakness and servanthood of the cross, with its denial of all self display, while pointing to the cross as the ultimate source of wholeness for the individual. It acknowledges that the kingdom and the powers of the kingdom have arrived and are with us now (including the gift and gifts of the Holy Spirit) and acts accordingly but it understands that the kingdom has not yet come in all its fullness.

HEALING AND RECONCILIATION

Throughout the Bible we find three predominant themes: creation, the fall, and God's plan of salvation through which the individual and ultimately the whole of creation are restored and reconciled with him. In Genesis, we read that at each stage of his creation God saw that it was entirely 'good' (see Gen. 1:4,10,12,18,21,25). When it came to the great climax of creation, when he created humankind in his own image as male and female, he viewed what he had done and considered it '*very* good'. In Genesis 1:4–31 the sequence is 'good . . . good . . . good . . . good . . . good . . . good . . . very good'. This sevenfold affirmation leaves us in no doubt about the essential goodness of the original creation, seven being the number of perfection. Thus we can see that sickness, like sin, is an intrusion into God's creation. It is neither part of his original purpose nor part of his ultimate purpose. In Genesis 3, we have a very simple but profound account of what seems to be, at least in part, a figurative description of the fall – the entry of sin into the world. Here the fall leads to separation and death.[26]

Sickness and the fall

We are not told when sickness originated but, throughout the Old Testament, sickness is connected with sin in general. Note that the Bible does not teach that those who are sick are greater sinners than those who are well but it does teach that sickness and sin are related: sickness like sin is an intrusion into God's good creation. It is a sign of our fallen mortality. Indeed Genesis 2:17 affirms that we 'surely die' because of sin. Also implicit in the Old Testament is the solidarity of the human race. Thus good (righteous) people suffer along with bad (unrighteous) people and bad people are blessed along with good people; we all belong together in the human family.

Evil events and circumstances do not have their origin in God. Sickness is, in a general sense, satanic in that it belongs to that part of reality that is opposed to God and his will. God remains sovereign, however, overruling this evil for his good purposes and satanic power is itself limited by God's sovereignty (Job 1:12; Mk. 1:25; Jn. 14:30–31).

Paul's attitude to his 'thorn in the flesh' illustrates these points (see 2 Cor. 12:7–10). We do not know exactly what his problem was,[27] but we do know that he had a painful disability that he described, not as a messenger of God, but as a messenger of Satan. He does not want to blame God, but he acknowledges God's sovereignty when he says that the thorn was given (by God, we presume) to keep him from being too conceited (v. 7). It remains, however, a messenger of Satan and he is the one to blame.[28] In this sense he sees his sickness or disability as 'satanic'. It is associated with the activity of the evil one, a consequence of the fall, not part of the perfect plan of the good God for his creation. It does not follow, however, that sickness is evidence of a specific sin in a person's life. Nor should sickness be regarded as evidence of demonic oppression or possession.[29]

A new order in Christ

Ralph Martin, a great New Testament scholar, describes the fall as 'the cosmic predicament': a disordered, travailing, impatient creation, racked by demonic opposition and containing alienated and disconsolate sinners, 'bereft in the universe and estranged from the holy God'.[30] There has occurred a dislocation, an alienation and a fragmentation in God's good creation with which we all must struggle. We have sickness, mental illness, death and our own sinful human behaviour – all the outcome of the entry of sin into the original perfect creation.

Martin points out that the main theme of Paul's writings is reconciliation through the bringing of a new order in Christ. The action of God is the key to this, particularly in the cross. Paul thinks about salvation in big terms: to him it means not only personal salvation (although that is a significant part of it), but 'a process of restoration that will one day . . . lead to a reclaimed universe, at one with its creator'.[30] The life of the early church was a sign that the process had already begun:

> The sign and pledge of that cosmic renewal have already been given in what was taking place in the apostolic community – deliverance from demonic forces, the forgiveness of sins and life in the fellowship of the Spirit under the lordship of the exalted Christ. One token in particular was evidence of the new age that, it was believed, had dawned with the post-Easter triumph of Christ and his new life in the Spirit. Barriers of separation were being broken down, not only between God and the sinful race of humankind, but just as impressively between the inveterately distanced groups in ancient society: Jew/Gentile; slave/free; male/female. Life in the society of the new creation, the church, was a marker of what God was accomplishing in the world at large, and this revolution in the microcosm of the church was treated as a foretaste and promise of God's plan to embrace the whole cosmos in his new order.[30]

The Church is thus a sign of what God is going to do for the whole universe. This process will, of course, involve judgment for the individual and the casting out of all that offends, but the overwhelming emphasis is on reconciliation. The Bible consistently teaches that somehow through the death of Jesus Christ everything is going to be put right; however, the final putting right will occur only when he comes to establish the kingdom in its fullness.

Fighting the fall

Because the effects of the fall are an intrusion into God's world, they are to be resisted. In Romans 8:22 we read that 'the whole creation has been groaning' in longing to be released. We as part of that creation, have had an innate longing to get rid of the effects of the fall since the beginning when man tilled the soil to get rid of the weeds (Gen. 3:17–19). We are to battle against the effects of the fall but we are to do it in the way of faith: in God's strength and according to biblical priorities. Paul did not automatically accept his thorn in the flesh. He resisted it and prayed to be delivered from it (Rom. 12:8). In the same way, we should not give in too readily to sickness or our own particular 'thorn in the flesh' sent by Satan. We must be prepared to resist it by praying for healing and by doing everything else we can to aid recovery.[31]

In this sense, we are fighting the fall when we pray to our Father and let our needs be known to him, including our need for healing. We are fighting the fall when we pray for grace to overcome temptation so that we can live God-glorifying lives. When viewed from this perspective, 'spiritual warfare' seems to be more about praying *for* ourselves and other people, even our enemies, than praying *against* Satan and his demons.

In the fight against the fall, Christ has achieved the decisive victory that brings everlasting peace: 'For God was pleased to have all his fullness dwell in him, and through him to reconcile to himself all things, whether things on earth or things in heaven, by making peace through his blood, shed on the cross' (Col. 1:19,20). Through his coming and especially his death, *shalom* (a Hebrew word meaning peace, wholeness and reconciliation) is to be restored to the universe. This has profound implications for the healing ministry. We are in need of healing because of the disorder of nature, the opposition of demonic powers, and human alienation. Although everything has not yet been fully restored, we can now experience forgiveness and a measure of healing and wholeness. Indeed we are assured that, whatever our present circumstances, God is working 'for the good of those who love him, who have been called according to his purpose' (Rom. 8:28). It is a foretaste of the ultimate reconciliation of the cosmos made possible through the gift of the cross.

HEALING AND THE GLORY OF GOD

Paradoxically, the symbol of the power of God is a weak and humble cross. We follow a crucified servant, not a superstar. What we need are God-glorifying, not self-glorifying, healing ministries: ministries that focus on God himself and leave people in no doubt whatsoever that he is our only focus. In Psalm 103:1–4 we find an interesting reminder of biblical priorities:

> Praise the Lord, O my soul;
>   all my inmost being, praise his holy name.
> Praise the Lord, O my soul,
>   and forget not all his benefits.
> He forgives all my sins
>   and heals all my diseases;
>   he redeems my life from the pit . . .

First, the psalmist rejoices in God himself and then he lists his 'benefits'. Because wholeness is being centred in God, our first need is not healing or any of God's blessings, it is God himself! Life for the Christian is being completely wrapped up in God and wholehearted praise and worship should flow naturally as an expression of our love and gratitude. The first benefit the psalmist mentions is salvation from sin. In our ministry we should place the first emphasis here too – on people having their sins forgiven and being reconciled with God. Next the psalmist talks about healing. As we have already discussed, Hebrew thought, with its emphasis on the person as a whole, did not make a clear distinction between the cleansing of the soul and deliverance of the body from disease. Both are part of one salvation. There is a certain priority, however: forgiveness first, then healing. Ultimately this means deliverance from 'the pit', that is, the pit of death.

Biblical healing begins with a concern for the glory of God. In reports of healings in the New Testament, it is often noted that people praised or glorified God because of them. We see one example of this in the story of the healing and forgiveness of a paralytic man. This man 'went home praising God. Everyone was amazed and gave praise to God' (Lk. 5:25–26).[32] But when ten lepers were healed, only one returned to Jesus to give praise to God (Lk. 17:12–19). Presumably the others did not give the glory to God. Were they preoccupied with the healing miracle itself? All ten were 'cleansed' (v. 17); only one was made whole (v. 19).

Jesus' ministry always brought glory to God, although he often had to resist a tendency in people to move away from this focus. In the book of Acts we find his disciples following his example, shrinking back from taking credit for the healing of the cripple at the gate called Beautiful (Acts 3). Peter asked: 'Why do you stare at us as though by our own power or godliness we had made this man walk?' (Acts 3:12). He then pointed them to the 'God of Abraham, Isaac and Jacob' (v. 13). The primary goal of our healing ministry also must be the glorifying of God's name.

Healings can be spectacular. If in our healing ministry we begin to witness remarkable, instantaneous cures, we may become overwhelmed. Success may go to our heads. The glory of God can easily be overlooked if our attention becomes focused on the miracle itself or on the human agent. We need constantly to remind ourselves and each other that every aspect of our healing ministry must give glory to God who alone has power to heal. 'Hallowed be thy name' is an appropriate prayer to pray in every circumstance we face. It is vital for those who participate in the healing ministry.

HEALING AND THE GOSPEL[33]

We have seen that healing ministries that are reflecting biblical theology will be comprehensive (addressing the needs of the whole person), kingdom-based, cross-centred and God-glorifying. In the gospel we find the key biblical concept that draws all these aspects of ministry together and guarantees their realisation. Understanding this is, I believe, crucial to having an effective healing ministry.

The dynamic theme of gospel, the gospel of grace that comes to us in Jesus Christ and by his Spirit, is central to the whole message of Scripture. Paul reminds us just how important it is when he says, '. . . even if we or an angel from heaven should preach a gospel other than the one we preached to you, let him be eternally condemned!' (Gal. 1:8). Yet he found it astonishing how easily distortion of the true message could happen (Gal. 1:6,7). Today some Christians seem to allow healing itself to become the gospel. They may attach so much importance to healing that the gospel emphasis on forgiveness seems all but forgotten. Others, in contrast, do not acknowledge any relationship between the gospel and a ministry of healing and either participate in a very limited way or choose not to be involved at all.

What is the gospel?

In simplest terms, gospel means 'good news', but the Christian concept of gospel goes far beyond that. In fact, the words used for 'good news' in Old and New Testament times had shades of meaning that are not familiar to us today.

The Hebrew word used in the Old Testament for good news (*besorah*) sometimes meant the good news itself but it could also mean the reward given for bringing the good news. The good news was regarded as having its own effective power. Bad news brought sorrow while good news brought joy (which might earn a reward); the news produced what it proclaimed.[34] The Greek equivalent of *besorah* is *euangelion*, the word subsequently used for 'good news' or 'gospel' in New Testament manuscripts. In the New Testament, however, *euangelion* takes on a very specific meaning – it becomes a distinctively Christian concept.[35]

The essence of the gospel (*euangelion*) is contained in just three words: 'Jesus the Christ'. He brings and proclaims the gospel. It is not an abstract idea. It is not really a doctrine. The incarnate Christ embodies it. He is the gospel. Without his death on the cross and bodily resurrection there is no good news – no gospel (1 Cor. 15:1–5). This 'good news' not only produces joy, it is life-changing! What it proclaims and produces through its message is original and its consequences are eternal.

The gospel is equated with the name of Christ and with the kingdom of God.[36] God's reign is ushered in by Jesus, the King. This kingdom becomes a reality, it arrives, in the incarnate Christ. There is the closest possible relationship, however, between the gospel of the kingdom and the Lord's death and bodily resurrection (2 Tim. 2:8). The kingdom arrives with Jesus but comes with power through the cross and resurrection. Thus the concepts of gospel and kingdom are inseparable from the cross, and Jesus Christ embodies both.

The gospel speaks of abundant grace towards those who are powerless: good news indeed for all of us but especially for those who are ill. Grace is the free and unique gift of God, the sovereign Father, to undeserving sinners (Rom. 3:24). It always comes through Christ and it is always given in abundance.[37] But judgment is also part of the gospel. The gospel looks forward to the coming judgment at the end of time; the Saviour is also Judge. The proclamation of judgment and the message of joy and God's grace belong together.

The word 'gospel' may also be used to summarise the whole of the Christian message. For example, the first four books of the New Testament, which are records of Jesus' life and ministry, have become known as the Gospels. Mark launches his account with the words: 'The beginning of the gospel about Jesus Christ . . .' Although the heart of the gospel is the story of the suffering, death and resurrection of Jesus, everything connected with this may be regarded as part of the gospel: 'It has the right to be so in virtue of its connection with Christ'.[38]

The power of the gospel

The gospel is dynamic; its effect is explosive. The gospel produces what it proclaims: 'in the very act of proclamation its content becomes reality, and brings about the salvation which it contains . . . Wherever it is proclaimed . . . this gospel is charged with power. It creates faith (Rom. 1:16f; Phil. 1:27), brings salvation, life (Rom. 1:16; 1 Cor. 15:2) and also judgment (Rom. 2:16). It reveals God's righteousness (Rom. 1:17), brings the fulfilment of hope (Col. 1:5,23), intervenes in the lives of men, and creates churches.'[39]

The gospel is not an empty word but effective power, which brings to pass what it says because our Creator God is its author.[40] Thus the proclamation of the gospel brings forth fruit; it imparts salvation. It produces the response of hearing and accepting, although obviously not in any automatic or magical sense. Through the dynamic operation of the Spirit and the genuine response of the listener 'the hearing of faith' is created, a process that involves repentance and leads to joy and wholeness (Rom. 1:16,17). This interaction between God and the individual is full of mystery; but it is clear that the full proclamation of the gospel itself influences the response in decisive (if mysterious) ways. What the gospel *is* (the message and Christ himself) is inextricably linked with what the gospel *does*.[41]

I am convinced that we need to present healing in the context of the central theme of Scripture: the gospel itself. We also need to keep the gospel central in our lives and in our preaching. Only then will our ministry be truly comprehensive. In the power and unity of the Spirit, it will contribute to the wholeness of both the individual and the Church. Our main focus must be primarily on the gospel – that is, on the crucified Lord himself – not on miracles or other signs and wonders. It is above all by the preaching of the gospel, the gospel of the kingdom, that God's name is glorified.[42]

The wonderful truth that God can and does heal is certainly 'good news' but it is not the gospel, and good news that is anything less than the full biblical gospel will not bring wholeness. It is only as we proclaim the gospel in its biblical fullness that our healing ministry will be both balanced and maximally effective. It will not need to be emphasised unduly or boosted by human emotional energy or the involvement of any particular leader. Our ministry will receive all the thrust it needs through being supported and empowered by the gospel itself.

Notes

1.   See Appendix I.
2.   Many of the ideas in this section come from a chapter entitled 'The Whole Man' in G.C. Berkouwer, *Studies in Dogmatics. Man: The Image of God* (Grand Rapids: Eerdmans, 1962), pp. 194–233, which clearly is about the whole person, male or female. It contains a much more scholarly treatment of this important topic.
3.   Berkouwer, p. 196.
4.   Berkouwer, p. 195.
5.   See R.S. Pine-Coffin (tr.), *St Augustine's Confessions* (London: Penguin, 1961), p. 21.
6.   G. Pidoux, *L'homme dans l'Ancien Testament* as quoted in Berkouwer, p. 215. Berkouwer decries attempts to depreciate the human body, 'which came to the fore in theology under the influence of Greek thought, and which showed itself not only in the theory of salvation from the body as from a lower form, but also in the practice of asceticism' (p. 203). He also points out that the contrast between the Greek *sarx* (and *sōma*) and *pneuma* in Paul's thought is not a contrast between the body, as the seat of sin, and the spirit, above sin (p. 205). On this issue John Stott writes: 'What Paul means by the 'flesh' (*sarx*) is our fallen nature or unredeemed humanity, everything that we are by birth, inheritance and upbringing before Christ renewed us. Because our 'flesh' is our 'self' in Adam, its characteristic is self-centredness'; see J.R.W. Stott, *The Cross of Christ* (Leicester: Inter-Varsity Press, 1986), p. 242; this and all subsequent quotations used by permission.
7.   From the Gk. *holos* meaning whole. Note that I use the term 'holistic' here in a specific way that is distinct from its usage in relation to secular holistic philosophy.
8.   John Bright writes: 'The Old Testament is illumined with the hope of the coming Kingdom, and that same Kingdom lies at the heart of the New Testament as well. But the New Testament has introduced what we might call a tremendously significant change of tense. To the Old Testament the fruition and victory of God's Kingdom was always a future, indeed an eschatological thing . . .

"Behold, the days are coming". . . But in the New Testament we encounter a change: the tense is a resounding present indicative – the Kingdom is here! And that is a very "new thing" indeed: it is gospel – the good news that God has acted!'; see J. Bright, *The Kingdom of God: The Biblical Concept and its Meaning for the Church* (Nashville: Abingdon, 1984), p. 197. Thus Paul can announce, '. . . now is the time of God's favour, now is the day of salvation' (2 Cor. 6:2; cf. Is. 49:8).

9.   From Bertold Klappert in *The New International Dictionary of New Testament Theology*, Vol. 2, by Colin Brown, p. 385; copyright © 1976, 1986 by the Zondervan Corporation. This and all subsequent quotations used by permission of Zondervan Publishing House.

10. Or the 'already' and 'not yet'; see G.C. Berkouwer, *Studies in Dogmatics. The Return of Christ* (Grand Rapids: Eerdmans, 1972), pp. 96–139, esp. p. 110. George Ladd taught this concept at Fuller Theological Seminary for many years; see G.E. Ladd, *Crucial Questions about the Kingdom of God* (Grand Rapids: Eerdmans, 1952) and *The Presence of the Future* (Grand Rapids: Eerdmans, 1974). Note that, in terms of general teaching on eschatology, I do not hold Ladd's premillennial view that there will be a literal reign of Christ on earth for a given period (a 'thousand' years) following the coming of Christ. I favour Berkouwer's view that the millennium in Revelation 20 refers to the present reign of Christ; Christ is already reigning in his millennial kingdom, which extends from the time of his coming until his return. The vision of Revelation 20 is not a narrative account of a future earthly reign but a vivid picture of the reality of salvation in Christ as a backdrop to the reality of suffering that continues as long as the reign of Christ remains hidden. It is part of the New Testament presentation of the return of Christ in the context of hope and encouragement for the persecuted Church. See Berkouwer, *The Return of Christ*, pp. 291–322, esp. p. 307.

11. Paul G. Hiebert in J.R. Coggins and P.G. Hiebert (Eds), *Wonders and the Word: An Examination of Issues Raised by John Wimber and the Vineyard Movement* (Winnipeg: Kindred, 1989), p. 130. This and all subsequent quotations used by permission.

12. In those days, dramatic, immediate healings were especially important as signs that the kingdom had arrived in Christ. See Art Glasser in Coggins and Hiebert, pp. 100f.

13. C. Peter Wagner, *Church Growth and the Whole Gospel: A Biblical Mandate* (San Francisco: Harper & Row, 1981), p. 4; this chapter includes an interesting analysis of the sequence of events that previously had prevented him, and perhaps many other Evangelicals, from fully appreciating biblical teaching on the kingdom.

14. From M. Cassidy, *The Passing Summer: A South African Pilgrimage in the Politics of Love* (London: Hodder and Stoughton, 1989), p. 258; copyright © 1989 by Michael Cassidy; this and all subsequent quotations reproduced by permission of Hodder and Stoughton Limited and William Neill-Hall Limited. See also

pp. 256–260. The kingdom of God is inextricably bound up with the person of Jesus and it is only in this sense that the future kingdom is present; see Klappert, pp. 383,386. Klappert also notes 'Jesus' claim that the verdict to be passed on men in the final judgment is already determined by the attitude they adopt to himself in the present age [Mt. 10:32] . . . the presence of the kingdom of God in the person of Jesus faces the individual with a clear-cut decision' (pp. 383,385). The notion of the kingdom is a grace concept – God gives the kingdom and we enter it in response to grace; see Karl L. Schmidt in G. Kittel (Ed.), *Theological Dictionary of the New Testament*, Vol. 1 (Grand Rapids: Eerdmans, 1964), p. 587.

15. The author of Revelation uses highly symbolic language, drawing on Old Testament images, to express the perfection and joy of the future kingdom.

16. C. Peter Wagner, *How to Have a Healing Ministry Without Making Your Church Sick* (Eastbourne: Monarch, 1988), p. 100f.

17. See P.G. Hiebert in Coggins and Hiebert, pp. 130–133.

18. Peter Wagner in discussing the Christocentric nature of the kingdom suggests that Jesus himself refused to claim that he was the king because he knew it would lead to misunderstanding, to an incorrect emphasis on a domain rather than a dominion; see Wagner, *Church Growth and the Whole Gospel*, p. 4.

19. For example, many songs associated with contemporary healing ministries focus on power and victory arising out of Christ's death with little, if any, acknowledgment of his suffering on the cross.

20. Stott, p. 240. Stott continues: 'An overemphasis on the "not yet" leads to defeatism, an acquiescence in continuing evil which is incompatible with the "already" of Christ's victory'. No doubt, such acquiescence – or failure to enter into the victory of Christ achieved on the cross – would also undermine our effectiveness in ministering to the sick.

21. P.G. Hiebert in Coggins and Hiebert, p. 139. Hiebert believes that some of John Wimber's teaching at this point has been particularly weak. Referring to Wimber's early writings (e.g. 'It's God's nature to heal not to teach us through sickness. Sickness is not generally beneficial'), he points out that there is no place in such a theology 'for seeing death as positive, as going to meet the Lord, or for godly dying, in which Christians look forward in peace to being with Christ and their departed loved ones'. Following his own experience of serious illness, there seems to have been a shift in Wimber's position: 'I have looked death in the face . . . Since that time I have frequently reflected on the place of suffering in the Christian life, trying to understand why God allows it and what it accomplishes. I am now convinced that one of the best ways to equip ourselves to deal with suffering is to have considered the purpose of suffering in the Christian life before we have to face a personal crisis. Understanding what Scripture teaches about suffering won't remove our pain, but it will provide a context for trusting God in the midst of trial'; see J. Wimber, *Kingdom Suffering* (London: Hodder and Stoughton, 1989), p. 6.

22. See chapter entitled 'The place of suffering in Christian experience' in L.B.

Smedes (Ed.), *Ministry and the Miraculous: A Case Study at Fuller Theological Seminary* (Pasadena: Fuller, 1987); quotations are from pp. 51–54. This and all subsequent quotations used by permission.

23. Henry W. Frost, *Miraculous Healing: A Personal Testimony and Biblical Study* (London: Evangelical Press, 1951; reprinted 1972) provides an interesting historical record of aspects of this debate.

24. Stott, pp. 244–245.

25. In Christ, we become a 'new creation' (2 Cor. 5:17). See, also 2 Cor. 4:10–11. Commenting on the latter passage Colin Kruse writes: 'On the one hand he [Paul] is daily subject to forces which lead to death, but on the other he is continually upheld, caused to triumph, and made to be more than a conqueror by the experience of the risen life of Jesus in his mortal body' (cf. 2 Cor. 1:8–10); see C. Kruse, *Tyndale New Testament Commentaries: 2 Corinthians* (Leicester: Inter-Varsity Press; Grand Rapids: Eerdmans, 1987), pp. 107f.

26. For a more detailed treatment of this subject see G.C. Berkouwer, *Studies in Dogmatics. Sin* (Grand Rapids: Eerdmans, 1971).

27. Many suggestions have been made as to the nature of Paul's 'thorn in the flesh'. These fall into three main categories: spiritual opposition, persecution, or physical or mental illness. Most commentators favour the view that it was some kind of physical illness.

28. In both the Old and New Testaments, Satan has no power other than that allowed him by God. Satan is allowed to harass Paul, but his action is made to serve God's purposes, which are always good; see Kruse, pp. 205–206. In a chapter entitled 'The Mystery of Providence', Donald Carson writes: 'God stands behind good and evil in somewhat different ways . . . God stands behind evil in such a way that not even evil takes place outside the bounds of his sovereignty, yet the evil is not morally chargeable to him: it is always chargeable to secondary agents, to secondary causes. On the other hand, God stands behind good in such a way that it not only takes place within the bounds of his sovereignty, but it is always chargeable to him, and only derivatively to secondary agents'; from D.A. Carson, *How Long, O Lord: Reflections on Suffering and Evil* (Grand Rapids: Baker Book House, 1990), p. 213; copyright © 1990 Baker Book House Company and Inter-Varsity Press. This and subsequent quotations used by permission.

29. The Bible sharply distinguishes between sickness and demonic possession. I will return to this important point later (see Chapter 5, *Casting out Demons: a Biblical Perspective*).

30. Ralph Martin, *Reconciliation. A Study of Paul's Theology* (Atlanta: John Knox, 1981), p. 46. Used by permission of Harper Collins Publishers Ltd. Note that the process of cosmic reconciliation will involve the great upheaval of judgment when all that offends is discarded (Mt. 13:41,42) and the destruction of the heavens and the earth as we know them and the bringing into being of 'a new heaven and earth, the home of righteousness' (2 Pet 3:10–13). Martin comments that Paul frequently mentions his personal reconciliation with God, his

Damascus road experience, which led to reconciliation with fellow Christians.

31. John Koenig, Charismata: *God's Gifts for God's People* (Philadelphia: Westminster, 1978), p. 136; this and all subsequent quotations used by permission. Koenig warns against accepting our pains too courteously; it was only with time that Paul learned that his thorn was a 'gift'. He suggests that Paul's initial resistance is recorded in Scripture to alert us to 'the danger of masochism. Healing is always a possibility; not all thorns are "given" to last.'

32. See also the raising of the widow of Nain's son (Lk. 7:11–17); the healing of the woman who had been infirm for eighteen years (Lk. 13:10–17); the healing of the blind man in Jericho (Lk. 18:35–43).

33. For a fuller treatment of many of the ideas in this section, see articles on 'gospel' by Gerhard Friedrich in G. Kittel (Ed.), Theological Dictionary of the New Testament, Vol. 2 (Grand Rapids: Eerdmans, 1964), pp. 721–736, and Ulrich Becker in C. Brown (Ed.), *The New International Dictionary of New Testament Theology*, Vol. 2 (Grand Rapids: Zondervan, 1976), pp. 107–115.

34. The second meaning of *besorah* ('reward for good news') does not carry into the New Testament although the concept of the good news producing what it proclaims certainly does; see Friedrich, pp. 721,725.

35. In the Old Testament the use of the equivalent word is secular; however, the Old Testament as a whole foreshadows the New Testament gospel and, because it bears witness to Christ, is part of it; see, for example, Rom. 1:1ff, 1 Cor. 15:1ff and Rom. 16:25ff; Friedrich, p. 730. See also Mk. 1:15; Mt. 3:2ff. Becker notes that, in New Testament times, the word *euangelion* already had a quasi-religious meaning in the Hellenistic world, especially in the imperial cult. 'Good news' about the god-emperor (about his birth, coming of age, enthronement, decrees and acts, for example) was equated with 'long hoped-for fulfilment to the longings of the world for happiness and peace'. His birth was regarded as bringing blessing to all men and restoring 'the shape of everything that was failing and turning into misfortune'. He was seen as a saviour, as one who would make wars cease and create order everywhere. 'The proclamation of this *euangelion* does not merely herald a new era: it actually brings it about. The proclamation is itself the *euangelion*, since the salvation it proclaims is already present in it'; see Becker, p. 108. Becker suggests that, in the early churches, gospel terminology developed 'by analogy out of that associated with the "gospel" of the imperial cult, though also in conscious opposition to the latter' (p. 110f).

36. Mt. 19:29; Lk. 18:29, cf. Mk. 8:35; 10:29; also Mt. 4:23; see Friedrich, p. 729.

37. See Rom. 5:1–2; 1 Cor. 1:4; Eph. 2:7 and Rom. 5:17; 2 Cor. 4:15. James Moffat has said of Paul's writings: 'Over and over again he speaks of "grace abounding", far surpassing in power any contrary force of evil, flooding life with a lavish wealth of hope and strength . . . When Paul thinks of grace, it calls up before his mind God pouring into human life His marvellous favour, his language vibrates with passionate gratitude as he surveys the working of it amid

the poverty and weakness of life'; see J. Moffat, *Grace in the New Testament* (London: Hodder and Stoughton, 1931; New York: Long and Smith, 1932), p. 179.

38. From G. Kittel (Ed.), *Theological Dictionary of the New Testament*, Volume II, Geoffrey W. Bromiley, trans., © 1964 Wm. B. Eerdmans Publishing Company, Grand Rapids, Michigan, p. 730. This and all subsequent quotations reprinted by permission of the publisher; all rights reserved. The fullest descriptions of the gospel in Paul's writings are found in Rom. 1:1–4 and 1 Cor. 15:1–8 (see also Rom. 2:16, 16:25; 1 Tim. 1:11; 2 Tim. 2:8).

39. Becker, p. 111,

40. Friedrich, p. 731. See also Becker, pp. 111,113: '. . . this gospel is no invention of man (Gal. 1:11) . . . not a human word but the word of God (1 Pet. 1:12) . . . [Its message is] a word charged with power in the present so that it cannot be fettered by human chains (2 Tim. 2:9).'

41. See Becker, p. 111. The content and the proclamation of the preaching of the gospel are one. It is both 'the gospel he promised beforehand through his prophets in the Holy Scriptures regarding his Son' and also 'the power of God for the salvation of everyone who believes' (Rom. 1:2f,16).

42. There are many different ways of preaching the gospel, of course, and preachers need to be careful that their presentation of the gospel is appropriate and relevant to their audience. It is of the utmost importance that all preaching, including teaching to the church, be undergirded by the proclamation of what God has done through Christ's life, death and resurrection (see *The safeguard of sound biblical teaching* in Chapter 11).

Chapter 3

Healing and the Miraculous

A comprehensive healing ministry will acknowledge that all true healing comes from God. It will also teach that God may choose to bring about healing by a whole range of possible means, including some that may be regarded as miraculous. A balanced understanding of miraculous healing is therefore an essential ingredient in an effective healing ministry.

At one extreme, we may place so much emphasis on miraculous healing that we neglect other sources of healing, such as appropriate medical treatment. If we take the opposing view and dismiss the possibility of miraculous healing altogether, we also deprive ourselves of part of God's loving provision for us. What we really need is a biblical and theologically-sound understanding of miraculous healing.

WHAT IS A MIRACLE?

In simplest terms, miracles are events that involve a suspension of the established laws of nature. Some people would also regard as miracles ordinary events that are spectacular or providential in their timing: for example, 'coincidences' that have such profound and beneficial effects on our lives that they seem to be orchestrated by God. Norman Geisler, a contemporary Christian apologist, defines a miracle as:

> . . . a new *effect* produced by the introduction of a supernatural cause . . . a divine intervention into, or an interruption of, the regular course of the

world that produces a purposeful but unusual event that would not (or could not) have occurred otherwise. The natural world is the world of regular, observable, and predictable events. Hence, a miracle by definition cannot be predicted by natural means.[1]

This is a useful definition provided we recognise that supernatural occurrences, including miraculous healings, should not unquestioningly be attributed to *divine* intervention. Satan treacherously uses 'all kinds of counterfeit miracles, signs and wonders' to deceive the unwary (see 2 Thes. 2:9, for example). This is why some Christians prefer to use the more specific term 'divine healing' rather than 'miraculous healing' to refer to the times when it is *God* who is intervening in a special way 'bypassing the natural processes of the body and the skills of doctors and nurses'.[2] I agree that we should be encouraging an openness only to miracles that come from God; however, provided that is clearly understood, as in the present context, I prefer to use the term 'miraculous healing'. For me healing from every legitimate source is, in a sense, divine; it is a gift from God, whether he chooses to provide it miraculously or otherwise.

DO MIRACLES HAPPEN TODAY?

Many Christians have experienced or witnessed something out-of-the-ordinary in relation to healing. Books and articles describing amazing, 'supernatural' healings have been appearing in a continuous stream in recent years as a result of growing interest in the healing ministry. Some represent the grateful testimonies of those who have been healed. Some are the reports of reputable witnesses to healings. Others are no more than collections of unverified and unverifiable anecdotes. While some stories are well-reasoned and well-documented, others seem embarrassingly naive, coloured by wishful thinking, an unhealthy enthusiasm for the spectacular or allegiance to a particular healer or approach to healing. How can we be sure the 'healings' described are really miracles? How can we separate fact from fantasy, genuine miracle from counterfeit?

Reports of healings in contemporary Christian literature are frequently presented within the framework of Charismatic–Pentecostal teaching and practice, even those presented by authors who are avowed Evangelicals. The healings I am about to describe generally took place in more traditional Evangelical settings.

Some years ago, I experienced a remarkable healing myself. Following a heavy cold, I became quite deaf. Despite emergency surgery, I suffered an 'irreversible' loss of hearing. I was told there was a slim chance of improvement but warned that unless this happened within two weeks my hearing would be permanently impaired. Much prayer was offered on my behalf, several weeks went by with no change in my condition and I began resigning myself to the fact that I would need a hearing aid. Some weeks later, my wife and I thought we noticed some improvement but we were not sure. Imagine our joy when tests revealed that my hearing had returned to normal. I have had no problem with deafness since. 'Your being a religious man, we'll have to call this a miracle', my doctor remarked.

I have seen other people healed 'miraculously' and my files contain many letters from people who believe they have received healing through prayer at services or seminars I have conducted. For example, a woman confined to a wheelchair for several months following a stroke walked unaided the day after we prayed for her. On another occasion, we prayed for a girl with a marked curvature of the spine. To her doctors' amazement, her spine straightened. X-rays clearly document the change. Of course, I also have letters from people who did not appear to be healed.

The pastor of a Baptist church shared the following stories with me and gave me permission to use them. A member of his congregation had suffered from an agonising degeneration of the spine for some fifteen years. When drugs could no longer provide relief, electrodes were implanted in her spine and connected to a 'black box' that sent electrical pulses to her nervous system to counter the pain. Her suffering was still intense. Eventually, several years ago, she arranged for the pastor and the elders to pray with her for healing. She turned the 'black box' off just before the prayer meeting and never turned it on again! Within a few days she was running without pain, even up stairs. Her doctors, naturally sceptical, put her through a number of tests, not expecting to find any real change in her condition. Within six months, however, they removed the electrodes, thoroughly convinced that she no longer needed them. She seems to be completely cured.

A child from the same church developed a serious eye infection and was rushed to the Children's Hospital. There was genuine concern that the infection would spread to her brain and kill her within hours. The pastor, unaware of the child's illness, was at the hospital on other business. He was alerted to the situation by a nurse, another church member, who had seen him arrive. In a public waiting room, after asking permission of both mother and child, he simply placed his hands on the little girl's shoulders and asked Jesus to make her better. She was admitted for treatment and her recovery was rapid and complete. Within two days her doctors were so surprised by her progress that they questioned their original diagnosis; however, the seriousness of the situation was subsequently confirmed by the results of tests requested at the time of admission.

I cannot lightly dismiss these stories. They represent the personal testimonies and first-hand accounts of people whom I consider to be reliable witnesses. In many instances, medical records support the claim that something exceptional has happened. Are they really examples of miraculous healing? Many Christians would readily accept them as such, especially among those who are eagerly expecting miracles to happen through the power of the Holy Spirit. But possibly just as many would be sceptical, especially among those who hold the view that miracles and other signs and wonders belonged only to the ministry of Jesus and his apostles. They may believe, like Calvin, that 'such works have ceased, having fulfilled their function in establishing the gospel'.[3] They would say there is always a natural explanation for unusual events but sometimes our lack of knowledge prevents us from understanding what is happening. Alternatively, some people may be reluctant to accept the above examples as miracles simply because insufficient 'evidence' has been presented to convince them.

This raises an interesting question: is it ever possible, on the basis of objective evidence, to be one hundred per cent certain that a miraculous healing has occurred? Probably not.[4] Is this a problem for the healing ministry? I do not believe so. In fact I would argue that proving (or disproving) miracles ceases to be a major issue when we gratefully acknowledge *all* healing as a gift from God. Becoming too caught up in such quasi-scientific concerns may even be counterproductive (see *Facing the facts* in Chapter 11).

Clearly, I am not suggesting we should totally deny the possibility of miracles just because they are so difficult to prove beyond a shadow of doubt. On the other hand, I am not advocating unquestioning acceptance of every enthusiastic testimony of miraculous healing. Such blind belief seems inappropriately naive and leaves the Church open to justifiable criticism. This unquestioning attitude is most damaging when it is mistakenly regarded as a sign of faith in God and promoted as a virtue.

Somehow we have to find a balance between these two extremes: inappropriate belief and inappropriate disbelief. The former denies the value of our God-given ability to reason, the latter denies the healing power of the Spirit.

MIRACLES AND THE WESTERN WORLD VIEW

According to Peter Wagner, 'Believing is seeing. If you have already decided that God does not heal today, it will be impossible to prove to you that anyone has been healed through prayer.'[5] Therefore for him the key question when assessing claims of miraculous healing is 'whether this account is backed by the type of evidence that indicates that accepting it as valid would be a reasonable response for one who assumes that such a thing is possible'.[6] In similar vein, Colin Brown points out: '. . . having once settled his convictions about the possible, the skeptic demands a great deal of evidence and argument in order to change them. He more readily attributes unverifiable reports of miracles to lack of knowledge on the part of the reporter, credulity, the inflamed religious imagination, or sheer deceit, than allow them to shake his convictions.'[7]

In our secular society many people are closed to, or do not expect, miracles. Charles Kraft has written extensively on this issue in a book entitled *Christianity with Power: Your Worldview and Your Experience of the Supernatural*.[8] He is convinced that we are blocked from experiencing widespread New Testament 'power Christianity' by our western world view with its underlying assumptions that channel, limit and focus our perspective. For him 'power Christianity' includes miraculous healing.

Many Christians unconsciously adopt world views that are very much like those of non-Christians around them, views that are more a reflection of western culture than scriptural truth.[9] Typically their focus is on the natural rather than the supernatural world. Their tendency is to think of an autonomous world created by God but now controlled by the laws of nature. Disease and accidents are explained in purely naturalistic terms as if God did not exist. The mindset is technological. As a result, materialism tends to dominate: '. . . now our real religion is science, and our priests are the scientists'.[10] Reason (rationalism) has become the main means of understanding reality; emotion and the spiritual realm tend to be suppressed or denied. Also featuring in this world view are individualism and independence, leading to self-centredness and a sense of isolation.

Having a world view helps us to categorise, and so understand, reality. Our perceptions of reality, however, are largely the outcome of what we have been taught to see. Because culturally approved ways of seeing are rewarded, we learn to perceive selectively and tend to accept things that are in line with early teaching. As Paul reminds us, we see truth only partially (1 Cor. 13:12).

Our world view can thus become a trap for us. If a particular expression of God's activity does not fit into any of the categories in our own world view, we may fail to recognise it. Thus, if we have never encountered miraculous healing before, our tendency will be to deny it as a possibility. It will be especially difficult for us to accept this new phenomenon if we are feeling emotionally vulnerable at the time or if our temperament is naturally pessimistic or conservative. The strength of our will, peer pressure and social norms may also influence our reaction.

The perception in the west is that everything (even God) behaves like a machine. In non-western societies everything works like a human. Westerners tend to describe events in terms of intermediate causes (for example, bacteria and viruses) whereas other societies refer to ultimate causes (gods, spirits, etc.). Neither approach is sufficient in itself and the popularity of the New Age movement is indicative of an increasing western dissatisfaction with intermediate causes. Kraft says that we need to recognise both the strength of our drive to find a rational explanation for everything and the difficulty this creates for us:

> Even though we freely admit that God and his works are beyond our comprehension, there is something within us that won't quite accept that as the final conclusion. We want to know . . . Our drive to understand is not evil in and of itself. But when that part of us is too much in control, we are not able to appropriate faith. Too much of a drive to understand robs us of our ability to trust God and to release ourselves to receive whatever he has for us, whether or not we can understand it . . . We can't explain it so we reject it . . . Satan can be very clever in the way he takes such good things as our ability to reason and uses them to cripple us.[11]

Liberty comes when people are released from the bondage of having to understand everything.

LESSONS FROM HISTORY

Throughout its history, the Church has struggled to find a balance between overcredulity and scepticism.[12] Nevertheless, scholars seem to agree that some Christian expectation of miraculous divine intervention in life existed almost continuously from the time of the apostles to the Reformation.[13] Then came a strong movement away from this belief, largely as a reaction against the superstition, exaggeration and wrong emphasis on miracles that was prevalent in the Roman Catholic Church at that time. Calvin protested, '[They] allege miracles which can disturb a mind otherwise at rest – they are so foolish and ridiculous, so vain and false!'[14]

I believe that, in part at least, this kind of reaction underlies the now widely held belief that the age of miracles is past – that miraculous healing, along with other signs and wonders, should be regarded as a unique feature of the apostolic church. It is interesting to note that many of the influences that shaped this view and strengthened it at the time of the Reformation are more historical and secular than theological.[15] Paul Hiebert describes the way in which the Renaissance reintroduced neoplatonic dualism into western thought, with its dichotomy between spirit (God, angels, spiritual beings) and matter or nature (humans, animals, plants).[16] Science became less and less dependent on a concept of God and western thinking became increasingly secularised.

According to Hiebert, many westernised Christians were left with 'spiritual schizophrenia'. Liberals reduced their stress by interpreting miracles in naturalistic terms. Conservatives accepted biblical miracles but affirmed a naturalistic interpretation of the world. Evangelism and social gospel were separated and a wholesale secularisation took place in the western Christian world.

The struggle continues today, creating heartbreaking divisions within the body of Christ. Sadly, within the Church, we still find some whose gullibility and abandonment of reason belong more to a medieval than to a contemporary world view. Today, as in the past, belief in miracles can easily lead people away 'from a sober and responsible faith to superstition and exploitation, from liturgical prayer to quasi-magical tricks'.[17] In contrast, some Christians, in reaction against alleged miracles 'so foolish and ridiculous, so vain and false', are completely denying the possibility of miracles and adopting a world view that does not allow them to perceive God's Spirit at work. Both these extreme viewpoints dishonour God and hinder the healing ministry.

THE OMNIPOTENCE OF GOD

I believe that it is vital for us as Christians to reaffirm that the supernatural is part of reality. We need to remind ourselves that God is *God*. He is truly omnipotent. The great Creator of the universe is not restricted by human reason or by the laws of nature he set in place. We need to change our perspective 'on a sizeable segment of reality'[18] so that we become entirely open to the miraculous. I do not mean we should suddenly start claiming that every unusual event is a miracle but we should begin to include the miraculous as an option on our list of possible explanations. Accordingly, underlying our prayers should be a quiet confidence that God is able to heal in a miraculous way, together with a peaceful acceptance of the fact that he may not always choose to do so. He remains sovereign in all things. In this context, it is helpful to remember that, although the healings recorded in the Bible were generally immediate and complete, miraculous healing may happen in other ways; for example, it may come gradually or provide only temporary relief.

As we open ourselves to the possibility of miraculous healing, there is always a danger we may become overly dependent on the instantaneous and the spectacular. We must not allow our belief in miracles to blind us to the fact that often God's healing comes through less sensational means. We need to have a concept of a God-permeated cosmos in which ordinary healings are as divine as miraculous ones:

> A miracle is not a sign that a God who is usually absent is, for the moment, present. It is only a sign that God who is always present in creative power is working here and now in an unfamiliar style.[19]

The apostle Paul reminds us of our utter dependence on God's continuous creative power; it is 'in him we live and move and have our being' (Acts 17:28). Thus, for example, whether the restoration of a damaged spine comes about through prayer alone or through skilled surgical intervention, it is ultimately God's creative power that is at work.

The Church has a long tradition of ministering to the sick. Countless petitionary prayers have been offered on behalf of those who are ill. The following 'Prayer for a sick Child' is found in *The Book of Common Prayer*, first published in 1662:

> [Deliver] him in thy good appointed time from his bodily pain, and save his soul for thy mercies' sake: that, if it shall be thy pleasure to prolong his days here on earth, he may live to thee, and be an instrument of thy

glory . . .[20]

And the following assertion is found in 'A Prayer for a sick person when there appeareth small hope of recovery':

> We know, O Lord, that there is no word impossible with thee; and that, if thou wilt, thou canst even yet raise him up and grant him a longer continuance amongst us . . .[20]

Such prayers, which grew out of Reformation thinking, are surely more than trite words of comfort. To me they convey a strong sense of belief in an omnipotent, sovereign God who may at any time choose to intervene in miraculous ways to bring healing. Implicit in them is the genuine expectation that God will hear and heed them.

Today, whether we use an ancient or modern prayer book or whether we extemporise, we frequently ask God to do extraordinary things – to intervene in our lives in supernatural ways. We ask him to 'bless' leaders of the church or nation and our family and friends, to help someone find a home or a job, to give wisdom to doctors or skill to surgeons. We ask him to reduce someone's pain or to comfort them in their bereavement. Yet it often seems that we want God to respond, to intervene supernaturally, only in ways that are acceptable to us because they fit neatly within our world view categories. For example, we may genuinely want the sick to be blessed and healed but envisage this happening only through medical intervention or by a slight acceleration of the normal recovery process. We may not feel comfortable about, or may even strongly disapprove of, asking him to heal in an extraordinary way if he so chooses.

This attitude of unhesitatingly seeking and accepting God's intervention in many areas of our lives, while rejecting it in relation to miraculous healing, seems inconsistent and unnecessary to me. Yet it is distressingly prevalent. Because of this the healing ministry of the Church is impoverished and many Christians do not receive all the healing that God may have for them.

The gospel, through which we become new creatures in Christ, represents the ultimate revelation of God's miraculous intervention in the lives of men and women. As I will explain in the next chapter, inherent in the gospel is also the remarkable truth that God at times chooses to involve us in his mighty works. Through Christ and in Christ, ordinary people are enabled to do extraordinary things. This was certainly true in the days of the apostles. There is every reason to believe that it is also true today.

Notes

1. Norman L. Geisler, *Miracles and Modern Thought* (Grand Rapids: Zondervan; Dallas: Probe Ministries International, 1982), p. 13. Colin Brown discusses this issue at length in his book *Miracles and the Critical Mind* (Grand Rapids: Eerdmans; Exeter: Paternoster, 1984); all subsequent quotations used by permission. [Thomas V. Morris, in *Making Sense of it All. Pascal and the Meaning of Life* (Grand Rapids; Eerdmans, 1992), skilfully guides the reader through the fragments of thought contained in the *Pensées* of Blaise Pascal, 'a brilliant and profound Christian thinker' of the seventeenth century (p. 13). According to him, Pascal's perspective was this: 'If we want to think in terms of laws of nature, we can say that a miracle surpasses rather than violates them. Suppose it is a law that "wherever A then B." The theist always understands laws as restricted to the natural domain, so a full explanation of such a law should properly state that "wherever A, and nothing in addition to A, then B" or "wherever A, and God does not intervene to the contrary, then B" '; see p. 170.]

2. From John Wimber with Kevin Springer, *Power Healing* (London: Hodder and Stoughton, 1986), pp. 26,27; copyright © 1986 by John Wimber and Kevin Springer; this and all subsequent quotations reproduced by permission of Hodder and Stoughton Limited.

3. Brown, p. 17. Brown bases this comment on his study of relevant classical texts and fully documents his sources. He maintains that Luther and Calvin 'both believed that the age of miracles is past'; see Brown, p. 19. A popular variant of this view is that, while God may still work miraculously, the miraculous gifts manifested within the New Testament church, such as the gift of healing (see Chapter 4), have ceased.

4. Even scientists acknowledge that they have to settle for less than this degree of certainty in their work. By international agreement, a hypothesis is generally regarded as 'proven', at least for the time being, when the level of confidence that it is correct (based on statistical analysis of supporting data) reaches ninety-five per cent. A more complex aspect of this issue is raised by Colin Brown. He maintains that miracles cannot be the object of scientific investigation. They are intrinsically supernatural events – they occur outside the natural order – and science can only deal with nature as it is left to itself; see Brown, p. 292.

5. C.P. Wagner, *How to Have a Healing Ministry Without Making Your Church Sick* (Eastbourne: Monarch, 1988), p. 239.

6. Wagner, pp. 241f. Many Christians, however, would be reluctant to come to this 'reasonable response' of acceptance on the basis of the 'evidence' that seems to be sufficient for Wagner (p. 242).

7. Brown, p. 282.

8. I am indebted to Charles Kraft for many of the ideas expressed in this and the following four paragraphs; see C.H. Kraft, *Christianity with Power: Your Worldview and Your Experience of the Supernatural* (Ann Arbor: Vine Books,

1989).

9.	A scriptural world view sees God, who is the Creator and Sustainer of all things, as ordinarily working in the world in ordinary ways – what we call the 'laws of nature' (e.g. Ps. 104:24–30; Acts 14:17); it also sees God, who is the Redeemer, as sometimes working in the world in entirely extraordinary ways – what we would call 'miracles' (e.g. Ps. 105:26–41). Neither way is more God-like than the other; both reveal his wisdom and power. In contrast to the western understanding of things, biblical explanations more often concentrate on primary rather than secondary causes (e.g. Deut. 32:39; Is. 45:7).

10.	From *Christianity with Power, Your Worldview and Your Experience of the Supernatural* © 1989 by Charles Kraft; p. 32. Published by Servant Publications, Box 8617, Ann Arbor, Michigan, 48107; this and all subsequent quotations used with permission. It is important to realise that a biblical world view can accommodate science. It has the germ of the scientific world view in it. God is the God of truth and reality and in so far as science truly seeks reality it is quite compatible with biblical understanding; however, a solely scientific world view is inadequate to deal with the totality of life. [See, for example, George Smoot and Keay Davidson, *Wrinkles in Time* (London: Little, Brown and Co, 1993), a book about recent developments in astronomical understanding, which reminds us that there are questions in the realms of religion and philosophy that science is not equipped to answer; see pp. 291ff. It also proposes the following link between religion and science: 'The religious concept of creation flows from a sense of wonder at the existence of the universe and our place in it. The scientific concept of creation encompasses no less a sense of wonder' (p. 297).]

11.	Kraft, p. 48.

12.	As Colin Brown notes, 'Testimony to the miraculous was no less difficult to believe for the educated person in the second century than for his or her twentieth-century counterpart'; see Brown, p. 18.

13.	For example, see L.B. Smedes (Ed.), *Ministry and the Miraculous: A Case Study at Fuller Theological Seminary* (Pasadena: Fuller, 1987), pp. 35ff. This issue is also discussed by Colin Brown, Charles Kraft and Peter Wagner; see above. The Reformation, which began with Luther in Germany and led to the establishment of the Protestant churches, took place during the sixteenth century.

14.	A longer quotation (with source) is given in Brown, p. 15.

15.	The strengthening of this idea during the Reformation is described by Colin Brown (see pp. 13ff). He also notes that more than a millennium before the Reformation, Augustine (354–430 AD) speculated as follows: '. . . our predecessors, at a stage in faith on the way from temporal things up to eternal things, followed visible miracles. They could do nothing else . . . on the other hand, miracles were not allowed to continue till our time, lest the mind should always seek visible things, and the human race should grow cold by becoming accustomed to things which when they were novelties kindled its faith' (pp. 7f). He also points out, however, that Augustine, towards the end of his life, wrote the following retraction in a document intended to set right any errors he had committed: 'But what I said is not to be so interpreted that no miracles are believed to be performed in the name of Christ at the present time' (p. 8). Augustine, Luther and Calvin all recognised the danger of overemphasising miracles to engender or bolster faith and decried this practice.

16. P.G. Hiebert in J.R. Coggins and P.G. Hiebert (Eds), *Wonders and the Word: An Examination of Issues Raised by John Wimber and the Vineyard Movement* (Winnipeg: Kindred, 1989), pp. 110–113. The Renaissance, which marked the transition from the medieval into the modern world, was a time of great revival of art, letters and learning in Europe during the 14th, 15th and 16th centuries.

17. Smedes, p. 39.

18. Charles Kraft refers to this process as a paradigm shift; see Kraft, p. 82, and also Smedes, pp. 40ff. In his enthusiasm for such a paradigm shift to occur, Kraft expresses reservations about the term 'miracle' being applied to healings (see pp. 101–115). He claims that, because it implies an intervention or interruption of what is 'normal', this is the terminology of 'semi-deistic' views. Jesus acted as though healings were normal happenings and disciples were expected to do what he could do. He says Jesus is here advocating a 'new normalcy' for his disciples. There are no 'miracles' in the kingdom – only normal events resulting from people obeying God: 'The big sign and wonder is that we have been admitted into Gods family' (p. 103). Healings and other powerful events are 'only miracles to those whose definition of normalcy is tied to the earth . . . The concept of miracle as we ordinarily understand it is not helpful to us as we strive to see and relate to things as Jesus taught us' (p. 115). Contrast this with the view of Colin Brown (see Brown, p. 283), which echoes that of Pascal (see Note 1): 'The very idea of a miracle presupposes both a uniformity of events and the occurrence of something so unexpected and unusual that it defies explanation in terms of nature taking its normal course'; to him miracles are inherently 'unnatural'. There is an element of truth in both views. As Christians, we do not have to start regarding miracles themselves as 'natural' events – they are truly beyond the laws of nature – but we do need constantly to be open to the possibility of miracles, so that this way of viewing the world becomes 'natural' in the sense that it is normal for us.

19. These ideas are expanded in Smedes, pp. 40ff; quotation from pp. 48f.

20. *The Book of Common Prayer and Administrations of the Sacraments* (London: Eyre and Spotiswoode, 1966), p. 210. Interestingly, a more recent prayer book is much less forthright in its acknowledgment of the possibility of miracle; see prayer for 'one believed to be suffering from an incurable disease' in *An Australian Prayer Book* (Sydney: Anglican Information Office, 1978), p. 573.

Chapter 4

The Holy Spirit and His Gifts

While I am aware that recent emphasis on the Holy Spirit and spiritual gifts has brought new life to many individuals and churches, experience has taught me that it may also lead to tragic and hurtful divisions. No matter how controversial we may perceive these topics to be, however, we cannot simply ignore them. If we do so, we are neglecting a significant part of New Testament teaching. I believe that a sound biblical understanding of the Holy Spirit and his gifts, including healing gifts, is essential to a balanced and comprehensive healing ministry.

The Bible, especially the New Testament, has a great deal to say about the Spirit of God. We read about being born of the Spirit, baptised with (or in) the Spirit, filled with the Spirit, sanctified by the Spirit. We read about gifts and fruit of the Spirit. My aim in this chapter is to provide an overview of biblical teaching on these topics, focusing especially on aspects that are relevant to the healing ministry.[1]

THE GIFT OF THE SPIRIT

When we acknowledge God's right to rule our lives and become reconciled to him through Christ, we receive the gift (or the person) of the Holy Spirit. This gift is ours from the very moment of conversion. The Holy Spirit begins his lifelong work in us and we begin the great adventure of following Christ. We become 'born of the Spirit'; it is our beginning as new creatures, our 'baptism' in him (Jn. 3:5; 2 Cor. 5:17; Tit. 3:5; Jas. 1:18; 1 Pet. 1:3).

This amazing gift, the gift of the Holy Spirit poured out in unreserved and abundant measure on the whole Church, clearly comes as a result of Christ's death and resurrection. In Scripture, this link is illustrated by the fact that a gospel sermon on the death and resurrection of Christ is a major feature of the account of the Day of Pentecost (see Acts 2, esp. vv. 23–35). There we read: 'Exalted to the right hand of God, he has received from the Father the promised Holy Spirit and has poured out what you now see and hear.' All barriers to the lavish gift of the Spirit having been dealt with at the cross, the Father places his imprimatur on the offering of his Son by raising him from death and pouring forth the promised Spirit (cf. Jn. 7:39; 16:7).

The gift of the Spirit is offered to all who respond to the gospel. We read in the account in Acts that, on the day of Pentecost, Peter's Spirit-inspired sermon evoked the response: 'What shall we do?' His listeners were asking in effect: 'How do we find eternal life? How do we become Christians?' Peter replied: 'Repent and be baptised, every one of you, in the name of Jesus Christ for the forgiveness of your sins. And you will receive the gift of the Holy Spirit. The promise is for you and your children and for all who are far off – for all whom the Lord our God will call' (Acts 2:38–39).

The gift of the Holy Spirit was not promised and given only to these inaugural members of the Church; it is promised to every believer – past, present and future. As Christians we enter into the benefits of Pentecost and all the resources of God's omnipotent Spirit become available to us.[2] But this is only the beginning of an ongoing process. We need to continue to draw on the power of Pentecost or, as Paul expresses it, to go on being 'filled with the Spirit'.[3] It seems best, then, to speak of one baptism in the Spirit at the outset of the Christian life and many fillings.

When we receive the gift of the Spirit we begin to live as new creatures, with the potential – through the power of the Spirit – to act and react in ways that would otherwise be impossible for us. This is the natural outcome of our being 'transformed into his likeness with ever-increasing glory, which comes from the Lord, who is the Spirit' (2 Cor. 3:18). For this potential to be expressed, we need to be open to his miraculous working in our lives, including the diversity of gifts he provides.

GIFTS AND FRUIT OF THE SPIRIT[4]

The Holy Spirit chooses to work today, as when Christ was on earth, through the Church which represents the body of Christ. Christ himself is the head of this body and every Christian is a part of it (Col. 1:18; 1 Cor. 12:12–31). This means that everyone has a ministry – a unique and specific role in the life of the Church. We are truly the hands, feet and voice of Jesus Christ, not just to each other but to the world. It also means that everyone does not have the same role. If you are a hand you are not intended to be a foot and it is essential, for the sake of the body, that you fulfil your function as a hand. You can also be fairly confident that when you wake up tomorrow you will still be a hand. Thus finding the ministry (or ministries) you are equipped to fulfil is an important aspect of body life and an ongoing dynamic process. Your ministry will be an expression of your own particular gift or combination of gifts of the Spirit. Those with whom you share in ministry will be given complementary gifts. The body analogy presented in Scripture is a model of interdependence: 'If one part suffers, every part suffers with it; if one part is honoured, every part rejoices with it' (1 Cor. 12:26).

Spiritual gifts[5]

After we receive the gift of the Spirit, we are given at least one of the many gifts of the Spirit (or spiritual gifts) spoken of in the Bible.[6] These are the special abilities the Spirit of God gives to equip Christians to serve Christ, one another and the world. They are not given primarily for the sake of the individual, but for the building up of the Church – 'for the common good' (1 Cor. 12:7) – and ultimately for the glory of God and the extension of the kingdom.

Some twenty or more different gifts are mentioned in Scripture including gifts of prophecy, leadership, evangelism, teaching, administration, encouragement, serving and giving. Importantly, for the purposes of this book, also included are gifts of healing and other gifts relevant to the healing ministry, which I will describe in more detail later. We cannot earn these gifts – they are not meted out as rewards for faithful service – and we cannot decide which gifts we will have. They are grace-gifts, the work of the Spirit who 'gives them to each one, just as he determines' (1 Cor. 12:11). The Greek of the New Testament makes the intrinsic link between spiritual gifts (*charismata*) and God's grace (*charis*) very clear.

Acknowledging this link, Donald Carson writes: '. . . if we adopt *biblical* terminology, it is exceedingly difficult to think of any Christian as "non-charismatic" if all of us have received *charismata* ("grace-gifts") from God.'[7]

Spiritual gifts are not the same as the natural talents we are born with or the special skills we may develop through our own efforts. Certainly the Spirit may choose to work in power through some of these, and he often does so, but he is not bound to work within our limitations. It is not always the person who is most endowed with natural talents who is Christ's chosen one for a particular task, but the one who has been given the appropriate spiritual gift(s). So, even if we are not very talented, skilled or academically inclined, we need not think of ourselves as inferior parts of the body. We are each loved infinitely by our heavenly Father and gifted by the sovereign Spirit who seems to delight in giving gifts to very ordinary people and using them in remarkable ways in his service.

As we exercise our gifts we need humbly to acknowledge our Creator God. It is he who works in us. It is he who works through us. All our gifts and talents are given to bring glory to him and they can come to full fruitfulness only as we submit ourselves to his sovereignty. We need to remember that although we are his sons and daughters, we are also part of his fallen creation saved only by his grace. Our ministry needs to exalt *him*, not our own egos. It must be a means of extending the kingdom not advertising our power.

I want to encourage you to open yourselves wholeheartedly to the gifts of the Spirit, but I must also add a word of caution. Biblical teaching on spiritual gifts and the gifts themselves can be misunderstood and misused. In our humanness we can easily get things out of balance, especially when it comes to the more spectacular gifts.

Fruit of the Spirit

When the Holy Spirit is at work in our lives there are unmistakable signs, the fruit of the Spirit: love, joy, peace, patience, kindness, goodness, faithfulness, gentleness and self-control (Gal. 5:22f). It is quite inconsistent and unhelpful to seek the gifts of the Spirit but ignore the fruit. If we are not careful, spiritual gifts may become such a preoccupation that the more important ripening of the fruit of the Spirit is impeded.[8] *Every Christian is not given every gift, but all the fruit of the Spirit should be growing in every*

Christian. I say 'growing' advisedly because producing this fruit is a process of spiritual maturation that will continue in us until the day we die. Although we will never reach perfection in this life, lives that are open to the Spirit should generally be exhibiting his fruit. It is true that, even when we drift away from God and completely lose the fruit of the Spirit for a time, the gifts may remain and he may still choose to work through them (as in the early Corinthian church, for example). Nevertheless, living a holy life in response to God's grace is the essence of wholeness (see *Holiness and Abundant Living*, Chapter 6) and our gifts reach their full potential only when we are sincerely cooperating with God in their use.

Discovering your gifts

The New Testament does not give any specific recommendations about discovering your gift or gifts. It seems that if we genuinely want to serve God he will make our ministry clear to us. It is not something we have to worry about; however, asking the Father to help us discover our gifts and prayerfully encouraging each other to explore new avenues of service can be helpful.[9] Any individual or congregation embarking on this venture, however, needs to consider their primary motivation. It must be, 'How can I best serve Christ?' If it is, 'How gifted am I (are we)?' or 'Who has the most spectacular gifts?' then beware. The church is more likely to be damaged than edified.[10]

Our gift will be confirmed for us in several ways. One of the things about exercising our special gifts is that, generally, service becomes a delight rather than sheer duty or drudgery. It remains a burden (Jesus used the term 'yoke') but it is a light burden (Mt. 11:29,30). We may not get paid for exercising our gift, we may have to train hard, but when we use it we will experience a sense of fruitfulness, fulfilment and belonging and, generally, we will be able to cope. We will find others affirming us in this ministry and we will come to know that this is what we do best for God and for others.

On the other hand, we should not be concerned if we cannot define our gift(s) precisely. Being open to whatever gifts God bestows and exhibiting the fruit and the gifts of the Spirit naturally and unpretentiously are far more important than correctly identifying or categorising them.

SOME SPECIFIC GIFTS

In this section I describe just nine of the many different gifts we may receive from the Holy Spirit. Some are directly related to healing. Others are included because they have been given great emphasis in the contemporary healing movement.

Healing

There are some Christians whom God uses in a special way as channels of his healing grace, giving them a specific ministry of healing. As a result miraculous healings occur: healings that go beyond the limitations of human understanding and experience. Many regard it as significant that this gift is referred to in the plural in Scripture – 'gifts of healings' is the literal translation of the Greek in 1 Corinthians 12:9,28,30. While we do not really know the significance of this, it could be seen as an indication that a variety of healing gifts may be given. For example, sometimes such a gift may be comprehensive (that is, used in the healing of many different kinds of ailments) or it may be limited to a particular aspect of healing, such as emotional healing or healing of a specific medical condition.[11]

In its teaching on gifts of healing (and other gifts), Scripture places great emphasis on the Spirit and his sovereignty. The sixfold reference to the Spirit in 1 Corinthians 12:7–11 is particularly noteworthy. Those who have been given a gift of healing do not dictate the Spirit's use of it and there is no guarantee that healing will occur every time they pray for someone. The Spirit of God works through them using the gift as he sees fit. Because in his wisdom he does not always choose to heal, those who are given a gift of healing will generally witness a variety of results as they minister: instantaneous and gradual healings, complete, partial and temporary healings, and sometimes no discernible healing at all.

Intercession

Intercession is both a calling and a gift. God expects all Christians to pray for others but some Christians are called to a special ministry of intercession for which he gives them the grace (gift) they need in order to fulfil this ministry. It is a ministry that can be exercised at any time and in many different circumstances. It can be interspersed with everyday activities and the elderly and the retired can be involved. In fact, it is not unusual to observe this gift coming into its own in those whose activities are restricted by age or serious illness, thus enabling them to provide strong support for many other ministries. Intercessory prayer is a vital adjunct to the healing ministry (see *Healing and Prayer*, Chapter 8).

Exorcism

The gift of exorcism is the special ability that some Christians have to cast out evil spirits in the name of Christ and by the power of the Spirit. This process is referred to as exorcism (or deliverance). Exorcism is a genuine ministry of the Spirit but it is a gift that is often brought into disrepute by sensational reports or depictions of exorcisms in the secular media. While we should not be too quick to attribute illness to demonic possession, we do need to recognise that there are some individuals genuinely in need of the ministry of exorcism. We should therefore be thankful that some Christians are gifted by God in both exorcism and the related gift, discernment (see below). In appropriate cases, this can be of great benefit in bringing wholeness. The gift of exorcism needs to be exercised with caution and wisdom and always within the context of the body of Christ. There seems to be much confusion about 'casting out demons' as an aspect of the ministry of healing. For this reason, the next chapter is devoted to this vexed issue.

Word of knowledge

There are two interpretations of this gift: it can be a special ability given to some Christians enabling them to understand and absorb a profound knowledge of the Word of God and to share it with others;[12] or it can be a word of revelation from God. In the latter case there is clearly some overlap between this gift and the gift of prophecy.[13] The information obtained by revelation may be symbolic and open to a variety of interpretations, but it may also be of a very specific and factual nature. Many involved in the healing ministry place great reliance on revelations received through this gift to provide information about the illness or emotional state of the person receiving ministry.[14]

Undoubtedly this gift has a place in the ministry of healing (I see it as especially useful in the area of counselling[15]) and we should be open to it, as to all the spiritual gifts. I believe, however, that there is a tendency to overemphasise this gift in the contemporary healing movement. There is no mandatory link between healing and words of knowledge; healing can occur whether or not God chooses to reveal specific information about the person's condition to either the healer or some other person. It is also important to realise that such 'revelations' should be checked against Scripture and shared with humility as they can easily be erroneous (see *Testing the gifts*, below). Mistakenly assuming that every idea, dream or vision that comes into our minds (in response to specific prayer or otherwise) is 'a word from the Lord' can have disastrous pastoral consequences. Particular care is needed when we are communicating such 'knowledge' to those who are seriously ill.[16]

Prophecy

This gift is so multifaceted that many different definitions of it exist in the literature on spiritual gifts. The following is the working definition I use. The gift of prophecy, which is highly valued in Scripture (1 Cor. 12:28; Eph. 4:11), is the special ability and call that the sovereign Spirit gives to some Christians to receive and proclaim inspired authoritative contemporary messages to the world, the Church or to individuals. It brings a direct message from God. The New Testament prophet usually brought a specific word so that the Christian community and the individual believers might know God's will. This prophecy often included a revelation (1 Cor. 14:6) and it could bring about conviction of sin (1 Cor. 14:24f). The prophet by his direct messages from God spoke to Christians for 'their strengthening, encouragement and comfort' (1 Cor. 14:3; cf. Acts 15:32). The New Testament prophets were *forth*tellers rather than *fore*tellers, although on occasions there was a reference to the future.[17]

Prophecy is often expressed through preaching but it may also be communicated person to person or through the written word.[18] Modern prophecy may include a specific type of down-to-earth pastoral preaching with a strong element of exhortation that offers insights about issues within the local church. In another form, prophecy may be concerned with issues like unity, hunger, poverty, racism and warfare and be addressed to a wider audience. Merely commenting on contemporary life, however, is not prophecy. Inherent in all authentic Christian prophecy is an element of revelation. Inspired by the Spirit and centred in Christ, its relevance consists in its witness to him. Prophecy at its best will be the inspired application of specific truths of Scripture to the real world of our day.

Speaking in tongues and interpretation

Some Christians are given a special ability to pray directly to God in an unknown tongue. This is spirit to Spirit communication that bypasses the limitations of normal speech and the restrictions of the mind. Complementing this gift is the gift of interpretation: the ability to interpret the meaning of such utterances – not by giving a word by word by translation (the language of tongues may not even be interpretable in that sense), but by recognising and revealing the essence of the communication. One person may receive both these gifts (1 Cor. 14:13).

Speaking in tongues (glossolalia) is not *always* a sign that the Holy Spirit is at work. This phenomenon may be counterfeited and it can be experienced by non-Christians.[19] Nor is it a *necessary* sign of a second experience of the Holy Spirit (subsequent to conversion), an obligatory 'second blessing'. Christians who are granted this gift often do regard it as a special 'blessing' because it helps them praise and communicate with God with great liberty and joy in times of prayer.

When used in public, as in a meeting of the congregation, speaking in tongues must be accompanied by the gift of interpretation (1 Cor. 14). It then serves the same purpose as prophecy and as such must be subjected to testing (see *Discernment and wisdom* and *Testing the gifts*, below). Because it is one of the more conspicuous gifts, it can cause problems if misunderstood and misused. Paul found it necessary to provide guidelines to the church in Corinth and stern warnings against the overvaluing and inappropriate use of this gift in public meetings, noting that this could in fact hinder the spreading of the gospel.

Scripture makes it clear that speaking in tongues is an authentic gift of the Spirit (as is the interpretation of tongues). I therefore advocate an openness to both these gifts, but not an overvaluation.[20] Speaking in tongues is not singled out as one of the 'greater' gifts we are told specifically to 'eagerly desire' (1 Cor. 12:31; 14:1). If we are truly open to the Spirit, however, and whether we are involved in the healing ministry or not, we must be willing for him to give us the gift of speaking in tongues should he choose to do so. No one should be discouraged from 'desiring' this gift along with other gifts of the Spirit; nor should anyone be encouraged to seek it above all others.

It is important that Christians who lack this particular gift do not feel inadequate and discouraged. All the gifts are important for the corporate life of the church and the healing ministry also needs a diversity of gifts. Speaking in tongues should certainly not be regarded as a prerequisite for becoming involved in the healing ministry. There is no suggestion in Scripture that those with a gift of healing (or the other gifts that complement the gifts of healing in the healing ministry) *must* also have the gift of tongues.

If you have a genuine special gift of speaking in tongues be thankful for it and exercise it in humility, freedom and joy to the glory of God. If you do not, then ask God to help you and others recognise the gifts he has given (or is giving) you and use them in similar fashion.

Discernment and wisdom

Wherever there is prophecy there is likely to be false prophecy; anyone can claim to have a message from God. Similarly, speaking in tongues is not always an indication of the presence of the Spirit and those who claim to bring a word of knowledge may be mistaken. When writing about spiritual gifts, Paul emphasises our limited ability in this age to discern God's truth (1 Cor. 13:9–12). To help prevent the Church from falling into all kinds of error, the Spirit gives to some of its members special gifts of discernment, literally 'discernings of spirits' (1 Cor. 12:10), and the word of wisdom (see 1 Cor. 12:8 *KJVII*).

The person with the gift of discernment may often be able to discriminate between false prophecy (human error or a message from a false spirit) and a prophetic message from the Holy Spirit, between false motives and genuine motives, between genuine and counterfeit tongues – between the brother or sister who really has something to say in the Spirit and the one who just has to say something! They may also be able to discern the operation of demonic influences in people's lives.[21]

It is not easy to make such distinctions and, unless discernment is our gift, we are not particularly good at it most of the time. Bizarre behaviour is not necessarily a sign of demonic influence. Nor is speaking with enthusiasm, ecstasy or charisma a clear indication that a person is 'in the Spirit'. Even the fact that someone has a recognised gift of prophecy or word of knowledge does not guarantee that every insight they offer is correct and helpful to the Church. Continuous discernment is needed and the contribution of those who are specifically gifted in this area is essential.

The gift known as the word of wisdom helps to keep the Church pointed in the right direction. This gift must be seen not so much in terms of a sudden miraculous giving of wisdom or the ability to utter wise infallible sayings but rather as a settled attitude of mind that is inspired by God's Spirit. It entails a special kind of wisdom: a comprehensive understanding of God's purposes, as revealed in Scripture, that is centred in Christ and will lead the Church towards Christlike living.

TESTING THE GIFTS

Many in the contemporary healing movement place great emphasis on receiving revelations about a sick person's present or future condition when ministering to them. The reliability of such revelations thus frequently becomes a critical issue for those who are trying to come to terms with serious illness. Without a doubt there are occasions when members of the Church are given prophetic insights about someone who is ill, including whether or not they will be healed.[22] It is painfully easy, however, to confuse wishful thinking with prophecy and it is my experience that prophecy concerning our own well-being or that of friends is especially tricky. We need constantly to be aware of our human fallibility. [Excerpts from Robert Hillman's journal poignantly illustrate this important point (see Appendix III).]

As already mentioned, some Christians are given special gifts of discernment and wisdom but, being human, they are still capable of making mistakes. Michael Green has suggested some ten criteria for testing present day prophecy.[23] They may also be helpful in testing the validity of other forms of insight associated with spiritual gifts, for example, words of knowledge and 'discernments'. The following list is based largely on his suggestions:

- The *honour* test
  Does it glorify God (1 Cor. 14:25)? It should focus attention on him, not the speaker or a particular church or denomination.
- The *scriptural* test
  Is it consistent with Scripture (1 Cor. 14:37f; Deut. 13:1–4)?
- The *nurture* test
  Does it build up the church (1 Cor. 14:5,26)? Here we need to bear in mind that building up may demand loving admonition on occasions.
- The *love* test

Is it spoken with love (1 Cor. 14:1)?

- The *body* test
  Does the speaker submit to the judgment and consensus of others (1 Cor. 14:29f)? As prophecy should be tested by the body of Christ, a sign of authenticity is humility on the part of the prophet – not an authoritarian and unteachable spirit.

- The *self-control* test
  Is the speaker in control of himself or herself (1 Cor. 14:32f)? Order is one of the signs of the presence of the Spirit: 'For God is not a God of disorder but of peace' (v. 33).

- The *quantity* test
  Is there too much of it (1 Cor. 14:29f)? As Michael Green observes, the longer someone (or several in succession) speaks the more likely it is that his or her own ideas will become confused with God's word.

- The *lifestyle* test
  Is the life of the prophet sound (Mt. 7:15–20)?

- The *submission* test
  How does the prophet relate to the leaders of the church (Heb. 13:17; 1 Cor. 14:37)?

- The *outcome* test
  What is the outcome of the prophecy? Provided always that the prophecy is consistent with biblical teaching, confirmation is to be found in its fulfilment (Deut. 18:22).

This whole subject is full of mystery (see Appendix III).[24] We need to be open to the insights that come from the exercising of spiritual gifts, including words of knowledge, prophecy and discernment, but we also need to beware of the danger of relying more on the 'inner light' than the written Word. I have found through long experience in living with this Word and these gifts that there is often not much of a step between the inner light and the outer darkness. In this aspect of our Christian life we are particularly vulnerable to Satan's deception. Satan, in his guise as 'an angel of light' (2 Cor. 11:14), may even offer his own 'word of knowledge' (a prophecy that is true in the sense that it comes to pass) in order to trap or confuse the unwary (cf. Deut. 13:1f). Our safeguard is God's written Word and its message as revealed by the Spirit: the plain, clear meaning of his Word taken as a whole, with each passage considered in its proper context.[25]

SPECIAL AND GENERAL GIFTS

As well as special gifts of the Spirit (those I have just described and others) there are what I like to call general gifts – sometimes called Christian roles. These are not different in type from the special gifts, only in frequency and degree. They are part of our being transformed into the likeness of Christ.

For example, all Christians need to take on the role of 'evangelist' when confronted by an earnest seeker and they can do this in the Spirit's power whether or not they have a special gift of evangelism. Similarly, whether or not they are specifically gifted, all Christians should be encouraging and merciful. There is also a general role for the whole congregation in the healing ministry (Jas. 5:16): praying for each other and caring for each other in times of illness or mental and emotional distress. Sometimes God may grant remarkable healing in response to these prayers, but this does not necessarily mean that we have a special gift of healing.[26] In other words, at any time the Holy Spirit may choose to give us a particular gift briefly to achieve his purposes, but it may not be part of our continuing ministry to the Church.

We should be seeking to use our special gifts, whatever they may be, and giving priority to aspects of Christian service where they will best be used. This is good strategy in terms of the kingdom of God. In doing so, however, we should avoid opting out of other more general areas of ministry. 'Healers' should also be relating to other believers and to the world around them with the fruit of the Spirit. As Christians we are all called upon to minister to one another with love as the need arises: to give, to intercede, to help, to exhort and generally build one another up in a whole variety of ways, no matter what our special gift may be. From time to time the Spirit may surprise us by giving us a special measure of grace to do this, briefly providing us with a spiritual gift (or gifts) quite different from our special gift(s). Thus, general gifts and special gifts operate continuously in the life of the Church in complementary fashion as the Spirit determines.[27]

WORKING AS A TEAM

Spiritual gifts are not restricted to just one or two key people in a church. God shares them around in different combinations so that everyone is gifted to play his or her unique part. As we exercise our gifts, a sense of unity or team spirit grows and we benefit individually and corporately. The fact that our gifts differ is an act of grace in itself. We, as a body, need each other to function properly.[28] If any one gift is to have its maximum effect, then it must draw on the insights and skills that come with other gifts. As individuals within the body of Christ, we are as interdependent as the cells of the human body. Sound biblical teaching about spiritual gifts promotes unity among us by reminding us of our need for each other and our need for 'him who is the Head'.[29]

Michael Green, referring to the gift of interpretation of tongues, makes the following comments which may well be applied to all the gifts:

> If this is indeed a gift to build up the Body, then it is appropriate that its exercise should involve members of that Body moving forward tentatively in dependence on God and on each other. They may well not always get it right. But that, too, can lead to the edification of the congregation in patience, mutual correction, and love. Spiritual gifts are heady wine: there are sure to be mistakes and imbalances. But granted love within the Body, humility in those who exercise the gifts, and a reverent discrimination in those so gifted, growth will take place. Without risk, without experiment, there can be no life or growth.[30]

In relation to the healing ministry, it is clear that those with healing (or prophetic gifts) are not meant to be either a one person band or an elite group. They are to use their gifts humbly and appropriately, recognising the giftedness of all members of the body and valuing the many different ministries they perform. While some Christians may still need encouragement to accept the healing ministry as a valid ministry of the Church (and my hope is that this book will provide such encouragement), there are others who may need to be reminded that the healing ministry is not the only ministry of the Church. And it is certainly not its primary mission.

Generally, it seems that gifts of healing are to be exercised within the context of the local church along with other complementary spiritual gifts. This is certainly the context in which teaching about the ministry of healing is presented in 1 Corinthians 12 and James 5. I believe that in all churches those with known healing gifts (or other appropriate gifts) should be working with the elders[31] in a regular ongoing healing ministry to members of the congregation. Others in the congregation should also be involved in the healing ministry, with intercessory prayer being especially important.[32] This ministry ought to be as low key as possible, carefully avoiding sensationalism or anything else that would distract from the glory of God.

Some spiritual gifts are spectacular (healing gifts can certainly fall into that category) while others appear more mundane, but there is no reason for us to envy people whose gifts seem more spectacular than ours. We are one body, we all drink of one Spirit (1 Cor. 12:13), so we share in each other's achievements. Envy not only prevents us from affirming others in their gifts but also robs us of joy and fulfilment and, as we are all gifted, no one need be envious. Nor is there any cause for pride in those who seem to be particularly gifted. The gifts given to us are grace gifts, totally undeserved, not signs of spiritual superiority.[33] They are to be exercised 'with the strength God provides, so that in all things God may be praised through Jesus Christ' (1 Pet. 4:10,11).

Let us exercise our gifts in humble gratitude to God, acknowledging Jesus Christ – the definitive expression of his grace and provision for us. All the other gifts given to the Church come from that one gift. They begin at the cross, the ultimate symbol of sacrificial, unconditional giving.

Notes

1. For specific Bible-based teaching about the person and work of the Holy Spirit see James I. Packer, *Keep in Step with the Spirit* (Leicester: Inter-Varsity Press, 1984); M. Green, *I Believe in the Holy Spirit*, Revised Edition, (London: Hodder and Stoughton, 1985). While I do not necessarily agree with these authors in every respect, they offer much that is helpful.
2. It is appropriate that water baptism as a once-and-for-all event should be the sign and seal of this initiating experience of entry into the benefits of the day of Pentecost, which was itself a once-and-for-all event.
3. See Eph. 5:18b; the use of the present imperative of the verb 'to fill' in the original text makes Paul's meaning clear. After their conversion, many Christians experience a time (or even several specific times) when they become 'filled' or touched by the Holy Spirit in a specially memorable way. Some see a special experience of this nature subsequent to conversion, generally called 'baptism in the Spirit', as essential to growth in the Christian life. Many involved in Charismatic renewal and the contemporary healing movement hold this view, although others such as David Watson and John Wimber have rejected it; see D. Watson, *You are My God* (London: Hodder and Stoughton, 1983), pp. 60ff; J. Wimber with K. Springer, *The Dynamics of Spiritual Growth* (London: Hodder and Stoughton, 1990), pp. 139f.

    While acknowledging that many deeply committed Christians hold views that differ from mine, I believe that equating the gift of the Spirit with a second blessing or 'baptism in the Spirit' given only to some Christians is not supported by Scripture. I also see it as inherently divisive and spiritually unhelpful to the individual. Such teaching tends to divide the Christian community into two groups – first-class Christians (those who have the gift of the Spirit) and second-class Christians (those who do not). It tends to foster spiritual pride in the 'Spirit-filled' group, who despite their 'Spirit-filled' status are still capable of sinning, and envy or feelings of guilt or inadequacy in the 'Spirit-less' group. Such potential problems are heightened when some manifestation of 'spiritual giftedness' (e.g. speaking in tongues or prophesying) becomes the accepted sign of graduation from one group to the other and normative behaviour thereafter.

On the other hand, much division is also caused within the Church by those who deny the reality of 'second' (or subsequent) blessings that many Christians claim to have received. They are not to be confused with the once-and-for-all gift of the Holy Spirit at conversion, but they may be valid experiences of Christian growth. Such experiences are not a measure of spiritual maturity or worth; they are given by God as he sees fit to achieve his purposes. See also R.J. Hillman, *27 Spiritual Gifts* (Melbourne: JBCE, 1986), pp. 127–131.

4. For a more detailed treatment of this general topic based on biblical teaching, see R.J. Hillman, *27 Spiritual Gifts*.

5. Key teaching on spiritual gifts is found in Romans 12, 1 Corinthians 12–15 and Ephesians 4. In these passages, contrary to some current teaching on this subject, both special abilities and special ministries are presented as gifts of the Spirit. The emphasis seems to be on what people do rather than on the office they hold. It is probably correct to assume that each one who ministers (e.g. a teacher) will have a corresponding ability (e.g. teaching). On the other hand, the person in the role of minister of the Word may not have all the spiritual gifts relevant to that office, e.g. teaching, preaching, pastoring, evangelism. I have found it helpful to think of the gifts as either speaking gifts or serving gifts, as suggested by 1 Peter 4:10,11. The two types of gifts operating together are indispensable for the Church's life and witness, the serving gifts authenticating the speaking gifts.

6. Scripture teaches that 'the manifestation of the Spirit' or 'grace' is given to each one, the context making it clear that these verses are referring to spiritual gifts (1 Cor. 12:7ff; Eph. 4:7ff). Ephesians 4:11 suggests that the same person may receive more than one gift, in this instance, gifts that equip them to be pastors and teachers; see also 1 Corinthians 14:13 where the gift-mix is speaking in tongues and the interpretation of tongues. The Bible does not set a limit on the number of gifts an individual may be given and a great variety of combinations of gifts is possible. It seems they are not necessarily all given at the moment of conversion; see Note 11, for example.

7. [From chapter by D.A. Carson entitled 'The purpose of signs and wonders in the New Testament' in M.S. Horton (Ed.), *Power Religion: The Selling Out of*

the Evangelical Church? (Sydney: ANZEA; Amersham-on-the-Hill: Scripture Press Foundation, 1992), p. 94. First published in the USA by Moody Press, 1992.]

8. See chapter entitled 'New Wine from the Vineyard' by John Schmidt in J.R. Coggins and P.G. Hiebert (Eds), *Wonders and the Word: An Examination of Issues Raised by John Wimber and the Vineyard Movement* (Winnipeg: Kindred, 1989), esp. p. 70. While affirming a number of Vineyard emphases, Schmidt is concerned about a tendency within this movement to overemphasise certain spiritual gifts, such as healing and exorcism.

9. The more we understand and recognise our dominant gift(s), the more likely we are to move into appropriate forms of ministry where it (or they) will be used effectively. It may sometimes be necessary to try ourselves out in certain jobs before we discover whether or not we have certain gifts. Failure in a certain area may indicate lack of giftedness in that area; however, it may simply be due to lack of training. Be prepared to give yourself to years of training if necessary in order to fulfil your calling and to develop your best gift(s).

10. Interaction with other Christians, especially those who are spiritually mature, is an essential part of the process of discovering our gifts; see Hillman, pp. 124–126. Many of the gifts have associated temptations that Satan can use in his attempts to undermine our effectiveness as the body of Christ. For example, leaders can be tempted to build a power base, healers to gather a personal following, prophets to become dogmatic. We need each other's insights and encouragement, and loving admonishment.

11. While specialisation of gifts is not taught in Scripture, it does seem to happen. Peter Wagner's experience is of interest here. In 1979 he wrote: 'I do not have the gift of healing . . . I would love to do it. I have prayed for many sick people and to date have seen no miracles'; see C.P. Wagner, *Your Spiritual Gifts Can Help Your Church Grow* (Ventura: Regal, 1979), p. 105. Then in 1984, he claims, he received the gift of healing; see C.P. Wagner, *How to Have a Healing Ministry Without Making Your Church Sick* (Eastbourne: Monarch, 1988), pp. 53f. He believes that God has given him a special ministry to people who have back or joint problems. Charles Kraft suggests (and it is an observation I have often thought might be true) that specific ministries are often related to a specific healing in that person's life; see C.H. Kraft, *Christianity with Power: Your Worldview and Your Experience of the Supernatural* (Ann Arbor: Vine, 1989), p. 137. I do not, however agree with his accompanying assertion that every Christian is 'gifted to heal'.

12. See Wagner, *Your Spiritual Gifts Can Help Your Church Grow*, pp. 218ff, 230ff.

13. This aspect of the gift of word of knowledge is frequently and, I believe, incorrectly equated with the gift of prophecy (described in the next section). Others, like Peter Wagner, present it as a subset of that gift. He wisely comments that '. . . the label one gives to the phenomenon makes little difference in the long run for the growth of the church' and, we might add, to the healing ministry; see Wagner, *Your Spiritual Gifts Can Help Your Church Grow*, p. 231.

See also Green, *I Believe in the Holy Spirit*, pp. 229f. I prefer to make a clear distinction between these two gifts to emphasise that true Christian prophecy consists of much more than revelations of the kind that are now almost obligatory in some healing ministries.

14. It is this aspect of the gift that John Wimber and Charles Kraft refer to in their writings and use extensively in their healing ministries. See J. Wimber with K. Springer, *Power Healing* (London: Hodder and Stoughton, 1986), pp. 202–206; Kraft, pp. 157–161.

15. [Clifford Powell, a Christian psychologist, tells how he is learning to listen to God and to use possible 'words of knowledge' wisely and sensitively as he counsels; see 'Hearing God in the helping role' in *On Being*, March 1993, pp. 10–13.]

16. Charles Kraft, who says that experience with words of knowledge has 'blown his mind' more than any other aspect of power ministry, recognises that they can be and frequently are misused. He writes: 'The fact that we cannot always be sure we hear God clearly should keep us from using formulas such as, "God says you have done such and such", or, "God has told me you are to do such and such". . . . I find it far more loving to understate my certainty than to risk overstating it . . . Presenting what may be God-given insight tentatively is especially important if the insight is in a sensitive area . . . such a gentle approach subtracts nothing from the effectiveness of the ministry.' Often, he suggests, asking a simple question (for example, 'Is . . . a problem to you?') can be a helpful way of presenting an apparent word of knowledge; see Kraft, pp. 157,159f.

17. They prophesied concerning the coming age (Rev. 22:6ff) and their message about contemporary events sometimes was specifically foretelling; see, for example, Acts 11:27f; 21:10f. Even then, such future references were given so that God's people might conform their lives to God's will in the present, never to satisfy idle curiosity or encourage a preoccupation with the future.

18. Michael Green lists a variety of ways in which prophecy may come. He includes a revelation or a picture revealed to a church member, a 'word of knowledge' or insight from God into the situation, teaching, tongues with interpretation, and Scripture (in the sense that we find ourselves directed to some surprising verse of Scripture that proves invaluable); see M. Green, *To Corinth With Love: The Vital Relevance Today of Paul's Advice to the Corinthian Church* (London: Hodder and Stoughton, 1982), pp. 76f. It is this latter form of prophecy that I have found particularly helpful. On several occasions in recent years as I have faced difficult treatment, my wife and I have been encouraged by some specific verse or truth, understood within its biblical context, in our daily reading. The relevance of such passages of Scripture has seemed striking to us at the time. This seems to be one essential mark of prophecy: it is a very specific word from God addressed to the contemporary need.

19. Glossolalia can occur as a purely psychological response to religious emotion, Christian or non-Christian and in western and non-western societies. It may even be satanic and opposed to Christ (1 Cor. 12:1–3). Occasionally, it may be

an expression of non-religious emotion. It may be artificially induced in a group where it is encouraged and expected and where it gives status in that group. For example, the danger of counterfeiting the gift (by imitation) may be particularly strong when it is implied that those who do not speak in tongues are immature Christians or relatively ineffective in 'spiritual warfare' or praying for healing. See, for example, W.E. Mills (Ed.), *Speaking in Tongues: A Guide to Research on Glossolalia* (Grand Rapids: Eerdmans, 1986); J.P. Kildahl, *The Psychology of Speaking in Tongues* (London: Hodder and Stoughton, 1972).

20. The Pentecostal movement at the turn of the century, which brought renewed interest in miraculous healing, taught as a key doctrine that speaking in tongues was necessary for every Christian as a sign that they had been baptised in the Spirit. Many associated with the Charismatic renewal and healing movements today have moved away from this view about speaking in tongues, as Michael Green reports in the revised edition of his book, *I Believe in the Holy Spirit*; see pp. 288f. There is, however, still a great tendency to overvalue the use of this gift. For example, when outlining a model 'healing procedure' John Wimber includes praying in tongues; see Wimber, *Power Healing*, pp. 216–217. He does acknowledge that in theory this is not necessary but counters this by saying, 'yet . . . everyone I have met who is effective in healing prayer speaks in tongues', thus giving the overriding impression that the gift of tongues is a prerequisite for effective healing prayer. He also cites Romans 8:26 to support his claim for the special efficacy of such prayer. While tongues no doubt can sometimes be involved, the reference in this passage is almost certainly to the regular experience of every Christian who agonises in inarticulate prayer: his or her inner longings are brought by the Spirit to the Father according to the will of God 'with groans that words cannot express'. It is not necessary to pray in tongues in order for the Spirit to intercede on our behalf!

21. Discernment thus precedes exorcism, which should not be attempted without it. Note that in Acts 16:16–18, Paul showed a gift of discernment when he identified particular behaviour as indicative of demon possession. In this passage discernment and exorcism are twin gifts. Peter apparently also exercised the gift of discernment, in the sense of discerning what is false, in his dealings with Ananias and Sapphira (Acts 5:1–10) and Simon the sorcerer (Acts 8:18–23).

22. Dr David Lewis assesses the gift of 'words of knowledge' in his analysis of John Wimber's ministry; see D.C. Lewis, *Healing: Fiction, Fantasy or Fact?* (London: Hodder and Stoughton, 1989), pp. 129–161. While many of Lewis' examples are unconvincing, there seems to be a core that represents extraordinarily accurate revelations. These are generally very specific information about, or insights into, the situation of someone quite unknown to the recipient of the 'word of knowledge'.

23. Green, *To Corinth With Love*, pp. 77f.

24. In Acts 21, Paul's friends speaking 'through the Spirit' tell him not to go to Jerusalem (v. 4), but this prophetic word seems to be contrary to the will of God

(see v. 14). If Paul had been relying on prophecy to help him discern the will of God he would certainly have been confused! There is also mystery in another sense. God's decrees, passed on through a human instrument, are not a mechanically fixed fate; there is always openness to unstated possibilities (Jer. 18:7–10). Prophecy is not a matter of fate; it is subservient to grace, as it is to love (1 Cor. 13:8–10), and it can never be dissociated from faith. The altogether free Father always remains free to respond in grace to the needs and cries of his children. But more importantly he takes the initiative of grace to achieve his good purposes.

25. See Appendix I.

26. In an open letter to John Wimber written in response to his book, *Power Healing*, Alan Cole writes: 'I do in particular appreciate your desire to draw every member of your congregation into a general healing ministry, and to set it in the context of regular worship and fellowship. That seems to me to be exactly the pattern in James, and indeed in the rest of the New Testament if I read it aright. But I hope you won't forget that some people still have special gifts and calling to healing, as you have, which other Christians should not expect: otherwise, they will be gravely disappointed'; see 'On Healing' in *Southern Cross* (a publication of the Anglican Diocese of Sydney), April 1987, p. 12.

27. This is illustrated in Scripture in references to the gift of prophecy. While only some Christians are prophets (1 Cor. 12:29), virtually every Christian may prophesy (Acts 2:17–18). In the early church, there were groups of prophets who prophesied regularly (because they had a special gift of prophecy), although any Christian could prophesy from time to time as the Spirit of God moved him or her to do so. Only some Christians have the special gift of visioning faith (1 Cor. 12:9; 13:2), but all Christians are to have faith. For almost all the special gifts, there are general exhortations in the New Testament addressed to the whole church; for example, encouragement (1 Thes. 5:14; cf. Rom. 12:8); serving (e.g. Gal. 5:13; cf. Rom. 12:7); giving (e.g. Acts 20:35; cf. Rom. 12:8).

28. John Koenig suggests that one of the purposes of God in giving us spiritual gifts may be to put a fence around our pride; see J. Koenig, *Charismata: God's Gifts for God's People* (Philadelphia: Westminster, 1978), pp. 130f. Each of us receives only one or a few of the gifts. Thus we have to learn to be satisfied with what God ultimately gives us, not think of ourselves more highly than we should, and we must humbly acknowledge that we cannot fulfil our God-appointed role in the life of the Church on our own (Rom. 12:3–6).

29. See Eph. 4:15f. It is a tragic irony that the church has let the issue of the exercising of gifts become an often explosively divisive element in church life and teaching. This is not right; it does not bring renewal to our nation or Christ's love to our world. If we accept that it is our unity that confirms the reality of Christ (Jn. 17:23), we must ask the question: how much has the spread of the gospel been hindered by our misunderstanding of the Spirit and the way he works?

30. Green, *I Believe in the Holy Spirit*, p. 206; what Paul is pleading for at Corinth, he says, is risk coupled with control and love.
31. By elders I mean spiritually mature members of the congregation who have been appointed to leadership roles, whatever name they may be given in the various denominations; cf. Jas. 5:14.
32. See Jas. 5:16. Many different gifts are relevant to the healing ministry. For example, gifted pastors, teachers and encouragers may also make important contributions. Every Christian does not have a special gift of healing (see 1 Cor. 12:30) or directly related gift but all, whether elders or not, can be involved in a general way and may even occasionally be used by God as channels of miraculous healing (see *Special and general gifts*, above).
33. Without this understanding, comparing ourselves with other Christians who have special gifts different from ours can easily leave us feeling inadequate and threatened. Expecting others to have the gifts we have is another common misunderstanding. For example, it would be very inappropriate for those with special gifts of healing or the gift of speaking in tongues to give the impression that every other Christian should be able to do as they do, especially if they were to suggest (or unwittingly imply) that failure was a sign of some underlying spiritual problem or inadequacy.

Chapter 5

Casting Out Demons: A Biblical Perspective

Human beings are spiritual beings. We cannot live in a totally non-spiritual environment. Consequently, the secular materialism of western society over the last few decades has left us in a kind of spiritual vacuum. One response of the secular world has been to turn to the occult. We see its influence in everything from a reviving interest in cults that openly claim to worship Satan to the popularity of horoscopes and occult-based board games. Ghosts, spirits, mediums, demonic possession, 'exorcism' and Satanism are common themes in literature, music, films and TV shows. As though reflecting this trend, Christians too are now inclined to give more credence to the power of demonic forces than in previous generations.[1] In some ways this is perhaps timely – it is important for the Church to adopt an appropriate biblical stance on both demonology and exorcism – but it has also led to a degree of paranoia over such things. In particular, it has led to a disturbing tendency among some involved in the healing ministry to exaggerate the incidence of demonic possession (or demonisation) and the need for 'deliverance'.

The New Testament shows Jesus' ministry and death as a battle against personal evil forces. Although Christ triumphed over these forces in his death and resurrection, they remain active. One symptom of the continuing power of Satan is demonic possession. Exorcism, that is, casting out or delivering people from evil spirits, was clearly a ministry of the early Church (in New Testament times and beyond) and demon possession is a reality that missionaries in non-Christian cross-cultural situations have always had to confront.[2] Nevertheless, throughout much of the twentieth century, interest in these phenomena in the western Church has almost exclusively been associated with the Pentecostal and Charismatic movements. Now it appears that many within Evangelical churches are being challenged to re-evaluate their position. Evangelicals traditionally reject the liberal theology that dismisses the supernatural (both good and evil) in Scripture and history; they have always believed in the miracles of the Bible. Now many are becoming more open to present-day miraculous healing and ministries of healing. For some at least, this has also meant adopting a whole range of teachings on demonology.

In widely read and frequently quoted books, at teaching seminars held all over the world and in the Vineyard ministries he has established, John Wimber has placed great emphasis on healing the demonised, which he presents as a major aspect of the healing ministry and of spiritual warfare generally.[3] He is not necessarily the originator of all of the ideas he presents, of course, but he has been a very effective disseminator. I must admit that I am deeply concerned about some of the teaching he has popularised.

I want to make it clear that I affirm Wimber's dedication and enthusiasm and his ability as a communicator and motivator. I respect his integrity and good intentions. Nevertheless, I do not believe that every aspect of his ministry has been helpful.[4] On the one hand, he has been used by God to encourage many within the Church to become open to the miraculous working of God's Spirit in our time. As a result of his ministry, at least in part, the Church has begun to break free from the excessive intellectualism that has held it captive for too long. On the other hand, his anti-intellectualism and, particularly, his lack of expertise as a biblical scholar have allowed him to accept uncritically and include in his teaching some concepts that are potentially damaging to the Church.

It is in the area of his teaching on demonology that this problem is most apparent.[5] Ironically, this is also an aspect of the healing ministry that especially needs the undergirding of a sound biblical theology in order to protect both those who minister and those who receive ministry.

OLD TESTAMENT CONCEPTS

Biblical scholars[6] stress the contrast between the lack of emphasis on demons in the Hebrew Old Testament and the emphasis on them seen later in both Greek and Judaistic traditions. In Greek popular belief the world was full of demons, beings between gods and men. They were spirits of the dead or ghosts and their work could be seen 'in the disasters and miseries of human fate. Through natural catastrophes they shook the cosmos. Above all they made men sick or mad.'[7]

The Old Testament discourages such a preoccupation with demons. Its focus is always on the one and only true God, Yahweh. For example, in the first chapter of Genesis, the heavenly bodies are simply called 'luminaries'. This is in marked contrast to the beliefs of surrounding nations, who looked on them as demons to be feared and honoured. Similarly, in the Old Testament angels are the mediators between God and humans, whereas other nations assigned this role to demons. Thus despite the enormous emphasis on demons in the Greek world:

> [The] whole sphere of demonology appears only on the margin in the OT [Old Testament] . . . It is particularly important to realise that the actual workings of destructive powers, which in the Gk. world are attributed to [demons], are in the OT ascribed to the rule of God . . . OT monotheism is thus maintained, since no power to which man might turn in any matter is outside the one God of Israel.[8]

While traces of the general popular belief in evil spirits are to be found in the Old Testament, there is no suggestion that individuals should have dealings with them even to ward them off.[9] In fact, conjuring up these 'spirits of the dead' was expressly forbidden.

Later, in the period between the Old and New Testaments and beyond, Judaism abandoned the strict reserve of Old Testament monotheism. Belief in demons became widespread, but the Jews never felt themselves as strongly threatened by them as did their neighbours. Demons came to be regarded as supernatural beings distinct from angels, not spirits of the dead. The scribes were steeped in belief in demons and had many names for them.[10]

NEW TESTAMENT TEACHING

In the New Testament, demons and evil spirits are mentioned more frequently than in the Old Testament, mainly in accounts of people who are demon-possessed; however, the New Testament continues basically in Old Testament succession. Generally there is a limited emphasis on demonic powers.[11]

While both pagans and Jews of that time 'tried to drive out the demons by magic, exorcisms and other magical practices, Jesus needed only his word of command (Mt. 8:16) . . . His dominion over these powers was a sign that the kingdom of God had come in his person (Mt. 12:22–28).'[12] And the New Testament gospel message is clear: through his death and resurrection Jesus Christ has already engaged the entire array of demonic forces in battle on our behalf and won! In this way the New Testament counters the fear of demons that had become prevalent in Jewish culture; it 'disappears because of faith in the triumph of Jesus Christ'.[13]

Thus, although the New Testament recognises the existence and ongoing influence of demons, it does not give them much emphasis. This strongly suggests that Christians of that day did not have the general interest in the powers of darkness that was evident in non-biblical writings. Nor did they have the commitment to the relative autonomy of demons of later Judaism; in the New Testament, demons are completely subject to Satan. Two kingdoms are clearly acknowledged, that of Satan and that of God, but there is 'no place for any special interest in the subordinate helpers in this conflict, whether angels on the one side or demons on the other'.[14]

The New Testament view is thus quite opposed to the Greek notion of attributing divine powers to demons and living in constant fear of them. Yet it does confirm the popular sense of something horrible and sinister in these servants of Satan. The New Testament bears witness to the victory won by Jesus over evil spirits – a victory that assures the Church that it will survive the temptations of the last days. We see that 'the [Old Testament] view of the demonic, namely, that the concern of Israel is with God alone, is fully maintained'.[15] In fact the New Testament revelation of God through Jesus Christ serves to clarify and expand this Old Testament truth.

The New Testament does teach that sickness is 'satanic' in the sense that it is aligned with Satan and against God's will for the universe. This is illustrated in Paul's description of his 'thorn in the flesh' as a messenger of Satan (see *Sickness and the fall* in Chapter 2). But Scripture does not teach that all sicknesses are the work of demons or due to 'demonisation' or demonic possession. In the New Testament, the latter term is used to indicate a very specific condition in which there is 'a destruction and distortion of the divine likeness of man according to creation. The centre of personality, the volitional and active ego, is impaired by alien powers which seek to ruin the man and sometimes drive him to self-destruction (Mk. 5:5). The ego is so impaired that the spirits speak through him.'[15]

SOME CURRENT IDEAS

There are important differences between the teachings of Scripture, as summarised above, and attitudes to the demonic associated with some contemporary healing ministries. An obvious point of difference is the current tendency to place strong emphasis on demons, which clearly conflicts with the restraint of both the Old and New Testaments. In his book, *Power Healing*, John Wimber strongly affirms – on what he believes are biblical grounds – the need for members of the kingdom to do battle with evil (including the devil and his demons) until Christ's return.[16] He claims that Christians are 'called to liberate territory for Jesus Christ, to take back ground from deceiving spirits who speak through hypocritical liars (1 Tim. 4:1–2)'. Exorcism (deliverance) is seen as an important part of this kingdom ministry. He acknowledges that 'the kingdom of Satan was decisively defeated through Jesus' death and resurrection' but also asserts that 'as we succeed in this warfare, the victims of Satan's power are released and the time for the ending of Satan's dominion and for the establishment of God's rule on earth comes near'.

I must admit that I have serious problems with Wimber's interpretation of Scripture on these issues. For example, 1 Timothy 4:1–2 is not a directive 'to take back ground' from deceiving spirits, as he teaches, only a warning about being misled by the hypocritical liars whose thinking is being influenced by them. The suggested remedy is sound teaching (v. 6), not exorcism!

I have a deep concern that such teaching may be creating confusion. It tends to obscure the fundamental scriptural truth that, although we are still living in a world where the kingdom of God is opposed by the kingdom of Satan, the outcome of this spiritual war is already decided. *Through Christ, through his death and resurrection, Satan and his demonic forces have already been defeated.* Waging and winning this particular battle is not up to us; victory for the kingdom of God does not depend on successful 'power encounters' between Christians and demons.

Like John Wimber, many involved in healing ministries give strong emphasis to dealing with demons. For example, Peter Wagner also believed it was necessary to include a chapter on demons in his book on healing because he considers that anyone who begins a healing ministry will sooner or later probably be confronted with demons.[17] Charles Kraft suggests that 'deliverance' ministry should be 'a normal part of our seeking to do the works of Jesus' in a context that indicates he is encouraging every Christian to be involved.[18] With deliverance ministry being promoted so enthusiastically, we need to remember that ministering to people who are under the evil influence of Satan (or releasing the 'oppressed') does not necessarily mean delivering them from demons.[19] Sometimes it may mean taking steps to alleviate a situation of injustice or abuse. And always at its heart is the gospel message about the Son of God who truly sets us free (Jn. 8:36). Through his death and resurrection, he offers freedom from the oppression of Satan himself. Generally, we are to pray *for* people in need of help, not *against* Satan and his demons.[20] Jesus' prayer for his disciples was not a confrontation with Satan to ward off his attacks on them, but a request to the Father that they be protected from the evil one (Jn. 17:15).

In recent years, many Christians seem to have become quite fascinated by demons and demonology. We read about hierarchies of evil spirits, with lists of names of demons assigned to specific aspects of temptation or destruction.[21] Some argue for the existence of territorial spirits, spirits allotted to specific geographical regions, and the need for Christians to confront them as part of spiritual warfare.[22] Once again we are in an area that is full of conjecture and confusion. Scripture teaches clearly that a demonic host exists, but there is no valid biblical basis whatsoever for such detailed descriptions. Great caution is needed when dealing with this extra-biblical teaching.

I am very concerned when I hear of twenty-week courses being run by some churches on hierarchies of demons and how to deliver people from them. It did not take Satan that long to work out how much damage he could do by moving the focus of Christians away from the living Christ and the power of his Spirit towards himself and his cohort. I know of one church in which the well-meaning pastor became involved in deep conversation with the very demons he was attempting to exorcise. He summoned them, talked to them, listened to them and passed on the information he received to others. As a result his life and the lives of the young people he led were shattered. A church was split, families were destroyed, faith was extinguished and individuals were left psychologically scarred. It is as though this church, through pastoral error, had opened itself to deceptive and dangerous teaching from the father of lies himself.

I cannot say it too strongly – Christ should always be the focus of our ministry. He is the enabling power, he is the all-wise, all-loving leader in our work for him and his words are there in Scripture for our feeding. In a ministry of exorcism we ignore this at our peril. When he ceases to be at the heart of what we do in his name, we set ourselves adrift from our safe anchor and we are free to be taken wherever Satan chooses – always away from God and towards our destruction.

There is much about the subject of principalities and powers of evil that we do not understand. There are mysteries that may never be resolved in the present age. What we do know is that Jesus, in training the carefully selected band of apostles who were to establish his church (Lk. 6:13; Acts 1:2), did not teach them a methodology for directly waging war on Satan, demons or territorial spirits. He simply commissioned them to heal the demon-possessed, if they came across someone so afflicted, just as he himself had done. There is therefore no biblical precedent for many of the approaches to 'deliverance' and 'spiritual warfare' now being advocated as part the healing ministry in many churches.

I am not suggesting that Christians will never be called on to confront the forces of darkness in the name of Jesus in a specific way. To deny that possibility would be presumptuous and unwise. And if we are placed in this position we should be prepared to respond appropriately.[23] Certainly, we all need to 'resist the devil' when we are tempted. There does not, however, seem to be any biblical support for teaching that promotes actively seeking prayer encounters with demons as an essential part of Christian discipleship and the key to a successful healing ministry.[24] Again the main problem is one of overemphasis.

DEMON POSSESSION OR DEMONISATION

Scripture speaks of people being demon-possessed (Gk. *daimonizomai*). Many prefer to use the term 'demonised' instead because demons never have absolute control (possession); people always retain a degree of free will. Sometimes 'demonised' is used in a sense that seems to be equivalent to the New Testament idea of 'demon-possessed'. For example, members of the missionary organisation SIM define demonisation as 'an evil spirit taking control of someone in such a way that the evil spirit speaks through or otherwise affects the faculties or person of that individual'.[25] In many other contexts, however, it seems to be given a much broader meaning. Because of this, I prefer to use the term 'demon possession' when referring to the phenomenon described in the Bible, without implying complete loss of the individual's free will.

Some are now teaching that there are degrees of 'demonisation' ranging from mild to severe, a teaching which has serious implications. According to John Wimber,[26] in the 'severe' form (which may be described as demonic attack, assault or possession) evil spirits reside in and take over 'almost complete control of the person at will, even blotting out his consciousness', frequently giving unusual strength, projecting a new personality in him, a strong opposition to Jesus, speaking with alien voices and languages and producing immorality. This description is strongly reminiscent of New Testament accounts of demon possession and parallels the SIM definition of demonisation. Wimber admits that such cases are comparatively rare. More frequently, he says, people are 'moderately' demonised: suffering demonic influence, oppression, obsession or subjection.

Others, building on such teaching, present demonisation as a continuum ranging from low to high levels of affliction. For example, Charles Kraft says he finds it helpful to list 'demonic attachment' on a scale of 1 to 10. He claims that Jesus cast out demons with a strength of attachment at a level of 9 or 10, whereas most cases he regularly encounters are in the 1–3 category. He thus implies that demonisation can be a very subtle process.[27] In marked contrast to such teaching, the Bible presents demon possession as a category not a continuum. People are either possessed by a demon or demons (Gk. *daimonizomai*) or they are not; no one is ever described as being mildly or moderately possessed. So we find another aspect of teaching on demons which, although it has no biblical foundation, is being widely promoted and accepted as part of the healing ministry.

CAN CHRISTIANS BE DEMONISED?

On this question we again have a variety of viewpoints, with ambiguities in terminology no doubt adding to the confusion. A growing number in the healing ministry teach that Christians, as well as non-Christians, can be 'demonised'[28] but there is considerable disagreement about this.[29] Howard Brant sums up the SIM position as follows: 'Not all of us are agreed as to the degree to which evil spirits can affect believers . . . But no one would doubt that Satan and his demons do have power to influence believers, at least to the degree of serious temptation (Act 5:3ff).'[30]

We cannot dismiss the possibility that a Christian may be affected in some way by demonic influence. Presumably Satan uses many different strategies in his destructive attempts to lead believers away from God. The Bible, however, does not provide any clear example of a believer being demon-possessed or demonised and therefore in need of this kind of deliverance.[31] There is certainly no biblical foundation for teaching that demonisation of Christians (requiring casting out, 'rebuking' or otherwise confronting demons) is a common occurrence. Especially alarming is the tendency to present demonisation as a mild to severe continuum rather than an all-or-nothing phenomenon. Inherent in this notion is the implication that Christians are susceptible to very subtle forms of demonisation, which is clearly not consistent with Scripture. Christians who accept such unbiblical teaching will be far more likely to regard themselves and others as demonised or open to demonisation. In this situation, demon possession is no longer a deep distant hole into which the few may fall; it becomes an endless deepening trench into which virtually any Christian may stumble.

Sinning and involvement in the occult are often presented as entry points for demons, for Christians as well as non-Christians. Being sinned against has also been suggested as an entry point, with claims that sexual abuse and alcoholism are especially influential in this process and that in this way demons are passed from one generation to another.[32] A damaging and widespread misconception associated with this teaching is that people whose relatives or ancestors have been involved in occult practices or other activities considered likely to lead to demonisation, are *inevitably* demonised and in need of exorcism.

The latter teaching on demonisation is also without biblical foundation, and many suffer unnecessarily because of it. (It may also lead to an unhealthy preoccupation with searching for skeletons in family closets!) Perhaps this is a form of oppression more serious than the demonic oppression it aims to relieve. We need to acknowledge the reality of demon possession and clearly teach the potential danger of involvement in the occult (and the New Age movement). At the same time, we should not come to the conclusion that an individual is demon-possessed or under some demonic influence merely because they have had some such involvement in the past.[33]

The fact that it is not possible to demonstrate from Scripture that believers can be demonised does not necessarily discount the possibility, but it should sound a warning against the unbiblical overemphasis on demonology and deliverance ministry that is affecting the Church. It can be a source of great tyranny and anxiety, especially to new or immature Christians, robbing them of assurance of salvation (see *Casting out demons with caution* in Chapter 11).

SIN, SICKNESS OR DEMONISATION

John Wimber teaches that Satan attacks us through temptations, opposition (preventing the spread of the kingdom by diversions such as counterfeit supernatural gifts, accidents and sickness) and demonisation (getting a grip on people's personalities or physical lives). The latter, he says, can lead to habitual patterns of immorality that are not changed by repentance and are sometimes accompanied by violence.[34] Most Christians would readily agree with Wimber that Satan can and does attack us. It is when attention is focused on specific demons held to be responsible for individual sins, sickness and emotional disturbances that many become wary – and with good reason. Alan Cole expressed such concern in an open letter to Wimber in 1987:

> I am quite sure that the Bible never teaches that there are hosts of different demons, with different names – separate demons of defiance, adultery, anger, fear, and so on – unless you are using the phrase purely as a vivid metaphor to mean that these are areas where Satan attacks us, and where we may be in bondage to him. If so, it is a dangerous and unbiblical metaphor to use, for simple souls will take it literally. If you were to 'divide up' Satan like this, you would have to 'divide' the Holy Spirit into spirits of holiness, power, love, sound mind, etc., in the same way.[35]

The unbiblical overemphasis currently being given to demons and demonisation is causing enormous confusion and unnecessary anguish.

This is of particular concern in the context of the healing ministry. Serious problems arise when it is too readily assumed that a demon (or assortment of demons) is the cause of a particular sickness, emotional problem or mental illness. In the Bible, we find that healing sometimes includes the casting out of demons, but often it does not.[36] Most illness is not due to demon possession, yet there are many Christians whose immediate response to illness is to rebuke the demon causing it. Some even view going to a doctor or taking medicine as yielding ground in the spiritual battle – a victory for the enemy.[37]

Charles Kraft correctly identifies emotional healing as an important aspect of the healing ministry. He says that 'many give [Satan] the opportunity to influence them by hanging onto such emotions as bitterness, unforgiveness, desire for revenge, fear and the like'.[38] He moves far beyond biblical teaching, however, when he claims a strong link between such 'inner problems' and problems with 'evil spirits' that require 'deliverance'. Once again it seems that giving the devil a foothold (Eph. 4:27) or succumbing to temptation is being incorrectly equated with demonisation. Confusion and fear abound when people start believing that certain emotions (such as bitterness, fear, anger) place the individual at high risk of demonisation. Some immature Christians exposed to such teaching live in a continuous state of tension: if I feel 'good' emotions I have God's protection, but if I feel 'bad' emotions (sometimes equated with sinning) then Satan or his demons can attack and hurt me or those I love. They have misunderstood, of course, but misunderstandings like this happen very easily when we focus too much on demons – especially to people who are emotionally unstable, anxious or superstitious. Believing that some emotions are intrinsically sinful and may be signs of demonisation also leads to unhealthy denial or suppression in some individuals.

In emotionally overstimulating environments where people are encouraged to abandon their objectivity and open themselves to subjective impressions, it is not uncommon for unusual behaviour to manifest itself. This is especially likely in situations where this has happened before and there is an expectation that it may happen again. Such behaviour may appear quite extreme and frightening at times both to the person concerned and to the average observer. For example, there may be shaking, crying or screaming, overwhelming feelings (fear, rage, jealousy, etc.), a desire to vomit, or the sensation of being paralysed or unable to stand. Such phenomena are sometimes observed by professional counsellors, psychologists and psychiatrists – both Christian and non-Christian in the course of their work.[39] Sometimes, of course, they may indicate demon possession or be observed during genuine exorcism, but it is important to realise that they can occur in the non-demon-possessed, in apparently psychologically healthy people without psychotic disorders. The unusual behaviour I have described certainly does not constitute proof of demon possession (or 'severe demonisation') and, for most people, casting out demons is not the appropriate response. In fact, many Christians who believe they have experienced 'deliverance' may not have been 'demonised' in the first place.

Many Christian psychiatrists and psychologists recognise demon possession as one possible cause of mental illness, but most would acknowledge that such cases are encountered only rarely and that diagnosis is difficult.[40] If teaching on this topic becomes distorted to the point where it is implied that all or most mental illness is a sign of demonisation, it can add immeasurably to the torment of sufferers and their families. It can also hinder the therapeutic process by preventing them from owning the true nature of the problem.

We can be reasonably certain that a person who is demon-possessed will exhibit sinful behaviour, but this does not mean that someone who is sinning is necessarily 'demonised'. Regarding sin as a sure sign of 'demonisation' is perhaps the most dangerous trap we can fall into through improper emphasis on demonisation. I believe that Wimber and others are unintentionally leading people towards this trap with unbiblical teaching about demons that tends to obscure the clear-cut biblical distinction between yielding to Satan's attacks in temptation and demon possession. The reality is that the Christian life is more about asking for grace to overcome temptations than praying against Satan and his demons or delivering people from them. I agree with Howard Brant's comments on this issue:

> We know of those who see demonic manifestations in all sorts of sins and shortcomings of the flesh. But we see no Biblical precedent for casting out demons of anger, lust, hatred of one's mother-in-law, etc. We know of deep crippling damage which has been done to Christians who have been dealt with in this way. We believe that the Biblical method for dealing with such sins is to repent and confess them to God. Any other teaching relieves sinners of their personal responsibility to confess their own sins to God (1 Jn. 1:9).[41]

In much present day teaching on demonisation I hear echoes of the garden of Eden: Adam blamed Eve, Eve blamed the serpent (Gen. 3:12,13). We can blame the demon who made us do it. From the very beginning, Satan has been using this ploy to keep people from owning their sin. Perhaps it is better to acknowledge that it was normal people like the Pharisees and Judas – not the demonised or demon-possessed – who were, and are, Satan's instruments of crucifixion.[42] Non-demonised people who give in to Satan's temptations are capable of every imaginable evil. Furthermore, the Bible teaches that evil thoughts come from the heart, not any external source.[43] We need to encourage accountability to God and each other, not victim mentality. On the other hand, it is very important that we recognise the reality and the seriousness of genuine cases of demon possession if we are confronted with them in ministry.

FINDING A BALANCE

In attempting to adjust our secular western world view to include the supernatural (see Chapter 3), we can easily overreact and give the supernatural (including demons) too much importance, adopting a primitive world view that is more animist than Christian. This may include being too ready to attribute sin, sickness or emotional disturbance to demons. Howard Brant provides some extreme examples:

> If we are not careful, we can become like the animist who sees spirits behind everything. The copy machine doesn't work; so you need to cast out the demon. You run the red light because the devil made you do it. And worse, you are ticketed by a policeman – a messenger of Satan to buffet you! This kind of thinking gives altogether too much emphasis to the demonic. It causes one to treat every natural phenomenon as if it were of diabolic origin.[44]

We live in a society obsessed with finding quick and easy solutions to complex problems. The 'instant fix' approach of driving out demons as the solution to all our difficulties may thus have particular appeal in our day.

Some present day notions of 'spiritual warfare' are dangerously close to dualism, a serious theological error. Dualism depicts two 'original forces', forces of good (led by God) and forces of evil (led by Satan) locked in eternal combat, and gives the impression that they are both equally powerful . . . Each can lose and gain ground, and the battle can go either way.[45] John Wimber does not want to teach dualism[46] and he repeatedly emphasises Jesus' triumph over Satan on the cross. [47] Nevertheless, a great deal of the teaching on spiritual warfare presented by him (and others) invites dualistic thinking. For example, we read: 'The expulsion of demons [in deliverance ministry] is a form of power encounter in which the kingdom of Satan is driven out by the kingdom of God'.[48] The growing emphasis on the notion of 'claiming territory' for God's kingdom is fraught with the same danger. The eminent theologian G.C. Berkouwer sounded a warning about this kind of thinking long before the present resurgence of interest in spiritual warfare. Describing the ease with which we may fall into the error of dualism, he wrote:

> [A] dualistic tendency may crop up in our thinking despite our rejection of every formal "dualism". This happens whenever the antithesis of God and evil is unconsciously set forth or experienced in a dualistic way. The idea of an "antithesis" may cause us, involuntarily, to think in terms of two "powers". These may be conceived of as unequal in theory but completely competitive in practice. Indeed, this tendency is present whenever we are struck by the apparent omnipotence or the infinite "scope" of the kingdom of darkness . . . The peril is then that we succumb to the hypnotic "powers" of evil and the curse of its ravages . . . Thereby we forget that something absolutely decisive has already taken place in this struggle . . . One could say that this battle still has an impressive scope and is loaded with wide and cosmic implications; but . . . *God's decision in the history of salvation has already been made.* For that reason the demonology of the New Testament is radically different from a dirge on the demons or a "demonization" of our living.[49]

When we begin to focus too much on Satan and his associates, our focus moves away from Christ. John Wesley, who often preached very strongly about sin, had to tell some of his followers that an overemphasis on sin was unhelpful. Similarly, while it is appropriate to recognise the fact of demons and their evil influence, it can be decidedly unhelpful to encourage an overenthusiastic interest in their activities. This could be done, for example, by running long courses on demonology or promoting an unhealthy interest in them through the way we write about them. All Christians are faced with a dilemma: '. . . on the one side, if we ignore our enemy, we cannot wage war effectively. But on the other, if we become unduly preoccupied with these issues, we will find ourselves detracted from our ultimate purpose or embroiled in paralyzing controversies.'[50]

In summary, we find a strong tendency in the teachings and practice of many involved in healing and deliverance ministries to depart from Old and New Testament restraint. Their overemphasis on demons may easily cause widespread unbiblical fear of demons especially among the young or immature, the superstitious or the unstable. In particular, their un-biblical teaching that Christians not only *can* be demonised, but frequently *are*, has far reaching consequences. The tyranny that it may bring to the vulnerable Christian is aggravated by teaching, in addition, that demonisation can be so subtle a process that 'most people who are demonised are not aware of it'.[51] Such teaching also shifts our focus away from the issue of sin as disobedience to God, which requires repentance and forgiveness, and away from the importance of the cross and the gospel of Christ for the individual. Such personal issues can easily seem insignificant when viewed in the perspective of a mighty cosmic battle.

I am not denying the reality of the demonic or the place of an appropriate ministry of exorcism in a comprehensive healing ministry. Some in ministry, especially in areas where overt or covert Satan worship is rife (and this now includes western as well as non-western cultures), may need to be particularly alert to this reality. Generally, however, our bias should be towards reluctance to attribute demon possession rather than a readiness to accept it as the most likely explanation. We need to remember: 'Biblically, spiritual warfare includes both resisting the devil as well as standing firm in our faith (1 Pet. 5:8,9). Often our struggle [does not consist] so much [in] a deliberate focusing on evil powers in conscious resistance as in living a life of disciplined responsiveness to the Lord, who has power over them.'[52] Our major focus should be Christ himself, not the kingdom of darkness.

Notes

1. Consistent with this is the great popularity of Frank J. Peretti's novels, such as *This Present Darkness* (Westchester: Crossway, 1989) and *Piercing the Darkness* (Eastbourne: Monarch, 1990), which depict the effects on the lives of human beings of a war raging between demons and angels; the human characters are given key roles in determining the progress of this war. Note that these are novels and should be read as fiction, as appears to be the author's intention, not as theology.

2. See Acts 5:16; 16:18; 19:12. The theologian Origen writing in the early part of the third century records that demons were driven out of many sufferers 'without any curious magical art or sorcerer's device, but with prayer and very simple adjurations and formulas such as the simplest person could use'; see C. Brown, *Miracles and the Critical Mind* (Grand Rapids: Eerdmans; Exeter: Paternoster, 1984), p. 337; also pp. 6,66. A paper by Howard Brant, entitled *Toward an SIM [The Society for International Ministries] Position on Power Encounter*, highlights the need for those in missionary service today to maintain

an appropriate scriptural perspective when dealing with the demonic. It summarises the findings of a study group of missionaries and national church leaders, supported by a group of theologians and several prominent pastor-teachers. It is available from: SIM, P.O. Box 7900, Charlotte, NC, USA 28241-8819, or SIM Australia, Locked Bag 2, Taren Point, NSW, Australia 2229. This and all subsequent quotations used by permission.

3. See, for example, J. Wimber with K. Springer, *Power Healing* (London: Hodder and Stoughton, 1986), pp. 111–138, and *The Dynamics of Spiritual Growth* (London: Hodder and Stoughton, 1990), pp. 178–192.

4. For a thorough, objective yet compassionate assessment of John Wimber's ministry see J.R. Coggins and P.G. Hiebert (Eds), *Wonders and the Word: An Examination of Issues Raised by John Wimber and the Vineyard Movement* (Winnipeg: Kindred, 1989). See also L.B. Smedes (Ed.), *Ministry and the Miraculous: A Case Study at Fuller Theological Seminary* (Pasadena: Fuller, 1987) and R. Alan Cole's open letter to John Wimber and accompanying article, written in response to Wimber's book *Power Healing, in Southern Cross*, April 1987, pp. 12,13.

5. [Sadly, John Wimber passed away on 16 November 1997, following heart surgery. He was only 63. It is right that we acknowledge here the very positive contributions he made to the healing ministry and the life of the Church; see especially the chapter by John Schmidt entitled 'New Wine from the Vineyard' in Coggins and Hiebert, pp. 69–84. We do not mean to place the blame for every unhelpful and unbiblical teaching about demonology and spiritual warfare at his feet; that would be quite unfair. Nor should he be held responsible for other people's misunderstandings and embellishments of teaching he presented. In any case, there were significant changes in his teaching in his latter years. For example, Wimber acknowledged that certain aspects of the teaching he presented in *Power Evangelism* were 'wrong'; see discussions with Wimber reported by Phillip D. Jensen (in what seems an unnecessarily confronting manner) in an article entitled 'John Wimber changes his mind', *The Briefing*, Issue 45/46, 1990, pp. 3–6; available from St Matthias Press, PO Box 225, Kingsford, NSW, Australia 2032. Yet, because for many years his own ministry and the associated Vineyard ministries so effectively promoted an excessive interest in demonology, across denominational boundaries and across the world, he has certainly opened the floodgates for the distortions and hurts that have inevitably followed.]

Jensen comments: 'None of us has to be right 100% of the time in order to teach. But the teacher is judged with greater strictness for the damage that he can do. We teachers must be clear on the basics, ready to admit error, quick to correct and withdraw misleading ideas, and willing to take responsibility for our faults. We must work hard to be accurate and to be accurately understood' (p. 6). These comments are, of course, applicable to anyone in a leadership role in the Church.

6. See, for example, Warner Foerster in G. Kittel (Ed.), *Theological Dictionary of*

the New Testament, Vol. 2 (Eerdmans: Grand Rapids, 1964), pp. 1–20 and Hans Bietenhard in C. Brown (Ed.), *The New International Dictionary of New Testament Theology*, Vol. 1 (Grand Rapids: Zondervan, 1975), pp. 450–454. I am indebted to these scholars for many of the ideas presented in this and the following section.

7.　Bietenhard, p. 450.

8.　Foerster, p. 11.

9.　Foerster, p. 11. See also Peter Ralphs's doctoral dissertation, pp. 17–18 (full citation in Appendix II, Note 1). He sees 1 Samuel 16:14–23 as the closest the Old Testament comes to an example of exorcism. An evil spirit torments Saul, but he gains relief and the spirit leaves him when David plays his harp. However, the spirit is said to be from Yahweh and is described as coming on Saul intermittently rather than as possessing him. Moreover, the playing of the harp by David is hardly an exorcism but rather a primitive form of 'music therapy' which soothes Saul's mental agitation.

10.　See Bietenhard, p. 451. Reviewing the complex system of belief in demons recorded in documents of the period between the Old and New Testaments, Peter Ralphs reports: " 'Their major function [was thought to be] the implementation of all kinds of wickedness, immorality, natural disaster, deformity, disease and death." T. Sol. [Testament of Solomon, which probably reflects first century Judaism in Palestine] records the story of an attack by the demon Ornias on a boy . . . The demon Murder is responsible for attacking premature and newborn infants, inflaming limbs, inflicting the feet and producing festering sores . . . The female-shaped demon Obyzouth, like Murder, kills newborn babies, injures eyes, inflicts dumbness, destroys minds and makes bodies feel pain . . . certain demons, the thirty-six heavenly bodies, describe themselves as causing all sorts of [specific] sickness and disease. This listing of human illnesses, as caused by demons, shows the extent to which demons and their activity were related to the everyday problems of sickness and death'; see Ralphs, p. 67; this and all subsequent quotations used by permission.

11.　There is no belief in spirits of the dead and, for the first time, angels and demons are clearly identified as opposites; see Foerster, p. 16; Bietenhard, p. 452.

12.　Bietenhard, pp. 453f. Demons also possess knowledge about certain things which they must express when confronted by Jesus; see Foerster, p. 19.

13.　Bietenhard, p. 452.

14.　Foerster, p. 18.

15.　Foerster, p. 19.

16.　John Wimber's biblical justification for his approach to spiritual warfare is presented in a chapter entitled 'Healing the demonised'; see Wimber, *Power Healing*, pp. 114–117. It rests heavily on a questionable interpretation of the following passage: 'The reason the Son of God appeared was to destroy the devil's work' (1 Jn. 3:8). He cites this as evidence that the kingdom of God is destroying the kingdom of Satan, meaning that it is now in the process of destroying it. Later this thought seems to form the basis for his general thesis that Christians (who are under the reign of God's kingdom on earth) are to be active in destroying the kingdom of Satan (by casting out demons, etc). But surely 1 John 3:8 is referring to what Jesus Christ has already accomplished through his incarnation, life, death and resurrection and to the freedom from enslavement by sin and Satan that the believer experiences as a result. In a subsequent book, Wimber argues unconvincingly from Ephesians 6:12 that while Satan is the ultimate enemy in the spiritual battle, Christians are more likely to have to deal with 'low-level' demons; see Wimber, *The Dynamics of Spiritual Growth*, pp. 187f. Charles Kraft's presentation of views similar to Wimber's about the need for Christians to reclaim territory for the kingdom of God is no more convincing; see C.H. Kraft, *Christianity with Power: Your Worldview and Your Experience of the Supernatural* (Ann Arbor: Vine, 1989), pp. 109–110. There is more than a hint of dualism in this kind of teaching. It is as though we are influential participants in a great cosmic battle that is still raging between God and Satan and angels and demons. The fictional works of authors such as Frank J. Peretti (see Note 1) have probably also played a part in reinforcing such thinking.

17. See 'Demons at Home and Abroad' in C.P. Wagner, *How to Have a Healing Ministry Without Making Your Church Sick* (Eastbourne: Monarch, 1988), pp. 179–206.

18. Kraft, p. 128.

19. In the Bible, 'oppression' and related terms are not generally used to denote demonic attack. In most contexts, oppression means the unjust treatment of one individual or group of human beings by another (e.g. Acts 7:19,34; Jas. 2:6; also Lk. 4:18 cf. Is. 58:6, 61:1), although we do read of a woman 'kept bound' by Satan for eighteen years (Lk. 13:16) and of people 'under the power of the devil' being healed by Jesus (Acts 10:38).

20. For example, if satanists are holding a convention in our vicinity, our response could be to pray for each participant asking that they be enabled to see through Satan's deception and come to know Christ. Contrast this with the 'spiritual warfare' approach of directly confronting the powers of evil in the name of Jesus. The latter gives too much acknowledgment to Satan; the focus is away from the loving Father and the gospel of Christ.

21. At least some of these are purported to be compilations of information obtained from demons during exorcisms, surely an unreliable and dangerous source; see Wagner, pp. 202–203. We also find John Wimber making a strange distinction between dangerous 'chained' demons and those who roam freely; see Wimber, *Power Healing*, p. 119. This is more akin to Jewish and pagan belief about demons in New Testament times than to biblical teaching about them.

22. See, for example, Wagner, pp. 196ff. He claims that demonisation and exorcism are important aspects of 'power evangelism' and that territorial spirits may be responsible for blocking a response to the gospel in areas where people are especially resistant to evangelism. The examples he presents are open to a

variety of interpretations and do not prove his claims; on the other hand it would be impossible to disprove them. They simply go beyond the parameters of Scripture to which we should confine ourselves. See also Wimber, *The Dynamics of Spiritual Growth*, pp. 186f. His use of a passage about a vision given to Daniel (Dan. 10) to support the notion of territorial spirits and the need to wage spiritual warfare against them is highly speculative and questionable. In this passage, an awesome messenger from God mentions a 'prince of Persia' who resists him and also a 'prince of Greece' (vv. 13,20), but it does not teach unequivocally that they are evil spirits who have specific power over these territories. Moreover, there is no suggestion that Daniel himself is to have any special dealings with them. While it may sometimes be helpful in ministry to get to know the background of an area, including the places where Satan's influence is or has been strong, I see no biblical basis for teaching that each 'satanic stronghold' is associated with a particular territorial spirit(s), who must be cast out before ministry can be effective.

23. Paul's encounter with the spirit-possessed slave girl in Philippi (Acts 16:16–18) supports this statement. The ministry of exorcism should not be entered into lightly (see *Casting out demons with caution* in Chapter 11).

24. It is interesting to note that in Ephesians 6:10–20 where Paul reminds the Ephesians that they need to the 'put on the full armour of God' (v. 11) in their struggle 'against the powers of this dark world and against the spiritual forces of evil in the heavenly realms' (v. 12), there is no suggestion that they are to wage war against these forces in the sense of launching attacks on them. Their armour is defensive, not offensive. For example, it is to enable them to stand their ground (v. 13) or 'stand firm' (v. 14) against 'the devil's schemes' (v. 11) and to protect them from 'the flaming arrows of the evil one' (v. 16). Having put on their armour, they are requested simply to 'be alert and always keep on praying for all the saints' and for the effective proclamation of the gospel (vv. 18–19).

25. See Brant, p. 6; cf. Foerster's interpretation of New Testament usage already quoted (see Note 15).

26. Wimber, *Power Healing*, pp. 123–127. Alan Cole in his open letter to John Wimber (see Note 4) draws attention to both the 'good' and the 'ungood' in this book. Writing of his particular concern about the chapter entitled 'Healing the Demonized', he supports Wimber's preference for the term 'demonized' but questions his interpretation of this phenomenon: 'I think you have gone far beyond Scripture here . . . Of course I do not deny the possibility and at times actuality of partial or total demonization, but I think that you have enlarged the category somewhat by an over-literalistic interpretation of the wording of Scripture, which may at times be only general or metaphorical'; see Cole, p. 12.

27. Kraft, p. 129f; Kraft does not indicate how he assigns people to these categories and it is not clear how they relate to Wimber's 'severely' demonised category.

28. See, for example, Wimber, *Power Healing*, pp. 127–130; Kraft, p. 129f; Wagner, pp. 189–196.

29. Among those who disagree are the (Pentecostal) Assemblies of God Church (as reported by Wagner, p. 190) and many others who generally have a strong belief in demonic activity as a present day reality (see, for example, Cole, p. 12).

30. Brant, pp. 5,6. He adds: 'We resolutely deny that Satan or any evil spirit can possess a believer in the sense of ownership. Believers belong to God. Jesus knows his own (Jn. 10:14). No one can take them out of His hand (Jn. 10:28,29).' His report includes the experiences of SIM missionaries who witnessed evil spirits speaking through professing believers. It seems these people had become involved again with worshipping Satan. When they repented and confessed their sin, they were immediately released. There may be a parallel here with the experience of the Christian whose testimony of repentance from involvement in the occult is recorded below (see Note 33).

31. Note that there are claims to the contrary, for example, see Wimber, *Power Healing*, pp. 129f. If we carefully examine Wimber's examples from Scripture of believers who were demonised, we find that none supports his argument: Saul does not seem to be presented as a believer but as apostate (1 Sam. 16:14); the 'daughter of Abraham' (Jewish woman) healed by Jesus and described by him as having been 'kept bound' by Satan (Lk. 13:10–16) is clearly not a believer living in the light of Christ's death and resurrection; in any case, this 'binding' is not necessarily demonisation. His description of Judas as a believer who was severely demonised based on Luke 22:3 is unconvincing. Surely he is Scripture's supreme example of apostasy. Nor is he described as demonised. Peter (Lk. 22) is certainly a believer but Wimber's suggestion that he (Lk. 22:31f) or Ananias and Sapphira (Acts 5:1–11) were demonised has no scriptural basis. Note that acting under Satan's influence in the sense of yielding to temptation, is not equivalent to being demonised.

32. See, for example, Wimber, *Power Healing*, pp. 130–132.

33. Dealing with the consequences of past involvement in the occult does not always require directly rebuking Satan or demons. Note, for example, that the apostle Peter did not recommend exorcism for Simon the sorcerer; he described him as a 'captive to sin', who needed to repent and seek God's forgiveness (Acts 8:9, 22–23). The following testimony also illustrates this point. I use it with permission: 'Many years ago I was influenced to join a secret mystical society. It claimed to be seeking truth and love, and in my ignorance I thought it was of God. In later years as I matured as a Christian I realised Satan was in it, masquerading as an angel of light, and had nothing more to do with it. I had not received any church teaching about the occult, demons or deliverance ministry at that time or prior to the experience that followed. Several years later, alone in my home and about to set the table for Sunday lunch, I suddenly became aware that in the past, through initiations and rituals, I had actually bowed my knee and my heart to Satan. I was horrified, literally stopped in my tracks, by the enormity of this. As I stood with knives and forks in my hands, my heart cried out to God in spontaneous prayer: "Lord, forgive me. I didn't know what I was doing. You know I love you and want to serve you with my

whole heart. I completely and utterly renounce Satan and all his works. I would never knowingly give allegiance to him." Then I had such an overwhelming sense of the presence of God that I instinctively bowed my head in awe and reverence. My eyes were closed so I didn't really see anything, but I had the impression that the room no longer had a ceiling and that light was streaming down on me from God in benediction. Something fluttered up from me. I didn't hear anything, yet it seemed as though angels were singing and rejoicing. The moment passed and I continued to set the table for lunch.' Was this a deliverance from the effects of the occult? If so, it was one that took place without directly addressing Satan, without fuss or use of a formula, without fear and without any dramatic physical manifestations. The focus was always on God, and Christ was central because the experience arose out of a maturing Christian faith.

34. Wimber, *Power Healing*, pp. 120–122.
35. Cole, p. 12.
36. See Appendix II; also Wimber, *Power Healing*, p. 122.
37. From time to time I have been urged to stop medical treatment by well-meaning Christians who hold these views; see, for example, a letter quoted in part in R.J. Hillman with C. Chamberlain, *There is Hope: For Those Who are Ill and Those Who Care for Them* (Sydney: ANZEA, 1992), p. 8.
38. Kraft, p. 129.
39. Outside this legitimate and controlled therapeutic context, it would seem very unwise for leaders to set up conditions likely to induce such states. It is not necessary to do so in order to identify those who are truly demon-possessed, and under such conditions non-demon-possessed Christians may become highly vulnerable, emotionally and spiritually. In particular, while not fully in control and in a highly suggestible state, they may become more open to Satan's deception. For example, he may offer them his own 'words of knowledge' to lead them or their church down his destructive paths. We need to remember that the fruit of the Spirit includes self-control and also that such experiences are not self-validating (see *Testing the gifts* in Chapter 4).
40. John White, commenting on the difficulty of correctly diagnosing mental illness due to demon possession, writes: '. . . the problem is compounded by the fact that in much insanity, hallucinations and delusions are woven out of the raw material in our memories. If our thoughts include the demonic, then we will hear "demonic" voices when we become crazy or have delusions about demons in and around us'; see J. White, *Masks of Melancholy: A Christian Psychiatrist Looks at Depression and Suicide* (Leicester: Inter-Varsity Press, 1982), p. 30.
41. Brant, p. 6.
42. cf. comment by P.G. Hiebert in Coggins and Hiebert, p. 119.
43. Reviewing biblical teaching about sin, G.C. Berkouwer writes: 'We are referred to the heart of man as the wellspring from which his sins flow forth (Mk. 7:21). When we listen to the Scripture we hear of the ways of sin which proceed from the "inside" to the "outside" (Mk. 7:23; Mt. 23:25; Lk. 11:39;

Joel 2:13). Yet there is no trace of a self-excuse in this kind of a statement . . . the reference to the "heart" eliminates the concept of an "origin" apart from man himself, for the heart is man in the center and the wholeness of his being . . . Precisely the heart of man is the "seat of his sin" and the gateway for expressing what is externalized in man's own sinful activity . . . No power of darkness causally "explains" our sin, and no inexorable force compels us to do evil . . . There is no unbounded power and work of the evil one; no seduction that is unrelated to the guilt of man . . . Only in our guilt and capitulation to the evil one is the power of evil irrepressible. Only in that way does an evil man become the "slave" to sin'; from G.C. Berkouwer, *Studies in Dogmatics. Sin*, Philip C. Holtrop, trans., © 1971 Wm. B. Eerdmans Publishing Company, Grand Rapids, Michigan; pp. 24f,112. This and all subsequent quotations reprinted by permission of the publisher; all rights reserved. See also Foerster's comments: '. . . the NT does not speak of individual seducing spirits . . . Evil thoughts come from the heart (Mt. 15:19) . . . To be sure, sin and the flesh are individual forces. Yet they do not come from without, like demons. They indicate the mode of existence of humanity itself, which is now sinful'; Foerster, p. 18.

44.	Brant, p. 12. And I know of one group of Christians who, on being plunged into darkness during Bible study, gathered in prayer over the spent light bulb. Happily, one down-to-earth member slipped out and bought a new one!

45.	G.C. Berkouwer devotes a whole chapter to this important topic in his book about sin. He writes: '. . . every dualism presupposes a fatal shadow which falls upon our world. That shadow is the shadow of an original evil in cosmic form, apart from man and apart from the sphere of his own responsibility. Thus the origin of sin lies in a lethal attack from the original "kingdom of darkness". That kingdom is set in opposition to the Father of majesty and his "kingdom of light". . . Dualism puts stress on man's fate, but not on his guilt'; see Berkouwer, pp. 70f.

46.	Wimber makes it clear that Satan is no god; see *Power Healing*, p. 117. He refers to him as a fallen angel, whose counterpart is the archangel Michael (cf. Rev. 12:7).

47.	See Wimber, *Power Healing*, p. 115 and *The Dynamics of Spiritual Growth*, p. 115.

48.	Wimber, *Power Healing*, p. 242.

49.	Berkouwer, pp. 71f.

50.	Brant, p. 3.

51.	See Wimber, *Power Healing*, p. 136. Prior to stating this he points out (pp. 132–136) that, despite the grim picture he has painted concerning the prevalence and power of demons, Christians have been given adequate resources for the spiritual battle against them and refers at some length to Ephesians 6:10–18. His inappropriate use of this passage in connection with demonisation (he seems to confuse Satan's attacks in temptation with demonisation) appears to give his claims biblical authority. It reinforces the impression that any Christian may be (and is likely to be) demonised.

52.	Brant, p. 7.

Chapter 6

Holiness and Abundant Living

When Jesus healed, he offered healing to the whole person.[1] He pre-sented the possibility of a completely changed existence, a new and abundant life. For many people in our western society, the good life is equated with vibrant physical health, high self-esteem and a bountiful supply of money, pleasure and adventure. The abundant life that Jesus offers to those who follow him goes far beyond this. At its heart is the rediscovery of our true place in creation through a life of holiness lived in union with him.

If we are to be truly effective in our healing ministry we need to be aware that there is the closest possible link between holiness, wholeness and health. In the Bible 'health' means well-being, soundness, life, strength and salvation, wholeness plus holiness – human life infused with the life of God and lived in close and constant relationship with him.[2] This is entirely consistent with the Bible's representation of the human person as a unity and totality. We are beings who cannot find wholeness apart from our creator God and the salvation and intimate relationship he offers through Jesus Christ. Although holiness does not necessarily ensure perfect health, it is an important yet often neglected aspect of the fullness of life proclaimed by Christ (Jn. 10:10). Before developing these themes I will present, in broad outline only, some biblical teaching about holiness.

WHAT IS HOLINESS?

The scriptural concept of holiness has many aspects and involves every level of our being: our thinking, our emotional responses and our actions. In essence it means being set apart, but it also means living a holy (that is, Christlike) life. 'Having at its root the thought of separation or apartness, it signifies, first, all that marks out God as set apart from men and, second, all that should mark out Christians as set apart for God', writes James Packer.[3] Referring to the latter aspect of holiness, he continues:

> Holiness, which means being near God, like God, given to God, and pleasing God, is something believers want more than anything else in this world . . . [It] is the fruit of the Spirit, displayed as the Christian walks by the Spirit (Galatians 5:16,22,25) . . . In relation to God, holiness takes the form of a single-minded passion to please by love and loyalty, devotion and praise. In relation to sin, it takes the form of a resistance movement, a discipline of not gratifying the desires of the flesh, but of putting to death the deeds of the body (Galatians 5:16; Romans 8:13). Holiness is, in a word, God-taught, Spirit-wrought Christlikeness, the sum and substance of committed discipleship, the demonstration of faith working by love, the responsive outflow in righteousness of supernatural life from the hearts of those who are born again.[4]

The following is a review of some of the teaching about holiness found in the Bible, organised under headings which refer to particular aspects of holiness.[5]

Begins with commitment

When Paul calls his friends in the church in Rome to present their bodies as 'a living sacrifice, holy and acceptable to God' (Rom. 12:1 *RSV*), he uses the familiar language of Jewish ritual but with new meaning. Instead of offering an animal as a dead sacrifice, they are to offer their bodies (themselves) as living (alive from the dead!) sacrifices. In Jewish ritual, the animal sacrifice was regarded as being handed over to God; so 'holy' signifies belonging to God. Furthermore, only unblemished animals were acceptable sacrifices. Thus the reference here is to holiness in its widest meaning: dedication and purity.

This offering of oneself as a 'living sacrifice' is an act of unreserved commitment, without which there can be no true holiness.[6] Packer writes: 'All the Christian's human involvements and commitments in this world must be consciously based on his awareness of having been separated from everything and everyone in creation to belong to his Creator alone.'[7]

Built on justification

Paul's plea for commitment and holiness follows on from his teaching about justification (Rom. 3–8, esp. 3:23–26; 4:5–8; 5:18,19). For Paul, justification means God's act of forgiving the sins of the guilty and regarding the guilty sinner as just or righteous. It is given freely through faith in Christ and cannot be earned by good works. It results from the death of Jesus, God's sinless Son on our behalf, as our representative – his shed blood redeems us, that is, frees us from the condemnation and death penalty our sin should bring.[8] It is as though the judge in the law court acquits the defendant, declaring him righteous in his eyes – as if without blemish (see above) – not because he is innocent but because his penalty has already been paid.

Thus justification depends on God's grace, Christ's death and on faith, not on our goodness (or good works). Until we get right with God (are justified) by acknowledging what Christ has done for us, we can never live holy lives. Justification is the *declaration* that a sinner is right with God, that is, has come into a right relationship with him, it does not mean making the sinner right with God in the sense of a transformation to a holier state. The latter process is known as sanctification. Our growth in holiness (or sanctification) is the result of justification, never the cause.

I am aware that holiness is a concept about which Christians have differing doctrinal views and therefore some may disagree with what I am saying at this point. I am convinced from Scripture, however, that holiness is an ongoing process, not (as some have taught) a state acquired instantaneously as a 'second blessing' subsequent to conversion.[9]

Based on union with Christ

The life of holiness involves much more than this legal 'no longer liable for sin' declaration from God. It is the justified sinner's personal relationship with Christ – a matter of union with him. This is the theme that Paul introduces immediately after passages about justification when describing the way of holiness in his epistle to the Romans.[10] The life of holiness is not primarily about following a set of commands. It is a new state of being that results from our being one with the crucified and risen Lord.

'For if we have been united with him in a death like his, we shall certainly be united with him in a resurrection like his', writes Paul. We are to count ourselves 'dead to sin and alive to God in Christ Jesus' (Rom. 6:5,11 *RSV*). As Packer comments:

Any idea of holiness as manful refusal to do all that one most wants to do must be dismissed as the unregenerate mind's misunderstanding. True holiness . . . is the Christian's true fulfillment for it is the doing of that which, deep down, he now most wants to do, according to the urging of his new, dominant instincts in Christ. The fact that few Christians seem to be sufficiently in touch with themselves to appreciate this does not alter its truth.[11]

Brought about by the Holy Spirit

Holiness is not a matter of self-effort. The life of holiness is completely dependent on the Holy Spirit.[12] As Paul says: 'And we all, with unveiled face, beholding the glory of the Lord, are being changed into his likeness from one degree of glory to another; for this comes from the Lord who is the Spirit' (2 Cor. 3:18 *RSV*). This difficult verse is really a description of the life of holiness. It refers to the progressive change which the Holy Spirit brings about in the life of the Christian. Our part in this is to make ourselves available for change and instruction and to accept the discipline of developing 'holy habits' as the Spirit enables us.[13]

As we open ourselves to him, he changes our hearts and the way we view our world, affecting every aspect of our lives. He initiates these changes in many different ways. For example, he may influence us through personal prayer or reflection, study of the Word or the sacrament of communion, through our own or another's circumstances, or through the ministry of members of his body. He will constantly delight and surprise us with the creativity of his interaction with us.

Bound up with moral law

Jesus assured his followers that he did not come to abolish the Law and the Prophets (the guiding principles by which God's people had previously lived) but to fulfil them, and he warns against relaxing even the least of the commandments (Mt. 5:17–19).[14] Thus, although the formerly-binding ceremonial law was fulfilled and made redundant by Christ, the moral law remains. Indeed, the ten commandments are affirmed in the

New Testament with deeper insights. Holiness is not a matter of outward conformity to laws or commandments, however, not even those given by God. Holiness is bound up with obedience to the law that is written on the heart of every Christian (Rom. 2:15; cf. Jer. 31:33).[15] United with Christ and in the power of the Holy Spirit, we live by the inner spirit of the law. This is much more demanding (Mt. 5:21–22,27–28), but also much more liberating, than the written law interpreted and followed literally. As Packer reminds us: 'Increase in holiness means, among other things, an increased sensitivity to what God is, and hence a clearer estimate of one's own sinfulness and particular shortcomings, and hence an intensified realization of one's constant need of God's pardoning and cleansing mercy.'[16]

Blessed by love

As Christians we are to understand the law in the context of love and grace. All of the moral law can be reduced to two commandments: to love God and to love one's neighbour as oneself (Mk. 12:29–31). The Old Testament presentation of the ten commandments indicates that the children of Israel are to keep them out of gratitude for God's grace in redeeming them from Egypt (see Ex. 20:2–17). Similarly, the life of holiness is a life of love and gratitude for grace, the grace of justification – God's free acceptance and forgiveness of the undeserving sinner. Jesus said: 'If you love me, you will obey what I command' (Jn. 14:15). The love for him, which stems from being in union with him, will be reflected in a desire to please him, a willingness to obey his commandments and an openness to the working of his Spirit in our lives. These are all aspects of holiness. Love for God and others is the chief characteristic of the life of holiness (see 1 Cor. 13).[17]

HOLINESS BRINGS BLESSING

It is my understanding from Scripture that, in a general sense, holiness (that is, living the abundant life that Christ offers) promotes health in every aspect of our being and facilitates healing. In other words, holiness and wholeness are inextricably linked. There are exceptions to this general rule, however, as Scripture makes clear. Indeed, as I emphasise throughout this book, unless these exceptions are acknowledged we cannot have a balanced healing ministry. For example, Job was a holy man who succumbed to illness (Job 1:1; 2:3,7); Jesus taught the disciples that a particular case of blindness was not due to sin (Jn. 9:3); Paul's thorn in the flesh was allowed to persist (2 Cor. 12:7). It was not for want of holiness that these illnesses occurred or persisted. As I will explain later, holiness and suffering are also linked.

We must acknowledge, however, that the whole of Scripture abounds with teaching that indicates that the righteous are blessed and that sinners (eventually) suffer. Many Old Testament references to blessing need to be interpreted partly in terms of spiritual blessing. While they also need to be interpreted eschatologically (that is, in terms of the age to come), they must nevertheless be applied to present physical and material existence as well. In saying that, however, I want to make it very clear that I am not endorsing the seductive 'prosperity' doctrine that has attracted much attention in recent years. God is not bound to deliver health, wealth or other blessings in response to our good works, nor because we 'claim' them, no matter what Bible verses we recite, what formula we use when praying, or how much faith we muster. Holiness is the appropriate response to God's love, not the means of earning it. The many blessings we receive are an expression of his sovereign grace towards us, not a reflection of our worthiness.

A recurring theme in the book of Psalms, and in the Old Testament generally, is summarised in Psalm 1:

> Blessed is the man
>   who does not walk in the counsel of the wicked . . .
> Whatever he does prospers . . .
> Not so the wicked . . .
> For the Lord watches over the way of the righteous,
>   but the way of the wicked will perish.

The righteous are blessed and the wicked perish (see also Ex. 15:26, 23:22; Lev. 26:3ff; Ps. 128). The rest of the Bible is at pains to show that this is not a universal principle in the sense that it applies to every believer in every circumstance, but it remains a general principle.

It stands to reason that we must be better off living (as far as is possible in this fallen world) the lifestyle for which we were created: in relationship with God, in deeper and healthier relationship with others, our lifestyle reflecting our union with Christ in every aspect. There is now a wealth of literature showing a general correlation between an individual's choice of lifestyle and overall state of health, which I will not attempt to review here.[18] My present purpose is simply to affirm the general biblical teaching, first, that holiness enhances health and healing and, second, that neglecting God's call to holiness produces ill-health, as well as many of the ills of society, and can actually hinder the healing process (see Chapter 9).

The Old Testament book of Deuteronomy contains a list of blessings (and curses) promised by God to the children of Israel that are generally material in nature. For example, we read:

> All these blessings will come upon and accompany you
>> if you obey the Lord your God:
> You will be blessed in the city and blessed in the country.
> The fruit of your womb will be blessed,
>> and the crops of your land and the young of your livestock . . .
> Your basket and your kneading trough
>> will be blessed. (Deut. 28:2–51)

The close link between blessing and holiness, the ultimate aim, is made clear a few verses later: 'The Lord will establish you as his holy people, as he promised you on oath, if you keep the commands of the Lord your God and walk in his ways' (Deut. 28:9). Thus these material blessings have a condition: they flow from obedience – obedience that is an essential element of the life of holiness. Jesus himself follows this teaching of Deuteronomy when he says in the Sermon on the Mount: 'Seek first his kingdom and his righteousness, and all these things will be given to you as well' (Mt. 6:33). Commenting on this, one recent writer concludes:

> Indeed, it has to be so, because the good things of life come from the good and living God, and to cut oneself off from God is ultimately to cut oneself off from good things and from life. And it has to be so, for moral reasons: how could God ultimately let the world work in any other way? In the end Job has to be the exception and Deuteronomy the rule.[19]

It is nevertheless important that those involved in the healing ministry do not overlook examples of undeserved suffering in both the Old and New Testament. Both the righteous and the wicked suffer illness in this fallen world. An excellent treatment of the biblical material on this and related issues is presented in a book by Donald Carson, entitled *How Long, O Lord: Reflections on Suffering and Evil*, which I wholeheartedly recommend to you.[20]

HOLINESS MEANS SUFFERING[21]

The life of holiness the Spirit enables us to live is a life of blessing, love and peace (Gal. 5:22), but that does not mean it will always be easy.

Conflict is inescapable

Scripture makes it clear that 'everyone who wants to live a godly life in Christ Jesus will be persecuted' (2 Tim. 3:12). This means that there will be times when we are vigorously opposed.[22] Indeed when persecution does come, we ought, in a sense, to rejoice (Mt. 5:10–12; 1 Pet. 4:13), for here is the proof of God's work in us. (Note that Scripture is speaking of rejoicing in the ultimate hope that is ours, not about maintaining a perpetual smile on our faces despite our real feelings.) There is, however, no suggestion that we should be deliberately provoking persecution or generating conflict with others by behaving badly. On the contrary, as far as it is possible and as far as it depends on us, we should be trying to live truly at peace with everyone.[23]

Persecutions will inevitably come, however, as we try to live a Christlike life because 'the man without the Spirit does not accept the things that come from the Spirit of God, for they are foolishness to him, and he cannot understand them' (1 Cor. 2:14). Of course, human condemnation and mistreatment are not the only type of opposition we may encounter as we seek to walk in the way of holiness. All the struggles the Christian experiences as he or she wrestles against the evil principalities and powers that seek to destroy God's work (Eph. 6:12) are part of the conflict that besets us.

Longing for perfection

I have been greatly helped in writing this and the next two sections by the insights of John Koenig, which he presents in a book entitled *Charismata: God's Gifts for God's People*.[24] He writes of the vigorous joy and sense of fullness that seems to be the typical initial response of believers as they recognise the power of God at work in their lives, through both the gift and gifts of the Spirit. But he also acknowledges the 'groaning' that this giftedness brings, the deep sense of longing for full redemption that is introduced by the Spirit. Paul knew it well:

> Now we know that if the earthly tent we live in is destroyed, we have a building from God, an eternal house in heaven, not built by human hands.

> Meanwhile we groan, longing to be clothed with our heavenly dwelling,
> because when we are clothed we will not be found naked. For while we are
> in this tent, we groan and are burdened, because we do not wish to be
> unclothed but to be clothed with our heavenly dwelling, so that what is
> mortal may be swallowed up by life. Now it is God who made us for this
> very purpose and has given us the Spirit as a deposit, guaranteeing what is
> to come. (2 Cor. 5:1–5)

In this passage, as Koenig notes, the Christian life appears to be anything but tranquil. On the contrary, it exhibits anxiety and yearning for a
better condition. The gift of the Spirit 'guarantees' that a future home-
coming will take place, but at the same time creates dissatisfaction with
one's present state. We find a related passage in another of Paul's letters:

> We know that the whole creation has been groaning as in the pains of
> childbirth right up to the present time. Not only so, but we ourselves, who
> have the firstfruits of the Spirit, groan inwardly as we wait eagerly for our
> adoption as sons, the redemption of our bodies. (Rom. 8:22–23)

The work of the Holy Spirit 'makes us sensitive to afflictions we have
never been aware of; they point us to the anguished "not-yet" of God's
redemptive work. And that is not easy to take.'[25] Thus holiness means
having a heightened awareness of the dislocation, alienation and fragmentation that are the outcome of the entry of sin into God's original perfect creation.

Sharing in Christ's sufferings

Jesus has made it clear that being his disciple, following him in the way of
holiness, means self-denial. In a sense it means sharing in Christ's sufferings: taking up our own cross and being prepared to do so daily (Mt.
16:24; Mk. 8:34; Lk. 9:23). As Koenig comments, 'probably all three
Gospel writers want to allow their readers the possibility of understanding
the word "cross" metaphorically as the constant struggle to live a life of
discipleship to Jesus'.[26] Similarly, Jesus is probably not referring only to
physical death when he says 'whoever loses his life for me and for the gospel will save it' (Mk. 8:35). We should not forget, however, that for some
Christians taking up the cross has meant, and may still mean, martyrdom.

Paul writes: 'For it has been granted [lit. bestowed as a gracious gift]
to you on behalf of Christ not only to believe in him, but also to suffer for
him'.[27] The 'gift' of suffering for Christ's sake means standing up for
Christ through our lifestyle, whatever the consequences. It may also mean

much more than enduring opposition and persecution that are imposed on us by others. It may include internal conflict or 'overcoming inertia and fear from within'[28] and experiencing all kinds of hardship. For some it may mean coping with ongoing illness or disability, should God choose not to heal.

The cross for the Christian means taking up arms against satanic forces, wrestling 'against the powers of this dark world and against the spiritual forces of evil in the heavenly realms' (Eph. 6:12). The outcome of this struggle has already been profoundly affected by Christ's death and resurrection. By that history-changing event Satan was, in fact, conclusively defeated, but his activity in the world continues for a time as God allows.

> In their death gasp the hellish powers will wreak immense destruction – especially upon Christ's followers . . . Although they cannot finally prevail, the satanic forces will torment believers with every imaginable 'tribulation, or distress, or persecution, or famine, or nakedness, or peril, or sword'. . . . Every new charisma [gift], greeted with human thanksgiving to God, diminishes Satan's power, and Satan will not take that passively . . . In some mysterious way God's Spirit comes mixed through and through with the cosmic sufferings of Christ.[29]

As we discovered in the previous chapter, our role in the war against Satan has more to do with holiness – living a life of obedience to our Lord in the strength of his Spirit – than deliberately focusing on the evil powers themselves. We are indeed the objects of Satan's hatred but, more importantly, we are the focus of God's love.

When writing his letter to the Philippians, Paul was reckoning with the possibility of his death in the near future and acknowledging the suffering of the Philippians; nevertheless, 'the language of joy abounds . . . With almost every new thought Paul pauses either to blurt out his own joy or to encourage the Philippians in theirs.'[30] Paradoxically, it is in the midst of suffering that he writes about the peace of God which passes understanding – about contentment in each and every situation (Phil. 4:11–13). Koenig comments:

> To be a charismatic in the New Testament sense, one need not, indeed cannot, be constantly happy. On the other hand, precisely because the crucified Christ rules as Lord, every limitation, struggle, and pain becomes a potential messenger from God . . . Amazingly, there is joy in all this: a steady, durable joy as different from our culturally produced emotional

highs as plastic from fine oak.[31]

Thus holiness, while it may include suffering, does not mean having a sombre 'killjoy' attitude to life. It does not mean living in a constant state of euphoria, but neither does it mean being continually miserable. On the contrary, an important aspect of the life of holiness is a new freedom to enter into everyday life, enthusiastically and with a living hope. It means loving the Creator of this world and following the Christ who became a man, entered into life fully himself and promises his followers life to the full (Jn. 10:10).

Special gifts, special wounds

John Koenig offers an important insight when he claims that special giftedness is often accompanied by severe burdens.[32] He gives several biblical examples. Jesus' ministry (which was, of course, unique) involved the heavy gift of the cross; it was part of the 'cup' he accepted from the Father (Jn. 18:11). Jacob when he wrestled with the angel, received a blessing from the Lord and a limp; the blessing from the Lord lasted, I am sure, and so did the limp (Gen. 32:22,23). Paul's list of adversities is remarkable: flogged and beaten on many occasions, stoned, shipwrecked three times, adrift at sea for a day and night, and so on (2 Cor. 11: 24–28). As well as that he had his persistent 'thorn in the flesh' to contend with (1 Cor. 12: 7–10). He, like many people involved in the healing ministry, was a wounded healer.

In his second letter to the Corinthians, Paul is dealing with a Church with a very high regard for miraculous gifts, which was calling into question his apostleship. Yet he devotes only one sentence to the miracles that were the authenticating signs of his apostleship. He chooses instead to write at length about the most important sign of an apostle and, no doubt, a disciple: a humble awareness at all times and in every circumstance of utter dependence on God. Strength in weakness is his theme (2 Cor. 11:24–12:10). What Paul seems to mean by 'weakness' is an acknowledgment that we are morally and spiritually weak and utterly dependent on the Spirit of God in all that we achieve in the name of Christ. This dependence is not necessarily physical and, clearly, we should not be seeking physical weakness, or acting in ways likely to induce illness, in order to become more holy. On the contrary, we should be seeking in every way to maximise our physical, mental and emotional health and strength.

Indeed, one of my aims in writing this book is to help people to achieve this important goal.

Strangely, however, it is not unusual for a person in leadership in the Church and in the healing ministry to experience some physical problem or other ongoing difficulty.[33] Many will be familiar with the life of the Anglican preacher David Watson who, although suffering terminal cancer, was a powerful witness to Christ as he ministered in weakness especially in his last months.[34] His good friend John Wimber has also suffered serious health problems. Most of us can name someone who falls into this category.

I have often warned fellow Christians against rushing into a healing ministry without counting the cost. They may be called to witness in weakness. I have also assured them that, if this truly is their ministry, they will know the power of Christ in marvellous new ways. That has been my experience. On countless occasions I have not known whether I could cope with even the first fifteen minutes of a day's seminar (usually, on healing or spiritual gifts). Yet, again and again, I have been given special strength and abundant blessing has resulted.

The story of Samuel Zeller, a man who received an extraordinary gift of healing, has been a great source of inspiration to me.[35] He conducted a 'spiritual sanatorium' on the shores of Lake Zurich for people who needed to be renewed physically and spiritually. This man who was God's instrument in healing many others was himself afflicted with a condition that at any time could painfully take his life. He was well aware that he was being called upon to glorify God's name through his illness: 'Hallowed be thy name' was his constant prayer. Here was strength in weakness. In Zeller's comprehensive ministry, the kingdom of God was advanced and his name glorified by a humble servant of God, who walked as a wounded healer along the way of the cross.

THE HOLINESS OF GOD

Holiness is elusive. It can easily become distorted into pietistic self-righteousness or Pharisaism – the hypocritical holiness of the Pharisees that earned stern condemnation from Jesus. This self-centred holiness is to be avoided at all cost; it is in fact pseudo-holiness. The holiness we are to seek is the kind of holiness we see in God. 'You shall be holy, for I am holy' is a recurring theme of Scripture (Lev. 11:44,45, 19:2; 1 Pet.

1:15–16; cf. Mt. 5:48). The holiness of God and the hallowing of his name (treating God with due reverence because he is holy) must take priority over the holiness of the Christian.

The Lord's Prayer puts this principle into practice. We find, at the very beginning, a request that God's name will be hallowed (Mt. 6:9) but no request for personal holiness at all. The spotlight is the holiness of God. This focus is particularly noteworthy in view of Old Testament teaching that 'the holiness of God's name is bound up with the character and conduct of his own people'.[36] God's name is profaned and brought into disrepute (the opposite of hallowed) when his people do not live holy lives. Nevertheless, the emphasis in the Lord's Prayer is that God's name will be made holy, not a request for holiness amongst his people.

I see in this emphasis a reminder that Christ has set us the perfect example of holy living. During his earthly life he made it clear that his purpose was to glorify the Father. An overwhelming sense of awe and reverence for the holiness of God permeated every aspect of his being. Through God's grace, we too can experience the wonder of being creatures in proper relationship with our Creator. As we grow in this relationship, true holiness will be seen in us. It is as we focus on the holiness of God, as we follow Christ's example and centre on the glorifying and lifting up of his name, that we are made holy. To focus on the gaining of our own holiness, happiness or health instead of the reverencing of God leaves us open to a type of self-centredness, even though our sincere desire may be to lead a life that is pleasing to God.

How does biblical teaching on holiness relate to the healing ministry? We can say that holiness must be given priority over healing. In our enthusiasm for this important ministry of the Church, we must never lose sight of the fact that 'godliness' has priority over physical well-being (1 Tim. 4:8); without holiness it is impossible to see (or know) God (Heb. 12:14). We can also say that, in general, holiness promotes wholeness and healing yet, paradoxically, at the level of the individual it may mean either health or suffering, prosperity or hardship. For most of us it means a mixture of all these things. The way of holiness includes learning to live at peace within this tension: learning more and more to rest in the assurance of our omnipotent heavenly Father's love – whatever our circumstances.

While healing has an important place in contemporary ministry, the holiness of God and the honouring of his name must take priority over the healing and holiness of the Christian. Mindful that our reason for being is to bring glory to the Father, the primary motivation for healing should be the hallowing of the Father's name. In our own lives and in the whole of the healing ministry, we should be seeking healing only in so far as it is consistent with this priority. That is the way of holiness, wholeness and abundant living.

Notes

1. See *A survey of the healings of Jesus* in Appendix II.

2. John Wilkinson, *Health and Healing: Studies in New Testament Principles and Practice* (Edinburgh: Handsel, 1980). This is an excellent treatment of the biblical material by a person qualified in both theology and medicine. I consider this an important reference book and a classic on the subject of healing in the New Testament. Wilkinson points out that a key concept in the Old Testament is *shalom*, 'peace', which refers to wholeness in every sphere of life, while in the Gospels the term *sōzō*, 'to save', always refers to the whole person. Healing of the body is never purely physical and salvation of the soul never purely spiritual; both are combined in the total deliverance of the whole person.

3. From J.I. Packer, *Keep in Step with the Spirit* (Leicester: Inter-Varsity Press, 1984) copyright © 1984, p. 95; this and all subsequent quotations used by permission of Inter-Varsity Press and Baker Book House Company.

4. Packer, pp. 94,96f.

5. In preparing this section I have gained much insight and inspiration from Packer, pp. 103–115. [See also J.I. Packer, *A Passion for Holiness* (Cambridge: Crossway, 1992). This book was first published as *Rediscovering Holiness* (Ann Arbor: Servant, 1992].

6. Note the use of the Gk. aorist tense for 'present' indicates that it is signifying something that is done once and for all, which suggests that what Paul had in mind was a definite once-and-for-all act of commitment to Christ. He bases his appeal for commitment on the 'mercies of God' (v. 1), asking his readers to respond in this way in gratitude for the grace of God, which he has been expounding in the previous eleven chapters.

7. Packer, *Keep in Step with the Spirit*, p. 104.

8. Based on definition of justification in J.D. Douglas (Ed.), *The New Bible Dictionary* (London: Inter-Varsity Fellowship, 1962), p. 683.

9. As we have already discussed, to achieve his purposes the Spirit of God does at times come mightily upon the individual Christian in a way that has been described variously as a second (or subsequent blessing), a baptism in the Spirit or an infilling of the Spirit; see Chapter 4, Note 3. God may use such experiences to bring about growth in holiness by a deepening of our relationship with him. It is helpful to acknowledge this provided that we do not make the mistake of either (a) claiming in doctrinal terms, or giving the impression, that this is a necessary experience for all Christians (part of or almost as significant as

conversion) or (b) equating it with moving into a new state of existence that enables us to live lives of sinless perfection. Neither of the latter views is supported by Scripture. Packer, *Keep in Step with the Spirit*, contains some interesting comments on this issue; see pp. 121–169. [See also Packer, *A Passion for Holiness*].

10. See F.F. Bruce, *The Epistle of Paul to the Romans: An Introduction and Commentary* (London: Tyndale, 1963), pp. 67f.

11. Packer, *Keep in Step with the Spirit*, p. 108.

12. As we move from the realm of the Old Testament to the New Testament, holiness takes on a new meaning. 'The concept of holiness in the NT is determined ... by the Holy Spirit, the gift of the new age ... The sacred no longer belongs to things, places or rites, but to the manifestations of life produced by the Spirit'; see Horst Seebass in C. Brown (Ed.), *The New International Dictionary of New Testament Theology*, Vol. 2 (Grand Rapids: Zondervan, 1976), p. 228.

13. See Packer, *Keep in Step with the Spirit*, p. 109.

14. We may say that Jesus fulfilled the Law in the sense that he gave it its full meaning. He emphasised its deep underlying principles and the need for total commitment to it, with right attitudes towards God and others, rather then mere external conformity. The Christian's relationship to the Old Testament law is now determined by its fulfilment in Christ; the law must henceforth be viewed in the light of the Christ-event.

15. Note that Jesus issues a strong warning to those whose good works do not flow from such obedience ('doing the will of my Father'); he will call them 'evildoers' and reject them (Mt. 7:21–23).

16. Packer, *Keep in Step with the Spirit*, p. 106. [The latter was certainly Isaiah's experience when confronted with the holiness of God; see Is. 6. For further discussion of our ongoing need for repentance and forgiveness, see Packer, *A Passion for Holiness*, pp. 134–140; he sees this as a fruit of true conversion.]

17. [Drawing together the two themes of law and love, Packer writes: 'Law-keeping love is the epitome of holiness, though love in any other sense negates it. Law-keeping love is God's prescription for the fulfilling of our humanity. Any alternative to it pulls us, more or less, out of our proper human shape'; see Packer, *A Passion for Holiness*, p. 177.]

18. This correlation is acknowledged in both Christian and secular works. See, for example, Robert Claxton, *A Christian Doctor Speaks on Healing* (Sydney: Lancer, 1987). [Bill D. Moyers, *Healing and the Mind* (New York: Doubleday, 1993), esp. chapter entitled, 'Changing Life Habits' by Dean Ornish, pp. 87–113.] It is interesting to note that the laws God gave his people for cleanliness, eating and social interaction (as recorded in Leviticus) must have greatly enhanced their health, although I am not suggesting that the link between health and holiness can always be understood in such simple practical terms.

19. Chris Wright in *Daily Notes* (Scripture Union), Oct–Dec 1990, p. 42; the italics are mine.

20. D.A. Carson *How Long, O Lord: Reflections on Suffering and Evil* (Grand

Rapids: Baker Book House, 1990).
21. [Suffering is a very personal matter. What amounts to intolerable suffering for one person may be accepted as normal living by another. In very general terms, suffering has been defined as 'getting what you do not want while wanting what you do not get'; see Packer, *A Passion for Holiness*, p. 249.]
22. See 1 Pet. 2:20f; 3:17; 4:12ff.
23. See Rom. 12:18. The injunction in Hebrews 12:14 is to 'aim at peace with everyone and a holy life, for without that no one will see the Lord' *REB*.
24. J. Koenig, *Charismata: God's Gifts for God's People* (Philadelphia: Westminster, 1978), see esp. chapter entitled, 'The Gift of the Cross', pp. 128–145. Note that although the term 'charismata' usually refers to the specific spiritual gifts (see Chapter 4), Koenig seems to place in this category all gifts from God, that is, every expression of grace in the life of the believer.
25. Koenig, pp. 131f. Philippians 3 suggests to him that the Christian also experiences 'growing pains': 'It is a mark of Christian maturity (see Phil. 3:15) to be constantly on the move, always aware that one has not yet been perfected in grace, always "forgetting what lies behind and straining forward to what lies ahead" (vv. 12–13)'; see p. 141.
26. Koenig, p. 138.
27. Phil. 1:29 *RSV*; see also Rom. 8:14–18. Paul makes it clear that the many adversities he has experienced during his ministry as an apostle, including persecution, result from 'the death of Jesus' which he bears in his body (2 Cor. 4: 8–10) and that the struggle is an ongoing one for him (Phil. 1:30). Koenig derives the expression 'the gift of the cross' from the use of the word 'granted' (Gk. *echaristhē*) Philippians 1:29; see Koenig, p. 137. God may permit suffering as a grace gift!
28. Koenig, p. 137. It may be difficult for us to allow the Holy Spirit to change us in areas where we are fearful of change.
29. Based on Mt. 24:9–12; Rev. 12:13–13:7, 17:6; and Rom. 8:35 read in the light of vv. 36–38; see Koenig, pp. 139f. In the New Testament, allusions to our sharing in Christ's sufferings are often placed in the context of cosmic upheavals initiated by his resurrection.
30. Koenig, p. 144.
31. Koenig, p. 145. Suggesting that some Christians have come to seek happiness or the elation that may accompany the exercising of spiritual gifts to the exclusion of all other human experiences (see pp. 169–171), Koenig comments: 'In extreme cases one ends up saying something like . . . "Since I now find myself in the depths, God must have left me . . . What grievous sin have I committed? What must I do to bring them [emotional highs] back?" We might call this kind of thinking an "underinterpretation" of the charismata. It fails to recognize the charismatic presence of God at the heart of suffering and therefore rejects the gift of the cross. One gives up deep joy in order to chase after shallow happiness . . . In the New Testament a pneumatikos, or "spiritual person", is one who follows the Spirit's lead, particularly in his or her moral behaviour, not

one who constantly bubbles over with positive emotions'; see Koenig, pp. 170,171.

32. See Koenig, pp. 133–136.
33. In my own small way I believe that I embody the message I am seeking to present here. While being involved in the healing ministry and observing God's healing power at work and experiencing it in my own life over many years, I have not been cured of the cancer that has invaded my body. It seems strange indeed that one can experience daily the healing power of Christ, which holds back what doctors describe as a non-curable disease, yet not be cured.
34. D. Watson, *Fear No Evil: A Personal Struggle with Cancer* (London: Hodder and Stoughton, 1984).
35. Recorded by O. Hallesby in his book entitled *Prayer* (London: Inter-Varsity Press, 1961), pp. 103f.
36. See Robert A. Guelich, *The Sermon on the Mount: A Foundation for Understanding* (Waco: Word, 1982), p. 310. Guelich suggests that a desire and commitment to live a holy life to the glory of God can thus be seen as implicit in our request that his name be hallowed.

Chapter 7

Healing Comes in Many Different Ways

God is at work in every area of our lives. To relegate his activity to the miraculous alone is not just a heresy, but a danger to our wholeness. If we are to be as healthy as possible ourselves and as effective as possible in the healing ministry, we need to understand that God may answer our prayers for healing in many different ways. Our God reigns over the universe and is the author of everything that is good and beneficial to his creation (1 Chr. 29:11,12; Is. 41:10; 46:4). He is interested in each individual as a whole human being with physical, emotional, intellectual, social and spiritual needs. Therefore, God's healing work goes beyond instantaneous, miraculous healing and beyond mere physical healing. It reaches into every aspect of our lives.

A good general physician does more than diagnose a patient's illness and prescribe appropriate medication or treatment. He or she is also sensitive to the needs of the whole person and able to show this in appropriate ways. Similarly, those in the healing ministry should do more than dispense prayer and comforting words to the sick and dying. They need to be aware of the many other factors that are important to the general well-being of their 'patients', to draw people's attention to them and to recommend specialised intervention when appropriate.

The primary message of this chapter is that God's healing comes in many different ways. Elsewhere I have described in detail how my own struggle with illness brought me to an understanding of this important principle.[1] In this chapter, once more drawing on my own experiences, I illustrate the great diversity of resources available to those who are seeking God's healing for themselves or for others.

The general principles about healing presented here are just as important to those who provide ministry as to those who receive it, as indeed are most of the teachings of this book. We must embody what we advocate to others. And many of the recommendations are relevant to anyone wishing to maintain good health, not only to those in need of healing.

MEDICAL SCIENCE

When I was first diagnosed as having lymphoma and told that without radical chemotherapy I had only a short time to live, some well-meaning but misguided Christians advised me to forget medication.[2] They assured me that, provided I had sufficient faith, God would heal me. It seemed as though, from their perspective, rejecting medical science was the key to healing because it would provide God with convincing 'proof' of my faith in his power to heal me. I firmly believe that if I had followed their advice my life would have been unnecessarily shortened.

It is essential for those in the healing ministry to acknowledge that God can and does use medical science to heal and prevent disease. His good gifts to his creation no doubt include the discovery of remedies and treatments that are now available to provide relief or cure for many diseases. Medical science has its limitations, of course. Doctors are human, not infallible. Some are not as skilled or dedicated as we would like them to be and even the best are working with partial knowledge. Nevertheless, *I strongly urge anyone who is ill to seek medical assistance.*

I am concerned about a growing tendency for people, including many Christians, to treat doctors with suspicion and turn instead to 'alternative medicine' with its so-called 'natural' therapies. While some of these approaches may be helpful in certain cases, the claims of many are dubious. 'Success' stories often rest on very flimsy evidence. I see no good reason to accept blindly promises of healing from these sources while dismissing what medical science has to offer. Such therapies are certainly no more 'spiritual' than conventional medicine. In fact, many still have their roots so firmly planted in Eastern mysticism that it is debatable whether Christians should be seeking healing through these means.[3] Wisdom and balance are needed.

We must also beware of thinking that being healed by a miracle, rather than medicine, is somehow more virtuous or spiritual. We need to be open to both mundane and miraculous healing, seeking medical assistance as well as praying for healing, and we must ensure that this message is conveyed clearly to others through our ministries of healing. God alone is sovereign, and we need to acknowledge his presence in appropriate medical intervention as well as in miraculous healing: 'In and around and under the benefits of medical research and the healing arts is the sustaining, ordering, healing presence of the Creator and Redeemer of all things.'[4]

THE IMPORTANCE OF LIFESTYLE

To a large extent health and healing come to us through sensible living. It is especially important for Christians to acknowledge this. A quite proper emphasis on prayer and miraculous healing may cause us to overlook the marvellous in-built defence and repair mechanisms of the human body that are an important source of healing. Making appropriate lifestyle choices helps us to take full advantage of these God-given natural processes.

In my exploration of such issues, I came across a very helpful book by Robert Claxton, a Christian surgeon. Noting that the major causes of heart disease and cancer in the western world (smoking, poor diet, lack of exercise, excessive alcohol intake, and stress) are all preventable, he presents a list of simple rules for healthy living, which I commend to you.[5] Along with the usual recommendations about exercise, diet and so on, 'meaningful faith stance' is included. This is in complete accord with the major theme of the previous chapter. The life-changing choice we make when we come to Christ in repentance and begin to live a life of holiness in the power of his Spirit is fundamental to health and wholeness.

Adequate exercise

Exercise makes an enormous difference to health. I experienced this when I began exercising regularly years ago. Until very recently I walked many kilometres each week, often choosing to walk rather than drive and to use stairs instead of elevators. Despite progressive illness over the past ten years, many people have commented on my 'healthy' appearance. It never ceases to amaze me just how fit a terminally ill person can be and I never cease thanking God for allowing me to enjoy this degree of vitality. I believe that maintaining a sensible programme of exercise, to the limits but not beyond my physical capabilities, has helped extend my life and has contributed significantly to my sense of well-being throughout the years of illness. Exercise is a readily available and wonderfully enjoyable source of God's healing grace.

Those who are ill or have not exercised for some time should ask (or be encouraged to ask) their doctor's advice about the most suitable form of exercise for them. Although rest rather than exercise may be required in some cases, generally regular exercise will be beneficial. Walking on level ground is wonderful exercise for many people. Swimming is even better for most. Non-competitive exercise is recommended for those wishing to reduce their stress level (see below), as competitive exercise may have the opposite effect.[6]

Appropriate diet

A great number of questionable claims have been made about the importance of diet in the treatment of cancer[7] and other illnesses. I am not going to elaborate on this complex issue here, but I do want to draw attention to the general principle that eating well helps keep us healthy.[8] I am talking about diet in a very broad sense here, not about eating particular foods that are supposed to have medicinal qualities. What I am recommending is that you consider for yourself, and advocate to others, a long term change of eating habits amounting to a permanent lifestyle change. This can be especially helpful to people suffering from chronic illness, even if that particular illness is not usually considered to be diet-related. I am convinced that adopting a more appropriate diet has made an important difference to my own quality of life in recent years.

Of course, it would be quite irresponsible to encourage those who are ill to make major changes in their diet without their doctor's approval. For example, I am aware that the low-fat, low-sugar diet that I found helpful is not suitable for all cancer patients.[7] I am certainly not recommending the 'quack' diets that emerge as fads from time to time and are often enthusiastically recommended as cures for particular illnesses, including cancer. Their extravagant claims often have no scientific basis. They may also be very costly because they include unusual and expensive foods or involve the purchase of books, food supplements or other items. More importantly, because many of them are not well-balanced, they may actually be harmful.[9]

It is worth noting that 'healthy' food does not have to come from a health food store or be organically grown. Moderation is also a good principle. For example, certain vitamins in high doses are dangerous even to healthy people and those who are ill should be particularly wary of taking excessive amounts.

Reducing stress

One of the ways God has answered my prayers for healing is by showing me ways of minimising stress. I believe that these, together with other strategies for maximising my general health, have been important in helping my body fight disease. When my blood pressure became alarmingly high some years ago, I felt the need to do something about my stress level. The result was a great simplification of my work and lifestyle. Resting in the assurance that my salvation and acceptance by God depended on his grace, not my works, I reduced my workload, focusing on my two best gifts – teaching and pastoring (caring mainly for cancer patients). With the help of assistants to organise teaching missions, I was able to be useful in work in which I felt fulfilled without undue stress.

Now in retirement, I have found it necessary to learn to live within my human and spiritual limits as I seek to serve others. A sense of purpose is very helpful in times of health and especially in times of sickness but, if we are to avoid undue stress, it is important that our workload be adjusted to our capacity to cope. My own adjustment to ongoing illness has included a radical simplification of my life. It has become more ordered and less cluttered with belongings. My days proceed at a much less hurried pace. I attempt much less, but in some ways I think I achieve more that is worthwhile in terms of the kingdom of God. I am convinced that a simple, relaxed and ordered lifestyle is beneficial to everyone and especially to those who are ill. It is another of God's healing resources.

Part of the slowing down process for me has been the use of a technique for systematically relaxing the various muscles of the body.[10] I believe that the practice of relaxation, in combination with an unhurried, simple lifestyle, greatly reduces wear and tear on our bodies and can do much to promote healing. It is also entirely consistent with a restful, patient and meditative Spirit-filled life. Many different relaxation techniques are available and, generally, they are quite straightforward.[11] There are, however, some approaches that should be avoided. In recent years, the New Age movement has propagated a type of Eastern mysticism in its relaxation (or meditation) techniques that is tantamount to a 'religious experience' centred on self or 'the God within' rather than the God and Father of our Lord Jesus Christ. In such approaches, vague terms like 'spiritual forces within' and 'life energies' may be used. Jesus may appear to be honoured, but only as a great teacher or prophet, not as Lord. Any method for achieving relaxation or reducing stress that we adopt ourselves or recommend to others must be entirely consistent with the biblical gospel if it is to promote true wholeness.

Enjoying life

In recommending a disciplined, balanced lifestyle I do not want to give you the impression that I am advocating an unrelentingly serious attitude to life. Feeling healthy but miserable is not consistent with the abundant life that is ours in Christ. Indeed, one of the signs that we are growing in holiness is a new freedom to enter into everyday life. As Christians we have good reason to be down to earth. We love the Creator of this world and follow the Christ who became human and entered fully into life himself. Although we need to be careful about becoming too focused on ourselves and neglecting to love and serve God and others, there is great benefit in entering into life: enjoying our work, our healthy diet, our daily exercise, listening to music, exploring new hobbies and leisure activities. Fun and play belong to life and we can go on discovering new ways of participating. We can learn to savour life in all its aspects, from the appreciation of nature to a joyful expression of our sexuality in marriage.

I always encourage those who are ill to live life each day as fully as their limitations allow – one day at a time. Even when quite limited in health they can benefit from trying each day to use their imagination to do something enjoyable. Genuine laughter can be wonderful medicine. David Watson towards the end of his life wrote:

> Laughter is one of God's great gifts and a delightful means of relaxation. Life is not always very funny, and my own situation was far from humorous, but laughter can save us from the deadly snares of self-pity and self-importance. It can also act as a powerful antidote to disease by turning negatives into positives . . . Quantity of life is not nearly so important as quality, even for 'terminally ill' patients.[12]

While there is scientific agreement that a good diet, exercise and enjoyable leisure activities will help maintain health and prevent illness, the role of these factors in treating illness is less clear cut. My own belief, based on personal experience and my observation of others, is that making such lifestyle changes is also important in fighting disease and promoting a sense of well-being. Knowing that we are doing as much as we possibly can to help the healing process also strengthens us emotionally and psychologically. While doing this does not guarantee perfect health or recovery from illness, it should be recognised as another of the resources available to those seeking all the healing God has for them.

It is important for people who are involved in the ministry of healing to embody this message, especially those who are leaders. We need to develop healthy lifestyles ourselves and encourage others to do so but without becoming hypochondriacs or 'health freaks' or overemphasising this particular aspect of healing.

EMOTIONAL WHOLENESS

In human beings, the body, mind and emotions are combined to make a whole. True healing thus means healing of the person in every part. To many, the notion that emotional factors should be taken into account in cases of physical illness may seem strange, but a strong link between emotional and physical health is now widely acknowledged.[13] It is not my purpose here to enter into a debate on the role of emotional factors in the cause and cure of disease. I simply want to remind those who are ill and those who minister to them to take into account the importance of the emotions in the healing process. I believe people should be encouraged to explore ways of dealing with issues that may be adversely affecting their emotional well-being and wholeness.

Many people, including Christians, live lives that are remote from their inner selves. Below their surface personalities and behaviour, operating in the unconscious, lies a pool of pain, sin and hurtful memories dating from their earliest experiences. Accessing and dealing with such pain is not pleasant, so there is a natural tendency to push it down below conscious awareness where it remains to a large extent hidden. This process, which can continue throughout life, occurs, to some extent, in virtually everyone. We are all in need of emotional healing. As part of our fallenness, our infirmities extend into our thought processes and emotional responses. We develop a whole range of defences, ways of processing information that protect us from experiencing the pain of emotions associated with painful events or memories. The stress and strain of trying to avoid these feelings may influence us in ways that are often more obvious to other people than to ourselves.[14]

As Christians we pledge our entire being to the Father through Christ. Through the power of his Spirit, we begin a new way of living that will lead us to surrender more and more of our lives to his Lordship. This is the only way to true wholeness, a process by which every aspect of our lives is brought into balance and harmony in him. We cannot attain the full measure of wholeness available to us in this life unless we are prepared to let God lovingly search our hearts: 'Behold thou desirest truth in the inward being', the psalmist affirms, 'therefore teach me wisdom in my secret heart' (Ps. 51:6 *RSV*). He then goes on to ask God to heal him in his inner being: 'Create in me a clean heart, O God' (v. 10).

Because we are beings in whom physical, mental, emotional and spiritual attributes are linked, anything that affects us in one area of our lives spills over, either negatively or positively, into another. Anyone who is truly seeking God's healing should not overlook this important aspect of wholeness. It will mean coming to terms with the hidden part of ourselves. We will never experience perfect physical health this side of heaven; nor will we be perfectly whole emotionally. Nevertheless, we should be actively seeking healing in both these areas of our lives and be prepared to deal with difficult issues as they arise.

Christians have a particular responsibility to look for appropriate ways of resolving emotional issues. These interfere with the health of the body, which is 'a temple of the Holy Spirit' (1 Cor. 6:19). For example, we are told to 'get rid of all bitterness, rage and anger . . . along with every form of malice'; such things not only limit the healing that God would give us but also 'grieve the Holy Spirit of God' (Eph. 4:30–32).

Christians generally accept the benefits of medical science. Some, however, are dubious about psychology and psychiatry, which relate to emotional and mental health. They may see these areas of human knowledge as ungodly, dangerous or even satanic. Others may simply not recognise that there is any need for change in the way they behave or deal with their emotions.

I see the insights of psychology as part of the array of resources that may be used by God to bring healing, but I am also aware of a need for caution. We must certainly be wary of the humanist attitudes pervading much of secular psychology that give the impression we can achieve wholeness in isolation from God, without his forgiveness through Christ and the indwelling power of his Spirit. Samuel Pfeifer, a Christian doctor and psychiatrist, comments:

> Many modern psychotherapists, while stirring up the mud of a person's life, do not offer real help. The term 'sin' does not exist in their vocabulary. While trying to untangle the web of repressed conflicts, they themselves are repressing man's biggest problem, his separation from God.[15]

Some Christians also fear that psychology encourages an unbiblical focus on the self. They feel uncomfortable with its jargon – 'self-awareness, self-acceptance, self-esteem, self-development, self-understanding, self-reliance' – and its emphasis on assertiveness. They may think the words of Jesus himself support their attitude: 'If anyone would come after me, he must deny himself and take up his cross and follow me. For whoever wants to save his life [Gk. *psuchē*)] will lose it, but whoever loses his life for me and for the gospel will save it' (Mk. 8:34,35). I have given much thought to these matters over the years and come to the conclusion that, provided Christ is given his proper place, a well-developed self and appropriate assertiveness are attributes consistent with holy living.[16]

Ultimately, being true to one's real self means living under the Lordship of Christ to whom the core of self has been committed. It means first serving him in loving, free obedience and then serving others in his name, even to the point of being prepared to lay down one's life for them. But it does not mean having low self-esteem and a poor self-image or being a 'doormat'. In humble gratitude, the Christian stands at his or her full height as he or she is aware of being, in Christ, a unique, infinitely loved and gifted personality. Thus the hallmark of the healthy self is humility, but not self denigration. On the contrary, there should be a sober, realistic acknowledgment of strengths and abilities (Rom. 12:3). The healthy self will have confidence, in the strength of the Spirit, to assert itself when appropriate but, in true humility, it may also at times choose graciously to lay aside what the world may see as its rights for the sake of the kingdom.[17]

If looking to psychology in our search for healing causes us to ignore our need for God, our need to be in a right relationship with him through Christ, or to become self-absorbed, it will lead only to confusion and despair in the end. But this does not have to happen. We can receive great benefit from the many insights of psychology that are compatible with biblical truth. Most of the therapeutic techniques used by qualified practitioners, such as psychologists and psychiatrists, are not inconsistent with Christian faith and teaching, and many committed Christians are found in these professions, in which they have unique opportunities to minister.[18]

Unfortunately, the voice of the New Age movement is often heard in the debate on the need for emotional healing, making Christians wary. This, and related spiritual movements which advocate a 'holistic' (or 'wholistic') approach to healing, correctly discern that there is an interaction between the human mind, body, emotions and spirit, but they do not recognise the sovereignty of the One who is the source of true wholeness – Jesus Christ, the Redeemer. They seek instead a self-obsessed oneness with a pantheistic, impersonal universal force, celebrating and relying for wisdom on the 'God within'.[19] The Christian approach to healing should be holistic in the *biblical* sense; it should recognise the needs of the person as a whole and work towards the wholeness of the individual (see *Healing and the whole person* in Chapter 2). Clearly, I am not giving blanket approval to the whole range of techniques currently being promoted as 'holistic' medicine. I am convinced, however, that those who are ill should be encouraged to deal with emotional and behavioural factors that may be limiting healing or quality of life.[20]

Specialised counselling[21]

During my years of illness I sought the skills of specialist counsellors[21] from time to time. Although they did not unearth deep emotional problems, they were able to make suggestions that have been invaluable in improving my emotional well-being. Most people, whether or not they are ill, can benefit from the insights of a perceptive, well-qualified counsellor, psychologist or psychiatrist.[21] Although God can certainly use a non-Christian in this role, I believe it is most helpful when the counsellor is also a caring Christian. Our emotional and spiritual needs are very closely linked and Christian practitioners or counsellors can draw on the insights provided in Scripture and by the Holy Spirit,[22] as well as their professional training, to assist their patients and clients. As is true for every aspect of healing, our aim in seeking help of this nature should be not wholeness itself but, ultimately, to give more of ourselves to the glory of God.

Monitoring mental attitudes

Cognitive therapy is another tool of psychology that I have found very useful. We frequently compound our problems by self-defeating interpretations of what is happening. If we can correct these interpretations, our emotions will tend to become more appropriate to the circumstances and therefore more manageable. Those who are chronically ill often have low self esteem and a tendency toward self-defeating thinking. This is particularly true for many cancer patients. David Burns in his book *Feeling Good: the New Mood Therapy* encourages his readers to analyse their thinking and to replace self-defeating 'self-talk' with more rational attitudes.[23] For example, the self-talk of someone who has just failed an exam may be, 'I failed this exam, so I'll probably fail the whole course. I'm a terrible student. I'll never succeed in this profession. If I don't succeed, I'll be unhappy for the rest of my life. People will realise I'm incompetent', and so on. A much healthier response is, 'I failed in this exam, but that doesn't mean I'm going to fail the whole course, etc . . .' Deliberately choosing a more rational and self-supportive attitude is a helpful coping mechanism in every situation.

Healing through remembering

In order to be whole we need not only forgiveness for our sins but also healing of our hurts, hurts that may sometimes be buried, but still alive, deep in our memories. Some years ago I began to develop a procedure that I believed might help Christians, physically ill or not, to become more emotionally whole. I was influenced to a certain extent by both Arthur Janov, a secular psychologist, and Ruth Carter Stapleton, who presented a fairly unsophisticated Christian perspective on 'healing of memories', although I must admit I had reservations about the approaches of both these people.[24] What emerged is not a form of primal therapy or an attempt to replace psychotherapy or counselling. It is an approach based on prayer, in which we ask the Spirit of Christ to be with us and help us find healing as, in his presence, we recall some events from our past. I do not want to encourage a morbid preoccupation with the past. I am simply suggesting that it can be helpful for some people to take a brief look backwards, asking God to reveal anything that (with his help) they can and should be dealing with at that time.

I conducted sessions of this nature for several years, usually for groups but occasionally for individuals, and I am aware of others in the caring professions who have also found this approach useful. It may be very beneficial to those suffering from cancer or other serious illness. Generally, it should not be attempted without the guidance and support of a mature Christian leader, and a highly trained and experienced counsellor [21] should be involved either in the role of group leader or as part of the ministry team. Additional information about 'healing through remembering' sessions is provided in Appendix IVA.

Dealing with depression

The Christian community is not immune to the depression, stress and anxiety that are so prevalent in modern society. These emotional 'diseases', another consequence of the fall, will be experienced by many members of church congregations. They affect not only those who are physically ill but also those who may appear to be quite healthy. People with life-threatening illness or chronic illness or pain (especially cancer patients) often suffer from depression.

In some congregations, depression is considered a sin. It is regarded as the antithesis of the joy that is supposed to be the hallmark of the Christian. Of course, unconfessed sin may underlie depression and, in such cases, repentance and forgiveness are an essential part of treatment. There are many other causes for depression, however, and there should be no shame attached to acknowledging this condition and seeking treatment for it.[25]

I experienced deep depression for several years and found it harder to cope with than any of the severe illnesses I have suffered over the past twenty years. I am very thankful that I was never tempted to commit suicide during that dark period; however, I believe that I came to understand, in part at least, the unbearable feelings experienced by those who do. My problem turned out to be endogenous depression (due to a natural chemical imbalance) and with correct medication I experienced wonderful relief. I accepted this treatment gratefully as a gift from God.

In cases where medication is required for depression as an adjunct to appropriate psychological treatment, a whole range of non-addictive drugs is available. These affect people differently, even adversely in some cases, and sometimes several have to be tried before the right one for the individual is found. I believe that Christians diagnosed as having clinical depression should be open to the possibility of taking antidepressant medication if that is the treatment recommended for their condition. Good medical care, skilled psychological intervention and addressing spiritual issues all play a part in dealing with depression.

Of course, everyone sometimes feels depressed by the struggles, frustrations and challenges of life. This is to be expected as a part of normal, healthy living. But we need to be on the lookout for abnormal or unmanageable depression, in ourselves and those to whom we minister, and be ready to do something about it. Anyone who is seriously depressed should be urged to seek help from a psychologist or psychiatrist. If their depression is associated with serious illness, they may also find it helpful to join a suitable support group recommended by their specialist or a major hospital.

A WEALTH OF SPIRITUAL RESOURCES

As Christians we are privileged to have many resources for healing that are not available to others. These go far beyond specific healing services or ministries.

Prayer and meditation

I see prayer, both personal and corporate, at the very centre of healing. There is a connection between prayer and all the other means of healing described in this book. God can use any one of them, or any combination of them, to answer our prayers for healing. In answer to prayer he has provided me with caring and competent medical assistance; with people who have supported and strengthened me emotionally; with grace and stamina to endure distressing treatments or complete a task for him when my human strength was exhausted. And, on many occasions, he has provided me with a degree of healing that is beyond medical explanation. In addition, he has shown me ways of changing my lifestyle to improve my general health. All these factors have been important in helping me fight disease.

Throughout my illness, my wife and I have had a wonderful sense of being supported and carried along by the gracious love of God as people have prayed for us. Those who are ill will benefit greatly from praying with a special friend regularly and joining a small group for prayer and Bible study.[26] In the next chapter we will explore many aspects of praying for those who are ill. Here I will just make the point that prayer is the greatest of all resources for healing and possibly one of the most neglected. It is our means of direct communion with our Creator and Healer.

My own times of prayer have been a source of rich blessing all my life. One aspect of prayer I have found especially helpful is meditation. By this I mean a very specific kind of meditation: meditation on God's Word. This meditation arises out of union with Christ and it is God-centred, not human-centred.[27] Since becoming a Christian some forty years ago I have spent a great deal of time in daily prayer. Over the years my prayers have become more meditative. Often during the night or in the early morning I will reflect on various passages of Scripture, thinking deeply about them and of associated Scriptures and centring my thoughts on God. My favourite passages for this exercise of mind and faith are Psalm 23 and the Lord's Prayer. I have found that combining meditation with prayers for intercession, thanksgiving and confession provides a balance to my prayer life.

I do not recommend 'transcendental meditation' or meditation of the kind often associated with Eastern religions or the New Age movement; these are really self-focused rather than God-glorifying. It is my conviction that Christian meditation is more healing and stress-reducing than any other form of meditation.[28] Christian meditation does not find truth *within*. It responds inwardly to the truth that comes from *above*. When our focus in meditation and prayer is our love for God and our concern for others rather than ourselves, it becomes more, not less, helpful to us. These gains are, of course, by-products of the process, not ends in themselves. The more we pursue meditation purely for God's sake rather than our own the more therapeutic it becomes for us. Here we have another example of the divine paradox that to lose oneself to God is to find oneself immeasurably blessed.

During meditation, people often become aware of unresolved issues that can be brought to God for healing. This process may include the recognition of unhelpful or sinful attitudes in ourselves. The appropriate response then is true repentance and prayer for God's help in changing them. While the benefits of meditation go beyond this, such insights are part of God's provision of healing.

A prayer for wholeness

Several years ago, I began to develop an approach to meditative prayer that I have used, in various forms, each day since then. I had read about the Simonton team who ran a clinic for cancer patients in Texas, where they sought to combine conventional medical treatment with psychotherapy.[29] Working on the theory that the human mind can influence the healing process, a general theory for which I believe there is growing support,[13] they taught their patients to visualise in vivid images the shrinking of their cancer cells. This visualisation process was carried out in a relaxed, meditative state. I had, and still have, reservations about many forms of meditation and visualisation that are not thoroughly Christ-centred and Bible-based, such as those promoted by the New Age and related 'spiritual' movements, but I could see the value of involving the whole person in the healing process. I therefore sought to put this approach (a combination of meditation, relaxation and visualisation) into a thoroughly Christian context. The ' prayer for wholeness' outlined in Appendix IVB is the result.

The Word, sacraments and Christian fellowship

God's Word comes to us through reading the Bible and in the teaching and preaching of the Scriptures. This is one of the chief resources of spiritual, emotional and physical healing. His Word has power; it never returns to him empty (Is. 55:11). Personal Bible study and regular attendance at a group Bible study[26] should be part of the life of every Christian, not in any legalistic sense, but because this will bring great blessing. It will also provide essential 'training in righteousness' (2 Tim. 3:16) leading to growth in holiness and wholeness. Attending a church where the biblical message is faithfully proclaimed and clearly expounded is also an important healing resource.

David Watson, when facing death from cancer, found great strength and comfort in reading and reflecting on the Word:

> As I spent time chewing over the endless assurances and promises to be found in the Bible, so my faith in the living God grew stronger and held me safe in his hands. God's word to us, especially his word spoken by his Spirit through the Bible, is the very ingredient that feeds our faith . . . I found God's word to be a wonderful protection from all dreadful imaginings. Even on a human level the existence of anxieties and fears can

accelerate the disease and hinder the healing process . . . As I read or prayed through those psalms, I was conscious of my tensions unwinding, my fears disappearing, and once again I was aware of the Lord's love surrounding me.[30]

The sacraments of baptism and communion (the Lord's Supper) are 'visible words' through which God communicates his love for us.[31] They are visual ways of proclaiming the word of the gospel. Through them we celebrate all that the life and death and resurrection of Jesus Christ mean to us. They are therefore important sources of healing in every area of our lives. This may mean physical healing, or it may not. David Watson was not healed physically, but shortly before his death he was able to write:

> I took the bread and the wine, tokens of Christ's ultimate sacrifice for my sins and the guarantee of God's unchanging love and mercy. I knew that I belonged to him for ever. Not even death could separate me from his love . . . 'Lord, I'm yours. You can do with me whatever is your perfect will.' In that surrender I found his profound peace.[32]

God's healing often comes to us through fellowship: the meeting together of his people in worship, anywhere and anytime, not only at regular church services. The music associated with worship is also wonderfully uplifting. Watson comments:

> It is one thing mentally to believe the statement 'God loves you'; it is quite another to have a deep certainty of that within my heart and spirit. Yet that certainty is so crucial in times of crisis: a quiet, settled conviction and faith. I have found that such faith is encouraged (and it needs daily encouragement) partly by meditating on God's word of love in the Scriptures, partly by the expression of God's love through caring Christian friends, but perhaps mostly by the inward experiencing of God's love through sensitive and joyful worship.[33]

As we meet together we can receive the love and discipline we need to grow in faith and oneness. Thus we encourage each other in godliness and holiness, the essence of true wholeness.[34] Worship and fellowship may also be channels of miraculous healing, coming through corporate meeting with the living God and through the loving prayers of the congregation.

The elders and gifts of healing

We should be willing to receive the prayer of the 'elders' or leaders of the church when we are sick (see Jas. 5:13–16). Acting on behalf of the whole church, they play a special part in the ministry of healing. In James we read that the elders laid hands on people for whom they prayed, as did Jesus and his disciples on some occasions.[35] This practice, which may also include anointing with oil,[36] continues in many churches today.

We may choose to place our hands on the sick as we pray for them to identify with them, to focus our prayers and attention on them and to communicate the care and concern of Christ and the Church.[37] I have taken part in this ministry in many places throughout Australia and I have also been its recipient. I heartily recommend it to church leaders and to those who are ill. I have a large file of letters from people who believe they have received some degree of healing through this ministry. I also have some from people (apparently just as godly and full of faith) who have not been healed. Laying on of hands does not guarantee healing, but it is an important and biblical part of a holistic approach to healing and the ministry of healing.

As already discussed, some Christians are given a specific gift that enables them to serve as channels of God's healing (see Chapter 4). Through them he sometimes chooses to bring about instantaneous healing that is quite remarkable, but he may also use them to bring healing in less spectacular ways. Individuals who are gifted in healing have a special role in ministering to the sick within the life of the church, whether or not they are church leaders.

HEALTHY RELATIONSHIPS

Everyday life thrusts us into relationship with other human beings, with family members, other members of the body of Christ and the wider community. The ability to establish and maintain healthy relationships[38] is therefore an important aspect of wholeness and holiness and another factor that influences our health.

Learning to love

The children of Israel were commanded to love God with all their heart and their neighbour as themselves. Jesus gave the same message an added depth when he told his disciples to love each other with the self-giving sacrificial love he exemplified on the cross (Jn. 15:9–13). He commanded them to love one another so that their joy would be complete (v. 11). Fullness of life belongs only to those who love others. While

Christians have a special obligation to love their fellow Christians (Jn. 15:17; Gal. 6:10), they are called upon to love all their neighbours, even their enemies (Mt. 5:44; Rom. 13:9; Heb. 13:16). Love is a command, not an option, and we need both to give and receive it as part of a caring Christian community.

Any breakdown in a significant relationship, with other people or with God himself, can contribute to health problems. Simmering resentment, bitterness and ongoing anger rob people of wholeness more than almost anything else. It is common for people who discover that they are seriously ill to become angry with God for allowing them to suffer. The classic question *Why me?* is a natural human response and understandable; however, such anger needs to be expressed and worked through. If we ignore it and leave it to develop into resentment, it will eventually mar our relationship with God – the most significant relationship of all. Dealing with it may be a long process, requiring wise and compassionate pastoral support and/or counselling.[21]

It is important for those who are ill (and indeed all Christians) to acknowledge any breakdown in a significant relationship, whether it is their relationship with God or another person, and to seek reconciliation whenever it is appropriate to do so. Personal prayer, Bible study, the fellowship of other Christians and professional counselling can all play a part in the healing of relationships.

In improving my own relationships with others, I have been greatly helped by a secular approach to classifying personality traits.[39] Its aim is to help people appreciate the varying gifts of personality expressed by others. A number of broad categories of personality types have been identified that assist in predicting the way individuals will focus their attention, acquire information, make decisions and orient themselves towards the world around them. If we can see another's personality, and our own, as parts of ourselves that are to be accepted and understood rather than resisted and changed, marriages and other relationships can be transformed and liberated. At the heart of wholeness is the acceptance of ourselves and others as valuable in God's sight. This should be a natural outcome of accepting the gospel and learning to live in its light.

The marriage relationship

For those who are married, a good husband–wife relationship is a key issue, an important element of wholeness as well as holiness. Some researchers have even gone so far as to suggest that poor marital relationships can be a factor in the onset of cancer, and presumably any disease that is stress-related. I am not sure whether this has yet been established conclusively in scientific terms, but it seems reasonable to assume that developing and maintaining a good relationship with your spouse will improve your quality of life and may even influence the likelihood of recovery from serious illness. Scripture tells us that lack of consideration and respect for your partner may hinder your prayers (1 Pet. 3:7), including presumably your prayers for healing. Successful marriages also contribute to the health of both church and community.

The Bible makes it very clear that God is strongly for faithfulness in marriage and against divorce. Christians need to understand the basis for this. Otherwise, if problems arise in their marriage, couples may well find themselves grudgingly staying together just to be obedient to God, but hating his commands as too restrictive. There is physical, emotional and spiritual risk in such a situation and I see a need for sound biblical teaching on this issue throughout the Church.

God's commands arise out of his very nature; they are not arbitrary. His love for his children has always been, and always will be, a steadfast love (Heb. *hesed*; see Ps. 103:4, for example). The God of the Bible is the God who binds himself to Israel in an unbreakable covenant. He also binds himself to the Church in 'the new covenant' sealed by Christ's blood (1 Cor. 11:25). God's love is utterly faithful; he will never forsake us (Ps. 27:10). He is like a husband joined to a wife in an unbreakable covenant of love. Christian husbands and wives are called upon to reflect that love in their relationship with one another. Thus the loving character of God is the basis for Christian marriage. The faithfulness, kindness and unselfishness they show to one another arise out of this fundamental aspect of his nature, summed up in one simple statement in the Bible: 'God is love' (1 Jn. 4:8). Wholeness in ourselves comes when we try, with God's help, to reflect this kind of faithful love in all our relationships with others, but there is a special obligation for those who are married to be committed to loving their partner in this way.

Reconciliation

People make mistakes in relationships. We have all hurt or been hurt by others. Sometimes the bitterness of past hurts lingers to sour not only the relationship involved, but also every other relationship in our lives. Unfortunately, we are so conditioned to hide our hurts and sinful bitterness under a guise of sociability and tolerance that our wounds fester unattended. We thus place ourselves at risk of turning our unexpressed anger and pain into greater sin through slander, manipulation or even violence – and we may not even know we are doing this.

We can master the art of self-justification to such a degree that we no longer realise when we are lashing out at another or 'getting our own back' for a past hurt. The latter telling phrase suggests we somehow feel that, having been hurt, we are now owed something that needs to be repaid through revenge. David Seamands, in his book *Healing for Damaged Emotions*, looks at the parable of the unforgiving servant, who, having had his own outrageously high debt cancelled, demands payment of a paltry sum owed him by another servant and has him thrown into gaol when he cannot comply.[40] Seamands suggests that the servant who owed the huge amount of money did not understand that the debt was cancelled. Instead he was acting as though he had only been given an extension of time to pay, as though he still had to put pressure on others to pay up. Similarly, many Christians act as though they are not aware that the debt, the unpayable debt they owe to God, has been cancelled. They go on attempting to collect from those around them the fulfilment and satisfaction that is theirs in one relationship only – their relationship with the debt canceller, Jesus Christ. In the Lord's Prayer we pray, 'Forgive us our debts as we forgive our debtors', and yet we carry around anger and resentment over the debts we are owed as well as guilt about what we owe others.[40] Reconciliation should flow easily and naturally from hearts that are replete with God's riches in Christ.

When reconciliation is necessary and appropriate, what can we do to help achieve it? The obvious first step is that we must want it. Many of us have hugged our bitterness to ourselves for years, a deadly security blanket that may be hard to exchange for the uncertainty of attempting to do something about it. God, who takes the risk of loving us unconditionally, is our co-worker in any attempt at reconciliation, whether we see ourselves as the giver or the receiver of the hurt. We need to ask the Holy Spirit to give us insight into the nature of the problem, to show us his truth. We need to accept our own responsibility in causing damage to the relationship. This may mean coming to terms with some hard facts.

Although the other person may have wronged us, we are responsible for our own reactions at the present time. Our responsibility may not be much – in some cases, we may in reality have been the innocent victim – but whatever our mistakes we need to own them. In relation to childhood events, there should be no self-condemnation about the inevitably childish nature of our responses at the time; however, as mature adults, we can take responsibility for choosing whether we allow past anger and hurt to continue.

Owning our mistakes means we also have to forgive ourselves and learn to receive God's forgiveness. It would be tragic to go on living with the belief that we are in debt, like the servant in the parable, when through Christ we are debt-free. In fact, we should not go to ask forgiveness of another, or face another with our own hurt while we still hold our own guilt in our hearts. We need to be wrapped in the power of Christ's love to deal with whatever reactions we may encounter from the person we face. We cannot predict what will happen. It is only out of the sure knowledge of our emotional riches in Jesus that we can hope to truly resolve the issue, whether we need to forgive or to be forgiven, or both.

Reconciliation is face to face working through the hurt and pain. It is a process that is often helped by a third party, preferably a mature Christian. Indeed the Bible advises taking a 'witness' in cases where reconciliation is proving difficult (Mt. 18:16). We need to move past the facts of the wrongs themselves to the emotions that block our inner health and on to the words and actions that will heal. In situations where hurts have accumulated over many years, as for example, in a marriage or parent–child relationship, or in other difficult cases, it would be wise to consider asking the help of a skilled counsellor[21] to facilitate the reconciliation process.

It is important to acknowledge that full reconciliation between two parties is not always possible in this fallen world. Both must desire it and be emotionally capable of working towards it. Sometimes the person we need to be reconciled to is dead, absent, or for some other reason cannot communicate effectively with us. At this point a skilled counsellor may be able to help us work through the reconciliation process, at least in terms of dealing with our own feelings about the situation. An approach such as the 'healing through remembering' described in Appendix IVA may perhaps be helpful.

I cannot stress too strongly the link between individual wholeness and establishing and maintaining good relationships with others. In the same way that a cancer in one part of the body can cause distress to the body as a whole, so one poisonous relationship can affect every area of life, including our health. We say, 'So and so makes me sick', and sadly that may, quite literally, be true. If we are to receive all the healing God has for us, we need the liberating experience of reconciliation achieved through his Spirit.

In this chapter, I have attempted to show that those seeking healing have many options. We are not restricted to placing our faith entirely in medical science, on the one hand, or praying and waiting for God to perform a miracle, on the other. I see it as essential for those in the healing ministry to be aware of the many different ways in which God may provide healing and to be encouraging a biblical, holistic approach to both health and healing.

Notes

1. R.J. Hillman with C. Chamberlain, *There is Hope: For Those Who are Ill and Those Who Care for Them* (Sydney: ANZEA, 1992).
2. For excerpts from a typical letter, see Hillman, pp. 8f.
3. See Samuel Pfeifer, *Healing at Any Price?* (Milton Keynes: Word, 1988). This book by a Swiss physician and psychiatrist about various forms of alternative medicine provides much food for thought. He argues that some such therapies that in themselves do not appear to be inconsistent with Christian faith and teaching may nevertheless be quite inappropriate for Christians when administered by people who believe they are drawing on occult powers or in some way honouring 'foreign gods' as the source of healing.
4. L.B. Smedes (Ed.), *Ministry and the Miraculous: A Case Study at Fuller Theological Seminary* (Pasadena: Fuller, 1987), p. 48.
5. These include: adequate exercise, appropriate diet, adequate rest, no smoking, minimal or no alcohol, meaningful faith stance or philosophy of life, social involvement, healthy attitudes and relationships; see R. Claxton, *A Christian Doctor Speaks on Healing* (Sydney: Lancer, 1987), pp. 21,34.
6. Archibald Hart, *The Hidden Link Between Adrenalin and Stress* (Waco: Word, 1986), p. 103.
7. While a sensible diet will not guarantee protection from cancer, it can reduce the risk of this and other diseases, as about one in three cancers may be caused by diet-related factors. On the other hand, there seems to be no scientific evidence that any form of cancer can actually be cured or reversed by diet alone. A suitable diet is regarded as a very important part of the treatment of cancer patients. It helps them to maintain body weight, control symptoms and cope better with the damaging effects of treatments such as surgery, chemotherapy and radiotherapy. This information comes from booklets entitled *Good*

Medicine for Cancer Patients and Good Advice on Diet and Cancer available from the New South Wales Cancer Council, Sydney, Australia. Elsewhere, clinics or large hospitals should be able to supply similar material produced by government agencies.

8. The following rules about diet, provided by the New South Wales State Cancer Council, are sound advice for most people whether they are ill or not: include a wide variety of foods; eat plenty of wholegrain cereals and fruit and vegetables, especially cabbage (or related vegetables such as brussels sprouts, broccoli and cauliflower) and yellow vegetables; eat less fat, sugar, salt, and salt-preserved or smoked foods; avoid spoiled (mouldy) food; and keep your weight within healthy limits. A major cause of disease in the western world is the traditional diet, which is too low in cereal fibre and plant carbohydrate and too high in animal fat, salt and refined sugar; see Claxton, pp. 21,34. For further advice on diet, the following are recommended for Australian readers: Rosemary Stanton, *Complete Book of Food and Nutrition* (Sydney: Simon and Schuster, 1989) and *Eating For Peak Performance* (Sydney: Allen and Unwin, 1988) and Gabriel Gaté, *Family Food* (Melbourne: Anne O'Donovan, 1987), a recipe book commissioned by the Anti-Cancer Council of Victoria. Because there is so much variation in the composition and types of foods available throughout the world, readers living elsewhere should refer to reliable books published in their country or obtain information from local health authorities.

9. See, for example, Catherine Saxelby, *Food What's in It: A to Z of Food and Nutrition* (Sydney: Reed Books, 1989), pp. 103–106; the author is a consultant nutritionist.

10. The technical term for this process is Progressive Muscle Relaxation (PMR). I was introduced to such techniques many years ago when I read a book by Ainslie Meares, *Relief Without Drugs* (London: Souvenir, 1968). He was an Australian psychiatrist who used relaxation as an adjunct to the treatment of cancer patients. Archibald Hart, whom I was privileged to meet at Fuller Seminary, also encouraged me to try this method of reducing stress. His book *The Hidden Link Between Adrenalin and Stress* (see Note 6) was very helpful to me. The following is a procedure that I have used each day for many years:

Either seated or lying down, raise your hands above your head and stretch your whole body, while holding your breath for ten seconds. Then let your whole body go limp. Repeat this three times. Next, beginning at your feet, take each group of muscles in turn, contract them tightly and hold them for five seconds, then relax them before moving up to the next group. As you hold each group of muscles tense, try to keep the rest of your body relaxed. The last muscles to be treated in this way are those of your forehead and head. When you have completed this exercise, with your eyes closed and breathing deeply, begin to count down from fifty continuing to tell the various parts of your body, including your mind, to relax . . .

When I am relaxed, I often begin a special kind of prayer and meditation that has meant a great deal to me over the years (see Appendix IVB). Usually when this is complete I continue to count down until I drop off to sleep. Note that sleep, although obviously a good thing in its own right, does not necessarily assist the relaxation process and is not part of it. Some people find it more helpful to relax progressively from head to foot because they associate this downward movement with letting muscles 'drop'.

11. Many people find that gentle music has a relaxing effect, on its own or as part of a relaxation technique. Some health professionals now specialise in 'music therapy'.

12. From D. Watson, *Fear No Evil: A Personal Struggle with Cancer* (London: Hodder and Stoughton, 1984), pp. 27f,167; copyright © 1984 by Anne Watson; this and all subsequent quotations reproduced by permission of Hodder and Stoughton Limited and William Neill-Hall Limited. He also questions the use of the word 'terminal' in these circumstances, because it means the end of something: 'In reality, when the body of the Christian dies, the really wonderful journey has only just begun', he says (p. 167). This, in the context of Watson's book, is an expression of the future hope that sustains the Christian who is facing death (see *About present and future hope* in Chapter 11), not an unhealthy denial of pain and grief.

13. [Current ideas on this topic were reviewed in an interesting television documentary series and companion book produced in the USA; see B.D. Moyers, *Healing and the Mind* (New York: Doubleday, 1993).]

14. Anyone unfamiliar with these concepts may find it helpful to read Evelyn H. Peterson's book *Who Cares? A Handbook of Christian Counselling* (Exeter: Paternoster, 1980).

15. Pfeifer, p. 175. Emotionally healthy people correctly feel guilt because of sin in the same way that they feel pain when they injure themselves. To maintain health, however, this guilt must be dealt with as soon as possible through confession, repentance and affirmation of God's forgiveness, acceptance and love through Christ.

16. To illustrate this point, I offer the following comments on some of the ideas presented in an excellent book by psychologists David Jansen and Margaret Newman with Claire Carmichael, *Really Relating: How to Build an Enduring Relationship* (Sydney: Random House, 1989; revised edition). It is written from a secular viewpoint. The authors emphasise the importance of a well-developed self in establishing and maintaining good relationships, especially in marriage; this self is the core of the person – the real 'you' that is quite distinct from all other people (see p. 31ff). They say that what you are now results from your own unique nature, from past (especially childhood) programming and from strategies you have developed for coping. The great enemy of the true self is the 'pseudo self', the phoney or conforming, socially agreeable self. Growth in your person and in relationships depends on shedding the pseudo self (p. 42) and developing the real (basic, genuine) self. To do this you must develop self-awareness, self-acceptance, self-esteem, self-integrity, self-development, self-understanding, self-reliance, assertive skills and altruism and deal with self-

deception, self-programming and unfinished issues from the past (p. 46). Relationships can only succeed and result in tandem growth where both participants have a well developed and maturing self.

In assessing these ideas in the light of biblical teaching, I have come to recognise that the 'core of the person' Jansen and Newman write about is the self that is transformed and taken over by the Spirit of Christ when conversion takes place. This is new birth, being born of the Spirit (Jn. 3). Subsequently, 'I no longer live, but Christ lives in me' (Gal. 2:20). The Christian life, then, is a denial of the pseudo, self-centred self for the sake of Christ. It is a taking up of the cross (death to the old self) and a following of Jesus. The Christian's true self has to do with who he or she is in Christ, with everything that is true (not false) to Christ. Everything that is lacking in integrity or genuineness or allows the old non-Christ-centred life to dominate belongs to the pseudo self.

Jansen and Newman maintain that the key to really relating is assertive communication (p. 61ff). Its opposite, 'non-assertive' communication, puts self last, lacks confidence, self-esteem and self-respect and does not express very much of what is within; it expresses the pseudo-self. There is also 'aggressive' communication, in which self predominates but there is a lack of respect for self and others; it feeds on anger and promotes it. The assertive communication they advocate acknowledges the self of the other person as equal and is based on confidence and self-esteem. For the Christian, however, appropriate 'assertive' communication is more than this. It is controlled by the Spirit and marked by prayerful humility, maximum grace and minimum anger, self-control (as a fruit of the Spirit). It is also marked by a gentle confidence that is of God and is not destructive to oneself or the other person. Humility, but not low self-esteem, is appropriate for the Christian. We are to express ourselves as we are – fully in Christ. In some churches, non-assertive communication may be mistakenly extolled as a virtue, as evidence of humility, but this is false humility. Everything false (or pseudo) is incompatible with our high standing in Christ.

17. In this Jesus again sets us the perfect example. He who was willing and able to assert himself when necessary for the kingdom (Jn. 2:13–17) was also the One who, for our sake, 'humbled himself and became obedient to death – even death on a cross!' (Phil. 2:8).

18. [See, for example, Clifford Powell, 'Hearing God in the helping role' in *On Being*, March 1993, pp. 10–13; or an excellent series of monographs edited by Gary R. Collins, *Resources for Christian Counseling* (Dallas: Word, 1986–1991), in which the best modern approaches to counselling are combined with the biblical gospel.]

19. New Age healing is thus 'hollowistic' rather than 'holistic'; see Pfeifer, p. 178.

20. Robert Claxton describes an encouraging trend towards a 'wholistic' approach to medicine amongst health professionals (the terms 'wholistic' and 'holistic' are equivalent in this context): 'Two or three doctors may form a wholistic medical group, sometimes inviting non-physician health care professionals to join . . . . In addition there are some that have spiritual health care modalities and

ministrations – often operating from church premises . . . The goal of wholistic medicine is positive wellness rather than absence of symptoms . . . The responsibility for the patient's health rests with the patient as well as with the physician. Illness may indicate the need for a change of emotional response or lifestyle as well as providing an opportunity for positive growth in wellness'; see Claxton, pp. 32–34. See also *The Healing of Persons* (London: Collins, 1966) by Paul Tournier, a Christian doctor who was suggesting a whole person approach in 1940.

21. The term 'counsellor' needs careful qualification because it tends to be used rather loosely. I use it to refer specifically to people in the following categories: A. Registered practitioners, such as clinical psychologists and psychiatrists. Before they can practice they must be registered by the relevant professional body. This involves postgraduate training and several years practical experience under supervision to ensure competence. Note that (at least in Australia), while anyone can call themselves a 'counsellor', it is illegal for an unregistered person to use the title 'psychologist' or 'psychiatrist'; B. Other professional 'counsellors', who have relevant training in human behaviour as well as considerable skill in listening and offering helpful feedback. People in this category are generally trained to assist individuals in developing insights and coping strategies and should be able to do this effectively. They fulfil a useful role in helping people deal with relatively 'normal' issues, especially people experiencing difficulty coping. As they work with their client, more complex underlying issues or evidence of psychological disorder may emerge and a competent counsellor will be equipped to recognise this and refer the individual on to the appropriate professional, that is, to someone in the first category.

Of course, Christians who are not counsellors may be called upon, and should be prepared, to offer compassionate support to others under the guidance of the Spirit. Their role is more that of a loving friend or a brother/sister in Christ. For some who are specifically gifted as encouragers or pastors, this may be a special ministry. Ongoing expression of the love of Christ in these ways should be a normal part of the life of the church and be evident in all its dealings with the wider community; see John Mallison, *Caring for People* (Sydney: Unichurch, 1979). It is good for us to support and encourage each other through difficult times. It is good to say, 'I'll stand beside you in this, I'll listen to you, pray with you and offer you any insights from Scripture I may have'. People may want to see us as their 'counsellor' but, if we lack the appropriate training, it will be necessary at times to say, 'I'm sorry, I cannot be your counsellor. You are going to need someone with special training to guide you on that journey. But I'll be here to pray for you and encourage you through it all.'

It seems preferable to avoid using the term 'counsellor' when referring to people in supportive roles who are not in category A or B described above, and that includes most of us. If we lack specific training, we are not equipped to recognise issues that require referral for proper diagnosis and treatment. If we do not realise this, it is possible for us to add to people's problems instead of helping them. For example, by providing bandaid help to someone who is psychologically disturbed, we may delay them from seeking the expert assistance they really need, or we may give inappropriate, or even unhelpful, advice. In addition, we may have unrecognised emotional needs of our own that distort our perception of the situation.

I offer these suggestions as general guidelines only, recognising that the Spirit of God may sometimes choose to work in ways that go beyond human wisdom and that we need to be open to this possibility at all times.

22. See *Some specific gifts* in Chapter 4.

23. David D. Burns, *Feeling Good: The New Mood Therapy* (New York: Morrow, 1980). [See also Antony Kidman, *From Thought to Action. A Self-Help Manual* (Sydney: Biochemical and General Services, 1988).]

24. See Arthur Janov, *The Primal Scream: Primal Therapy: The Cure for Neurosis* (London: Abacus, 1973) and Ruth Carter Stapleton, *The Gift of Inner Healing* (London: Hodder and Stoughton, 1977). Flora Slesson Wuellner's book, *Prayer, Stress, and Our Inner Wounds* (Nashville: The Upper Room, 1985) appeared several years after I began leading such sessions. I also benefited from her insights.

25. See for example Archibald Hart, *Coping with Depression in the Ministry and Other Helping Professions* (Dallas: Word, 1984).

26. [John Mallison, *The Small-Group Leader: A Manual to Develop Vital Small Groups* (Adelaide: Openbook, 1996) is a valuable resource for those wishing to develop effective small group ministry in their congregations.]

27. Although it is emphasised in Roman Catholic tradition, most modern Protestant Christians are not familiar with the process of meditation and reflection. Martin Luther, however, indicated that he was no stranger to it: 'It often happens I find myself with such rich thoughts that I let the rest (of the reading) wait . . . I listen in silence and by no means hinder. For here the Holy Spirit himself is preaching . . . Let your own ideas go, be quiet and listen to him . . . take note of what he preaches and write it down and you will see miracles, as David says, in God's law (Psalm 119:18)'; quoted by Dennis Lennon in *Daily Notes* (Scripture Union), Oct–Dec 1990, p. 97. You may find the following books helpful: E.P. Clowney, *Christian Meditation* (Leicester: Inter-Varsity Press, 1980); Mark Link, *You: Prayer for Beginners and Those Who Have Forgotten How* (Niles: Argus Communications, 1976); and as an inspirational preparation for meditation, Andrew Murray, *Waiting on God* (Fort Washington: Christian Literature Crusade, 1978).

28. Many responsible therapists use meditation as an aid to stress reduction in the treatment of cancer patients, claiming that it has great therapeutic value. Note that it is often 'non-religious' meditation, not the Bible-based Christian meditation I am recommending; see Meares, 1968; [and J. Kabat-Zinn 'Meditation' in Moyers, 1993.]

29. Carl O. Simonton, Stephanie Matthews-Simonton, James L. Creighton, *Getting Well Again* (New York: Bantam, 1980). This book is described as a step-

by-step self-help guide to overcoming cancer for patients and their families.

30. Watson, pp. 39,47f.

31. Colin Brown, writing of Luther's view of the sacraments as signs accompanying and embodying the promises of God, comments: 'As such, they were like visible words, and as such they call for the response of faith'; see C. Brown, *Miracles and the Critical Mind* (Grand Rapids: Eerdmans; Exeter: Paternoster, 1984), p. 14.

32. Watson, p. 31.

33. Watson, p. 62.

34. Samuel Pfeifer sees the instruction in James 5:16 to confess our sins to each other and pray for each other as 'a rebuttal to the modern disease of isolation and loneliness. Christians need the fellowship of other believers. How many people try to solve their problems in their own little protective shell. They have no one to comfort or to encourage them, no one who would perhaps tell them: "What you are doing is not right". . . To them I'd like to prescribe: "committed involvement in a living fellowship of Christians". . . And don't be surprised when suddenly the ailment they have suffered from for so many years loosens its grip, and their depression lifts'; see Pfeifer, pp. 174f. Within each congregation will be some who are especially gifted in caring for others. This gift should be encouraged and developed; see, for example, Mallison, *Caring for People*, Note 26.

35. In the New Testament, healing is often, but not always, associated with the laying on of hands (see, for example, Mt. 9:18; Mk. 6:5; Lk. 4:40; Acts 9:17; Acts 28:8). Peter Ralphs comments: 'Overall, Jesus' action of touching the sick may be seen as an act of identification with the sufferer and as a stepping across the barrier of impurity associated with the sick. This is so especially with regard to those suffering from "skin disease", whose situation came under the regulations of Leviticus 13 regarding ritual purity (Mk. 1:41), and with regard to the dead (Lk. 7:14; 8:54). Touch may also symbolize the conveyance of blessing (Mk. 10:13,16; cf. Gen. 48:13,15,20)'; see P. Ralphs, doctoral dissertation, pp. 112f, cited in Appendix II. Hanz-George Schütz, noting the close connection between intercessory prayer and the laying on of hands in Scripture, suggests that this action 'bears witness to the church's conviction that their prayers which are founded on God's promises have been heard'; see C. Brown (Ed.), *The New International Dictionary of New Testament Theology*, Vol. 2 (Grand Rapids: Zondervan, 1976), p. 152.

36. See Jas. 5:14. Peter Ralphs points out that the disciples of Jesus are depicted as anointing the sick with oil (Mk. 6:13) but Jesus is never so depicted. The anointing appears to be symbolic rather than medicinal, perhaps symbolising the protection and blessing of God (see also Is. 61:3 where oil is a symbol of gladness); see Ralphs, doctoral dissertation, p. 115.

37. See Claxton, p. 18.

38. See Jansen and Newman, 1989. [Also Henry Cloud, *Changes that Heal: How to Understand Your Past to Ensure a Healthier Future* (Grand Rapids: Zondervan,

1992).]

39. I first came across this approach in a book entitled *Gifts Differing* by Peter and Katherine Myers (Palo Alto: Consulting Psychologists Press, 1980). The Myers-Briggs Type Indicator (MBTI) is a widely used personality assessment tool.

40. Mt. 18:23–35; see D.A. Seamands, *Healing for Damaged Emotions* (Amersham-on-the-Hill: Scripture Press), pp. 25–29. Another helpful book on this subject is Lewis B. Smedes, *Forgive and Forget: Healing the Hurts We Don't Deserve* (New York: Pocket, 1984).

Chapter 8

Healing and Prayer

Prayer is right at the centre of healing and the healing ministry. When we pray we communicate directly with our Creator–Healer and open ourselves to all the healing he has for us, through whatever means he may choose.

THE BASIC ELEMENTS OF PRAYER

What should be the motivation, the inspiration, the driving force for our prayers for healing? The Lord's Prayer, the model prayer Jesus gave to his disciples, contains profound insights into fundamental aspects of prayer, including prayer for healing. The truths it reveals encourage us to pray with confidence and provide us with a proper context for all our prayers.

The love of God

In the Lord's Prayer, Jesus taught his disciples to address God as Father, the 'love' word for God (Mt. 6:9; cf. Lk. 11:2). Love is the very nature of God and calling him Father expresses an intimate relationship with that love.[1] This is the reality and the relationship from which all true Christian prayer should arise: 'Father!' All the riches of the Father's heart and kingdom are available to us in that word.[2]

In addressing God as Father, we are in a sense acknowledging the Trinity, not as a formal concept, but as a dynamic relationship. God is first of all the God and Father of his only Son. We call God Father because we have become children of God through new birth or adoption into the family of God and receiving the gift of his Spirit. It is at the foot of the cross that lost prodigals return to the Father and are welcomed home (Lk. 15:20); it is by the Spirit he has given us that we call him 'Abba Father' (Rom. 8:15). Thus, in turning to the Father, we are sharing in the love relationship of Father, Son and Holy Spirit.

Right at the beginning of our communication with God, as we focus on our relationship with God as Father, the answer to all our prayers is guaranteed. No prayer will escape the Father's loving ear or heart. No problem is too large or too small for the infinite love and grace of the Father of our Lord Jesus Christ.

As Christians, it is our privilege to have a special loving relationship with God as Father. This knowledge is to permeate all our prayers. For example, how can we find the courage to go on to pray, 'may your name be hallowed, your kingdom come, your will be done', unless our prayer is directed to a loving Father? Having begun with 'our Father' we are in reality saying, 'may your loving Fatherly name be hallowed, your loving Fatherly kingdom come, your loving Fatherly will be done'.[3]

It is the love of the Father, the God who is love, that should motivate and underlie all our prayers, including our prayers for healing. Thus in the healing ministry of the church and in the healing ministry of the individual Christian, compassionate love should be the driving force. Those for whom we pray should sense this; those who pray should embody it.

The power of God

We pray to our Father 'in heaven'. In doing this we are reminding ourselves that he is transcendent, above and beyond all things, not that he is remote from us. Heaven is the place where God effects his rule on earth, the place where things get done. It is the place of God's throne: the place of power, where Jesus reigns through the Spirit at the Father's right hand. Undoubtedly, belief in the all-sovereign power of our Father in heaven strongly encourages us to pray. Because God is powerful we can pray in confidence. He is able to answer.

Yet the love of God, not the power of God, is to be the primary focus and motivator of our prayers.[4] Absolute power, unqualified by love, is to be feared; powerful love is to be sought and welcomed. God's power is qualified only by his love. Thus the opening words of the Lord's Prayer, 'Our Father in heaven', convey a wealth of meaning. They remind us that when we pray we are addressing and in fellowship with infinite and personal love and power.

In previous chapters, I have argued the need for the contemporary Church to 'rediscover' the omnipotence of God, to acknowledge that the Father who rules over all from his heavenly throne is no prisoner of the physical laws of nature. He is able to respond to the prayers of his children in remarkable ways, which include miraculous healings. In accepting this reality, however, we must be careful not to become too preoccupied with miracles. It is important to recognise that the Father exercises his power through the everyday, ordinary things of life as well as the miraculous.[5]

God is willing as Father to answer our prayers. He is capable of doing so because he is the One who reigns over all from his heavenly throne. And we affirm with Paul that, by the power at work within us, he is able to do 'immeasurably more than all we ask or imagine' (Eph. 3:20).

The glory of God

The Lord's Prayer continues with a request that God's name be glorified: 'Hallowed be your name'. According to Ezekiel, God's name is 'hallowed' when the nations acknowledge him as Lord; this will happen through God's people, as they are cleansed and given a new spirit that enables them to walk in obedience to his law.[6] Although God's name is hallowed through his people, however, it is only God himself who can accomplish this. Thus the passive voice is used: we pray 'hallowed be your name', not 'may we hallow your name'. Nevertheless, we do honour God's name by our godly character and conduct as we prepare for the coming kingdom.[7] To be a Christian is to long for the glory of God, to be jealous for the Father's name, to desire deeply that the nations will lovingly worship the Father.

We will never seek the glory of God as our first desire, never have a passion for the hallowing or the holiness of God's name, unless we come to prayer in a loving relationship with God as Father. Prayer for the hallowing of God's name comes naturally to the true lover of God and it must always be the first priority of those who pray for healing.

Professor Hallesby, the author of a classic book on prayer,[8] was particularly impressed by the prayer life of Samuel Zeller, the man who conducted a 'spiritual sanatorium' while himself suffering from life-threatening illness (see *Holiness means suffering* in Chapter 6). He had heard others pray with more emotion and more fervour, but he had never heard anyone pray like him. His prayers were quiet and confident. 'He knew God well, and for that reason he was confident', Hallesby writes. 'I do not believe that I have ever heard anyone expect so much of God and so little of his own prayers as he did.' He simply told God what was needed and left the rest to him. He had many people to pray for at each day's assembly, including the residents themselves and those who wrote to him from all over Europe. As Hallesby listened, he realised that although the requests were multitudinous, Zeller really prayed only one prayer: that the name of God might be glorified.

He did not hesitate to pray for instantaneous healing – if it would glorify God's name. But he also prayed that people should remain sick, if that would bring greater glory to God's name. The remarkable thing about this story is that what he prayed for others he prayed also for himself: 'Miracle-working prayer was not to Zeller a means of escaping tribulation; it was only a means of glorifying the name of God.'

Over the years, as I have prayed for my own healing, I have learned increasingly to pray in these terms. It is liberating to seek the Father's glory ahead of one's own healing, and to seek healing only in the context of his glory. I have found the Lord's Prayer a wonderful model to help me give glory to God in this process. In my times of intercession, I often pause and reflect on each phrase. When we dare to pray 'our Father' we can go on with great love and earnestness to pray 'hallowed be your name'. When we begin to desire from the depths of our being that God's name will be hallowed, then we are really moving in the direction of being Christlike. I have found that 'Hallowed be your name' is an appropriate prayer to pray in any circumstance, and especially in the healing ministry.

The kingdom of God

Jesus next prayed, 'Your kingdom come'. This second request of the Lord's Prayer is a logical extension of the first. We make God's name holy as we seek God's kingdom, his rule over all. We know that his kingdom has already come in Christ, the king, but it has not yet fully and finally arrived. That will be achieved when Christ returns at the end of the age.[9]

As we pray for the coming of the kingdom, we are reminded that the signs of the arrival of the kingdom included the healing miracles described in Scripture (Mt. 11:2–6). No doubt, present day healings (and conversions) are continuing signs of the presence of the kingdom. They are a taste of what will be when ultimate healing comes at the final consummation of the kingdom (Rev. 21:4). As we pray for the growth of the kingdom and its future consummation, we also pray for healing. This is the proper perspective: we are to seek the kingdom first, above all earthly needs (Mt. 6:33). Because prayer for healing offered within this framework is in line with God's long-term purpose for the kingdom, 'the healing of the nations' (Rev. 22:2), our requests for healing are often granted. Sometimes, however, as will be discussed later, God permits illness to continue in this earthly life for the sake of the kingdom.

The will of God

We are also to pray: 'Your will be done on earth as it is in heaven'. Note that again the request is in the passive voice, reminding us that to do God's will we are entirely dependent on him and his enabling Spirit. As in the first two petitions, there is both a present and a future aspect.[3] We earnestly desire God's will to be done today, but we also look forward to the coming age when the kingdom comes in all its fullness and God's will is at last done perfectly, on earth as in heaven, to the consummate glory of his name. Thus the hallowing of God's name, the coming of the kingdom and God's will being done are inextricably linked. There is also the closest possible connection between the doing of God's will and the Father who dwells in heaven. Jesus himself said: 'Not everyone who says to me, "Lord, Lord", will enter the kingdom of heaven, but only he who does the will of my Father who is in heaven' (Mt. 7:21).

In learning to subject our requests to the will of the Father we must be careful to avoid becoming fatalistic. It is fatalistic to believe that 'whatever will be, will be' and neither we nor our prayers can do a thing to change it. This fatalism is an entirely non-Christian concept.[10] We are not at the mercy of the clenched fist of fate. We are in the loving hands of the Father who always remains free to respond to the prayers of his children and reshape the course of events.

We know that sickness was not part of the Father's original will for his good creation. We know that it has no part in his coming kingdom. It is an intrusion into his good creation and the work of the evil one. It seems, however, that he may temporarily permit it, for his altogether good purpose.[11] It is this 'permissive' will we should be seeking; it will always be for our good, ultimately, and always for the good of the whole creation. God's will comes from his unique perspective. He alone knows what humanity really needs. When we pray that our immediate human needs be met, we are praying from a human perspective, a perspective that is really very limited. When we pray that God's will be done, we are praying a prayer of trust in his greater wisdom and unchangeable love for us. True prayer is not a matter of asking God to intervene to bring about the outcome we have already decided is the right or best way forward.[12]

The attitudes and priorities we find in the Lord's Prayer should be at the heart of all our prayers, including our prayers for healing. True prayer is always offered in the context of the love of God, the power of God, the glory of God, the kingdom of God and the will of God. And it is in this context that they are always guaranteed an answer (Jn. 14:14).

Within this framework, however, we are encouraged to go on to ask for our own needs to be met: 'Give us today our daily bread'. This is a remarkably down-to-earth request for God to supply our basic physical needs. It is a mark of our incarnational (down-to-earth) faith that the first request on our own behalf in the Lord's Prayer should be so ordinary and human. No doubt, our requests for healing fall into this category. Note that we need to ask for forgiveness as well: 'Forgive us our debts'. Prayer for forgiveness and prayer for healing certainly belong together (Jas. 5:15; Mt. 9:2). Then there is a request that we be delivered from temptation. To me this seems to represent a genuine seeking after holiness or true wholeness (see Chapter 6).

Thus, as we reflect on the Lord's Prayer, we discover that our first priority in praying for healing is not to ask for anything for ourselves or for others. We are to acknowledge above all the Father's love and power and come to him seeking first the Father's name, the Father's kingdom, the Father's glory and the Father's will. What applies to the individual applies also to the Church. The healing of the sick must not become the Church's first passion; rather, it should be a natural outcome of its devotion to God.

PRAYER THAT IS APPROPRIATE

Tim Geddert, in an insightful article on praying for healing, argues the need for a theology, and an attitude to prayer, that embraces the whole range of experiences that come in response to prayer.[13] Sometimes complete healing may be granted 'miraculously'. In other cases there may be no discernible healing at all. Geddert believes that the examples given in Scripture and the experiences of life are too diverse to be squeezed into a single model for prayer. He argues that we should pray for healing in different ways, depending on the circumstances. Of course, the Father's loving commitment to hearing and answering our prayers does not depend on whether we use the 'correct' approach or consciously adopt any particular approach at all. Nevertheless, we can benefit from considering different ways of praying. I have certainly found Geddert's insights on this subject helpful. The following represents a development of some of his ideas.

The perseverance (Job) approach

This is the basic approach to praying for healing. Unless the church is given prophetic insight that the sick person will be healed (see below), our prayers should reflect the attitude of Job. He did not know the spiritual circumstances of his situation.[14] He did not know when God was going to restore his health, if at all. He simply had to be patient and persevere.

The perseverance approach applies when neither the person involved nor the church knows when, or even whether, God intends to grant healing. Healing may come at a later time, as with Job, but it may not come at all during earthly life. Nevertheless, it is proper that the church pray for healing in these circumstances. Those who are sick should open their lives to all the healing God has for them at that time or in the future, while awaiting ultimate healing in the age to come. The church as it prays should encourage them in this. If immediate healing does not come, the sufferer is to persevere, not with anxiety, but with a sense of peace as they rest in God's will.

The prophetic (Elijah) approach

Geddert, reflecting on James 5:14–18, describes an 'Elijah model' for prayer. I like to call this the prophetic approach because it relates to the fact that Elijah had special insight into God's purposes. He knew why there was a drought and how long it would last. Then, when the appointed time arrived, he prayed for rain and it came (vv. 17,18).

Sometimes, the church is given prophetic insight, through the spiritual gifts of prophesy, words of knowledge or discernment, that someone is to be healed. Then the church can pray for healing and speak the authoritative word, 'Be healed!'

It is painfully easy, however, for sufferer, friends or family to confuse wishful thinking with prophecy. I have already discussed the need for safeguards to help the church and individuals distinguish between insights that are gifts of the Spirit and those that arise out of human need and imagination.[15] The former will result in joy, confidence and spiritual growth for the Church and the individual; the latter are likely to cause confusion, bitterness and disillusionment. Those in the healing ministry need to have a sound understanding of the role of prophetic insights and their correct discerning. Learning to pray in appropriate ways for healing depends on it. It is also a matter of crucial importance to people who are seeking to discover whether or not they are to be healed.

The Pauline approach

Although God sometimes gives specific guidance to the church that healing will occur, there are also times when he gives a prophetic word that he is not intending to heal. Then, another approach to healing prayer is needed. Paul represents all those believers who are afflicted with some kind of 'thorn in the flesh', some painful illness or trial that is a persistent source of irritation (2 Cor. 12:1–10). Such people are also called upon to persevere.[16] Unlike Job in the first example, however, they have received prophetic insight that healing (or complete cure) is not going to be given. Instead they are to rest in God's all-sufficient, sustaining grace, finding in this the strength they need to continue serving him faithfully despite their ongoing affliction.

There are three stages in the Pauline approach: the asking stage, the answering stage and the accepting stage. Paul had a problem, generally considered to be a physical ailment.[17] As he grappled to cope with this situation, he first had to ask for healing. Like our Lord in the garden of Gethsemane, he prayed three times to be delivered from his suffering. It was important for him not to accept his condition too readily. He did not see his disability as 'the will of God', simply to be endured. He saw it as 'a messenger of Satan' and he earnestly prayed to be rid of it. Whether he prayed on three different occasions or three times on one occasion does not matter. The point is that he persisted in praying for healing until God gave him a clear answer.

Jesus instructed his followers to ask in order that they might receive (Mt. 7:7). The form of the Greek verb used in this verse conveys the thought of something that is ongoing: 'Ask [and keep on asking] . . . for everyone who asks [and keeps on asking] will receive'. In the initial stages of illness, everyone should feel free to ask for healing and keep on asking. Indeed, if they do not, something may be radically wrong with their attitude to illness or to God. In their perception, God may be a punishing rather than a loving Father. They may see illness as the inevitable consequence of sin or even an atonement for it.

The second stage in this approach is the answering stage. God answered Paul's request for healing by saying: 'My grace is sufficient for you' (2 Cor. 12:9). The form of the Greek verb used to introduce this response indicates both an element of a certain event and an element of continuity. In other words, God's answer came at a particular time, when he spoke to Paul (in a prophetic word perhaps?), but that answer also continued to come. It was always the same consistent, comforting and challenging answer: 'My grace is sufficient [and goes on being sufficient] for you'. We must remain in the asking stage until God answers. There is then no longer any need to ask; his ongoing provision for us is his continuing answer.

Then comes the final stage: acceptance. As we have seen, it is important not to enter this stage too soon or too readily. We may feel that, like Paul, we have received God's answer, through some prophetic word, word of knowledge or discernment; however, we may be mistaken. There is always the danger that we will mistake an unconscious tendency to expect the worst for a prophetic word that we will not be healed. I have found that there is a bias in human nature against grace and against good news; healing seems too good to be true. Many people also hold the unconscious belief that they must suffer (and so be ill) for their sins. For many different reasons, we find it difficult to expect healing for ourselves. This puts us at risk of resigning ourselves to our illnesses too readily.

Of course, the promise 'my grace is sufficient for you' is universal for every situation, but in the context of Paul's story it has a special prophetic meaning for him that should not be applied indiscriminately to every Christian. I have no doubt that many earnest Christians have mistakenly endured pain or illness thinking it was their lifetime thorn in the flesh, when God's word was one of healing – through medicine, miracle, life-style change, or a combination of these. They ought to have been praying according to the patience or prophetic approach rather than the Pauline model of acceptance. In other words, it is tragically possible to misunderstand God's answer. All 'prophetic' words need to be tested carefully (see *Testing the gifts* in Chapter 4); we are just as capable of being overpessimistic as overoptimistic. It is especially important to seek the guidance of mature, discerning Christians before moving on to the final stage of acceptance of illness.

If someone who is ill comes to recognise that this Pauline approach is *truly* appropriate for him or her, it can lead to a great sense of peace and even joy. Such a person can say with Paul and countless other wounded people of God: 'But he said to me, "My grace is sufficient for you, for my power is made perfect in weakness". I will all the more gladly boast of my weaknesses, that the power of Christ may rest upon me. For the sake of Christ, then, I am content with weaknesses, insults, hardships, persecutions, and calamities; for when I am weak, then I am strong' (2 Cor. 12:9–10 *RSV*). This is the acceptance of grace. Those who are genuinely called, like Paul, to accept their thorn in the flesh can do so only because of God's all-sufficient grace. Nothing but God's grace can compensate for illness. We dare not try to bear it in our own strength or for wrong reasons. Grace alone brings peace and acceptance, because through it the power of Christ comes to us in our weakness.

The paradise approach

When death is imminent and healing lies only beyond the grave, another approach to prayer is required. Again, this must not be adopted too readily because prayer can change a seemingly hopeless situation (2 Kgs. 20:1,5). The time may come, however, when we need to surrender ourselves or our loved ones up to death and paradise. On just a few occasions, when I have been conducting seminars on healing, it has been discerned that a person for whom we have been asked to pray should perhaps be surrendered into the Father's loving arms and allowed to die in peace.[18] I think it may be possible for us by our prayers sometimes to keep those we love alive beyond the time when the Father would take them home. Lovingly surrendering them to his safe keeping at the appropriate time can result in great blessing. In the midst of our grief, we can rejoice with them in their imminent and ultimate healing.[19]

The four approaches to praying for healing I have described are not necessarily mutually exclusive.[20] Some people will move from one category to another as their situation changes. I am not claiming that these are the only models for prayer, or even that they are the best that can be devised. I am certainly not advocating set formulas for prayer. On the contrary, my aim in this chapter has been to emphasise the need for flexibility in the way we pray for healing, so that we can do justice to the wide-ranging examples found in Scripture and daily life. Ultimately, whatever approach we adopt, the most important issue is the attitude with which we come to prayer, not the words we use. If our attitude is right, our prayers (both spoken and unspoken) will flow naturally. In our ministry of healing, let us encourage those in our care to pray in appropriate ways for God's healing and sustaining grace in this life, as they await in peace their ultimate healing in the life to come.

WHAT MAKES OUR PRAYERS EFFECTIVE?

On the surface, prayer seems to have all the hallmarks of powerlessness, a state that is considered undesirable in this self-focused world. Those who resort to prayer are admitting that they cannot deal with the situation on their own. To unbelievers, prayer can seem like merely talking to oneself, withdrawing from reality and action and taking comfort in wishful thinking. While they may concede a limited benefit, in the sense that prayer provides a positive form of self-talk for those coping with difficulties, they may still regard it as powerless to effect any change in people's circumstances. In reality, however, prayer is one of the most powerful forces in the universe. As Christians who have experienced the love and power of God in our lives, we recognise this. Through prayer miracles occur, the lost are saved, the sick healed. It changes the course of history. The Christian prays to an all-loving, all-sovereign Father who has promised to hear and grant the prayers of his children. He in sovereign grace freely responds to the requests of his people.

The contrast between the apparent weakness of prayer and the magnitude of its influence becomes even more evident when we acknowledge that Christians do not know how they ought to pray (Rom. 8:26). In human terms, even fervent, specific prayer seems a pathetically futile pastime. When it does not know its own mind, how can it be worth anything?

Yet, in a sense, this helplessness is the very essence of prayer: 'It is the helpless soul's helpless look unto a gracious Friend'.[21] What is it that transforms prayer from an apparently futile and weak collection of human words and desires into a life-changing, history-changing force?

Is faith the key?

It is 'by grace through faith' that we are justified and saved. Similarly, all healing is part of God's general grace, a function of his unconditional love for us. For our ministry to be soundly based we need to keep the close relationship between grace and faith in perspective: while both are important, the emphasis should be on grace rather than faith, on God's loving movement towards us rather than ours towards him. This is true whether we are thinking about salvation or healing. Grace is not dependent on any effort on our part. Indeed, God may choose to work without any faith being exercised at all. Faith, however, will always be in response to God's grace.

All healing is an expression of God's grace, whether we perceive it to be 'miraculous' or not. Amazingly, this grace towards us continues even if we ignore or spurn him and refuse to have faith. In the Gospels, Jesus is reported as healing in response to faith on only a few occasions.[22] At times he healed people who in no way looked to him for it and quite apart from any faith on their part.[23] In any case, miracles are possible with faith as small as a mustard seed (Mt. 17:20). Jesus was more interested in the 'quality' of faith than the quantity. The people whose faith he commended understood the nature of God to be both powerful and loving and they placed their trust in him. Their faith was not in faith itself; that would be idolatry. Their faith was an expression of their belief in the person and nature of Jesus Christ himself.

We do not need a specific gift of faith to pray for healing. All true Christian prayer, prayer in the Spirit, stems from faith. We do not have to work up a lather trying to convince ourselves that God is going to respond in a particular way. We simply need to turn to God in our helplessness. The faith the Bible speaks about is essentially trust. This trust is in a loving Father with whom we have an intimate relationship.[24] It is a trust full of restfulness and serenity because of the greatness and the faithfulness of the God in whom it is placed. Healing depends on the One who is the object of our faith, not on the amount of faith we can muster.[25]

Often God's present will is unclear to us. Although a genuine prophetic word may sometimes be given, generally we do not know how much healing is to be given to an individual here and now. We can be sure that it is God's will for them to be healed and perfect in the coming age, but it is not necessarily his will for every Christian to be physically well in the present. He may, as we have seen, allow illness or suffering to continue in this life for his good purposes. So it is not necessarily a breakdown of faith to be unsure whether a person is going to be healed, but it is a sin to doubt God as our loving heavenly Father and to doubt his word. Our God has both the power and the mercy to bring healing at any time. We must understand, however, that we cannot manipulate his will to our purposes, either by making-believe that we are well or by following some kind of faith formula. Unless these pitfalls are avoided, the healing ministry can lead people into a 'new Christian magic'.[26] Healings and miracles can breed a sense of power that makes us feel like gods – beings with supernatural powers, possessing the secrets of controlling nature – or even God himself. Magic, the opposite of religion, coerces God and denies the fundamental ingredient of faith – submission.

We need to trust in the goodness of God, irrespective of our healing or lack of healing. By offering healing to all who have faith and implying that everyone can be assured of healing in this life, some in the healing ministry are unconsciously indulging in a spiritual worldliness. It is, in fact, a type of 'spiritual materialism' that values physical healing above all else. Without submissive, grace-acknowledging faith, we move away from wholeness and serenity towards disillusionment and frustration. The danger with this type of faith is that eventually our very belief in God himself, may come to depend on whether or not we are healed; we may need healing as evidence of God's existence and power. On the other hand, if we feel that God somehow needs evidence of our 'faith' in order to heal us, we may become exhausted by the effort of forcing ourselves to believe that we are getting better, despite evidence to the contrary. If we look at healing in this way, our lives become desperate as we try to rally 'enough' faith. Misunderstandings of this nature are tragic. They are likely to lead to anxiety, guilt and a sense of hopelessness that will be completely counterproductive to the healing process.

Clearly, there is more to effective prayer than the faith of the one who prays, no matter how intense and fervent that may be. How is it then that prayer can have such profound effects? What are the means by which this miracle takes place? Scripture reveals that Father, Son and Holy Spirit are all involved; prayer like every other aspect of Christian theology and practice is trinitarian. The loving Father graciously responds to the powerful intercession of both Son and Spirit on our behalf.

The intercession of Christ

Scripture appears to teach that guilt may keep our prayers from being heard and answered (1 Jn. 3:21–22, cf. Ps. 66:18; Prov. 15:29; Is. 59:2). In Christ, who 'always lives to intercede' for us (Heb. 7:25), we are assured that our guilt has been removed and we now have unhindered access to the loving Father. The one who prays for us before the loving Father and judge of all (Heb. 12:23) is the one who died to pay the penalty for our sins and rose victorious over death. His resurrection was the Father's 'yes' to the offering of his Son, the one perfect, sufficient sacrifice for the whole world. For those who are declared right with God through faith in the crucified Lord there is no condemnation. There is therefore no possibility of the Christian being judged guilty because Jesus Christ pleads our cause at God's right hand.[27]

The One who intercedes for us is the human Christ. He died as our representative and, having risen bodily from the dead, still shares our humanity. He is our 'brother', interceding for us and sympathising with us in our weakness (Heb. 4:15). He identifies with us and represents us before the Father. He is our mediator, our sinless representative.[28] But more than this. He is the fully human Son of God, but being one with the Father, he is also God the Son (Jn. 1:1,14). He is the perfect go-between because he is both human and God – the one and only God–man. The Son is in constant unbroken fellowship with the all-loving, all-sovereign Father. He is also in fellowship with us, especially when we pray. It is this mediation of One who truly represents both his fellow humans and God himself that guarantees the effectiveness of all our prayers.

It is helpful to picture the interceding Christ as 'enthroned' at the right hand of God (Rom. 8:34). He is not a supplicant pleading our cause before a reluctant Father. Christ's death did not win over a hostile God. The Father has always been generously disposed towards us. The Father initiated the offering of his Son, who willingly offered himself and is now enthroned as Priest–King. We can say that the Son asks what he wills from the Father who freely and lovingly gives. In fact we can say that our

Lord's life in heaven as Priest–King is his prayer for us. It is because of who he is and what he has done that all our prayers are heard and granted. His promise that whatever we ask in his name will be granted (Jn. 14:13–14) has been sealed and guaranteed by his death.

In the prayers of Jesus for his disciples, as recorded in the Gospels, we catch a glimpse of what the risen Christ continues to do for us. He said to Peter: 'I have prayed for you . . . that your faith may not fail' (Lk. 22:32). And for all believers, including those who would believe in him in time to come, he prayed: '. . . Holy Father, protect them by the power of your name – the name you gave me – so that they may be one as we are one . . . My prayer is not that you take them out of the world, but that you protect them from the evil one . . . Sanctify them by the truth . . .' (Jn. 17:11,15,17). We read of Stephen, who was greatly comforted in his dying moments by a vision of the glory of God and Jesus, as Son of man, standing at God's right hand (Acts 7:55). We can find great inspiration in the knowledge that he is still there as our representative praying for us, his present day followers.

When it comes to illness we, like the disciples, stand powerless to effect a cure.[29] We are totally dependent on the intercession of Christ in heaven. What we need as we approach the healing ministry is not great confidence in our own faith, abilities or gifts, but a deep humility that seeks only the glory of God the Father and gratefully acknowledges all that Christ the Son has done and continues to do for us.

The intercession of the Holy Spirit

While the intercession of Christ is taking place for us in heaven, we have an intercessor within us here on earth, the Holy Spirit. Jesus called the Spirit 'another helper'.[30] In many ways, not least in prayer, he gives the Christian a helping hand. John Stott writes: 'The Holy Spirit's inspiration is as necessary as the Son's mediation if we are to gain access to the Father in prayer'.[31] As the time approached for Jesus to return to the Father he prayed that we, his disciples, be given this helper to strengthen and counsel us as he himself had done (Jn. 14:16–17).[32] In other words, the Spirit continues the work of Christ within us.

We are told that the Spirit helps us in our weakness for 'we do not know what we ought to pray, but the Spirit himself intercedes for us' (Rom. 8:26).[33] As we have seen, the intercession of Christ overcomes the gulf between the creature and the Creator and the barrier between the sinner and the Holy One. The intercession of the Spirit overcomes yet another difficulty. Basic weakness threatens prayer long before it gets to heaven. We do not even know how to formulate our prayers as we should. Often we cannot put our deep desires into words. Many years ago Robert Haldane wrote:

> The people of God are often so much oppressed, and experience such anguish of mind, that their agitated spirits, borne down by affliction, can neither perfectly conceive nor properly express their complaints and requests to God. Shall they then remain without prayer? No; the Holy Spirit acts in their hearts.[34]

The privilege we have of communicating with God through wordless prayer is described beautifully in the words of a well-known hymn:

> Prayer is the soul's sincere desire,
>   Uttered or unexpressed,
> The motion of a hidden fire,
>   That trembles in the breast.
>
> Prayer is the burden of a sigh,
>   The falling of a tear,
> The upward glancing of an eye
>   When none but God is near.[35]

When prayer is sighed rather than said, the interceding Spirit turns it into communication with God that goes beyond words (Rom. 8:26,27). Identifying with the deep longings of human hearts, he presents them to the Father as 'unutterable groanings'[36] that are in accordance with the Father's will. Here again we are reminded of the importance of being motivated by the will of God as we pray. We have the assurance that 'if we ask anything according to his will, he hears us. And if we know that he hears us – whatever we ask – we know that we have what we asked of him' (1 Jn. 5:14–15). Because our weak, often unformulated, prayers are turned into prayer that is in accordance with the will of God they are not only heard, they are granted in God's best time.

The heart cries that are translated by the Spirit as unutterable groanings are part of the longing of the whole creation for the time when God will set all things right.[37] Some of our prayers *will* be answered in this life, although not always in the ways we envisage; however, it is in the resurrection glory of the age to come that we will see *all* our secret, struggling prayers finally answered to perfection.

As a result of prayer, some will be healed in this lifetime, some will not; here again is mystery. We live in a fallen world between Christ's first coming and future reign. In our 'creatureliness' and sinfulness we must continuously acknowledge that God's ways are far above our ways. We simply do not know in detail what his present will is in terms of healing and wholeness. He has revealed sufficient of his will to encourage us to be involved in a healing ministry and to pray with confidence for the sick. But we do not always receive a prophetic word about the healing of an individual. Generally, we must confess with Paul that 'we see in a mirror dimly' (1 Cor. 13:12 *RSV*). As we carry out our healing ministry, we agonise in prayer because we share in the fallenness of the whole creation and because we long for the coming of the final age (Rom. 8:21). In the meantime the intercession of the Spirit more than compensates for our ignorance and weakness. He turns our weakness into powerful, effectual prayer: prayer that is therefore always heard and answered. So we do not lose heart as we pray for the sick and participate in the healing ministry. Our weakness, ignorance and confusion are the very stuff of which effectual prayer is made.

We began this chapter by reflecting on the Lord's Prayer in which Jesus encourages us to address our prayers to 'our Father in heaven'. We now see that through the intercession of the Son and the Spirit our prayer finds its way to the throne of our loving Father in heaven. There his infinite love and power guarantee that our requests are heard and answered, according to his will, either here or in the life to come.[38]

Notes

1. Elsewhere in Scripture, the use of the phrase 'Abba Father' (see Mk. 14:36; Rom. 8:15; Gal. 4:6) illustrates the intimacy of the relationship between Father and Son, which we as his disciples share. The Aramaic word Abba is the familiar term by which children address their father, equivalent to 'dad' in English. Significantly, although the word is still used in the latter sense in Hebrew-speaking families, it is not the term used by Jews when addressing God as their Father; see F.F. Bruce, *The Epistle of Paul to the Romans: An Introduction and Commentary* (London: Tyndale, 1963), p. 167.
2. It is important to recognise that some people have great difficulty in relating to God as Father. For example, some may have experienced (or be experiencing) an unsatisfactory or damaging relationship with their earthly father. Others may reject the concept because they feel it suggests male dominance. This issue

is discussed in Charles Sherlock, *God on the Inside: Trinitarian Spirituality* (Canberra: Acorn, 1991); A.F. Kimel, Jr (Ed.), *Speaking the Christian God: The Holy Trinity and the Challenge of Feminism* (Grand Rapids: Eerdmans; Leominster: Gracewing, 1992).

3. In these three petitions, the Greek aorist tense is used indicating that a single completed event is being described; however, each petition also looks forward to a final fulfilment at the return of Christ and the final consummation of the kingdom. Note that these petitions, which seem to be closely related, all ask God to do something on his own behalf, in contrast to the next three, which are for 'us'; see Robert A. Guelich, *The Sermon on the Mount: A Foundation for Understanding* (Waco: Word, 1982), pp. 289–291.

4. In our day, great emphasis has been placed on prayer as an aspect of 'power healing' or spiritual warfare. We need to be careful, however, that a fascination with the power of God to perform miracles, or a perception of ourselves as his agents engaged in 'power encounters' with the forces of evil, does not become the primary motivator of our prayers. The emphasis must always be on love rather than power; see Francis MacNutt, *Healing* (Altamonte Springs: Creation House, 1988), pp. 151–153.

5. The Lord's Prayer reminds us that we are speaking to a God who is 'in heaven' and therefore sovereign at all times and able to use any means he chooses to answer our prayers for healing. We must beware of seeing God as a 'God of the gaps' who is needed only when we cannot account for what happens in any other way. As science explains more and more of what we formerly thought of as miraculous, this 'God' will be progressively reduced.

6. See Ezek. 36:23–27; God promises, 'I will show the holiness of [or hallow] my great name, which has been profaned among the nations'. The opposite of hallowing God's name is profaning it, by such things as idolatry, immorality and false oaths.

7. See Mt. 5:16 and *The holiness of God* in Chapter 6.

8. See O. Hallesby, *Prayer* (London: Inter-Varsity Press, 1961), pp. 103f. Quotations in this and the next paragraph are from p. 104.

9. These and other aspects of the theology of the kingdom are dealt with in more detail in *Healing and the kingdom* in Chapter 2.

10. If taken to extremes, the Calvinist emphasis on sovereign grace (God's right to take the initiative towards us) can lead some people to an absolute determinism that amounts to fatalism. They may lose sight of the fact that God is always free to respond to the prayers of his children.

11. These ideas have already been introduced and discussed (see Chapter 2). Francis MacNutt, commenting on praying for healing, writes: 'The best point of view, I think, is to see that God's normative will is that people will be healed, unless there is some countervailing reason'; see MacNutt, p. 256.

12. Howard Brant suggests that many people today want to change the Lord's Prayer to, 'My will be done in heaven as I want it on earth'. He adds: 'When we desire to see God intervene miraculously in the affairs of men or nature, we

come to our sovereign Lord and present our requests, not our commands, before Him. We are not demanding our rights, but rather exerting the privilege which He has given us to come before Him confidently in our time of need (Heb. 4:16).' From a paper entitled *Toward an SIM Position on Power Encounter*, p. 13; see Note 2 in Chapter 5 for detailed citation.

13. T. Geddert, 'We prayed for healing . . . but she died', in J.R. Coggins and P.G. Hiebert (Eds), *Wonders and the Word: An Examination of Issues Raised by John Wimber and the Vineyard Movement* (Winnipeg: Kindred, 1989), pp. 85–91. He describes three approaches: the Job model, the Elijah model and the paradise model.

14. In contrast, as we read this story we are taken to heaven and told what was about to happen and what God was doing (see Job 1:6ff).

15. See Chapter 4, especially *Testing the gifts*. We should be wary of relying on a private revelation in case we are deceived by a condemning heart (1 Jn. 3:20).

16. To this extent there is an overlap with the Job approach. There is also an aspect of the prophetic in this approach; God's word to Paul, 'My grace is sufficient for you . . .' (2 Cor. 12:9), given in response to his pleas for relief, appears to be a 'prophetic' word indicating that healing will not be granted.

17. Philip Edgcumbe Hughes comments: 'Is there a single servant of Christ who cannot point to some "thorn in the flesh", visible or private, physical or psychological, for which he has prayed to be released, but which has been given him by God to keep him humble, and therefore, fruitful, in His service? And is not this the case to special degree with those who have been called to be ministers of the gospel? Every believer must learn that human weakness and divine grace go hand in hand together. Hence Paul's "thorn in the flesh" is, by its very lack of definition, a type of every Christian's "thorn in the flesh", not with regard to externals, but by its spiritual significance'; see P.E. Hughes, *Paul's Second Epistle to the Corinthians* (London: Marshall, Morgan and Scott, 1962), pp. 442f.

18. As the following experience illustrates, we can never be dogmatic on this issue. Once, at the end of a church service, with the elders I prayed for a very seriously ill woman in her eighties, the mother of a member of the congregation. Her liver was failing and she was not expected to survive the night. To us it seemed that her time had come; we did not want her suffering to be prolonged. So we prayed according to the paradise approach. To her doctor's utter amazement (and ours), her liver began to function, she recovered and some years later is still enjoying a quite remarkable quality of life!

19. [In a letter of thanks to his doctor only a few months before he died, Robert Hillman wrote: 'I remain open to any natural, supernatural (quiet miracle?) or medical healing which God may give even at this late stage, but I am fully open to the probability that Paul's words apply to me: ". . . the time has come for my departure. I have fought the good fight, I have finished the race, I have kept the faith. Now there is in store for me the crown of righteousness, which the Lord, the righteous Judge, will award to me on that day – and not only to me, but also to all who have longed for his appearing" (2 Tim. 4:6–8).' Significantly, in his

first draft he crossed out 'possibility' and changed it to 'probability'. He spoke of a sense of being 'given' this passage of Scripture early in November 1991 and of needing to feel that people were willing to 'let' him die.]

20. The following is a brief summary of the distinguishing characteristics of each approach: (a) perseverance: the person does not know whether he or she is to be healed. Healing may come at any time. The patient is called to persevere; (b) prophetic: prophetic insight is given that the ill person will be healed in this life; (c) Pauline (acceptance): the person receives insight that he or she will not be healed but will have God's all-sufficient grace; (d) paradise: insight is given that the person is not to be healed in this life but is to die and receive ultimate healing. Ways in which they overlap were noted in Note 16.

21. This is the view of one of the best known exponents of Christian prayer; see Hallesby, p. 48.

22. Out of twenty-six accounts of individual healing in the Gospels, mention of faith is found only twelve times. It is clear that Jesus healed in response to faith in only five of these instances, although faith is sometimes implied in the title by which Jesus addressed the person or by the fact that they approached Jesus. See J. Wilkinson, *Health and Healing: Studies in New Testament Principles and Practice* (Edinburgh: Handsel, 1980), pp. 42f.

23. See Peter Ralphs, Appendix II. In reviewing the role of faith in the healings of Jesus, he concludes that faith is important in healing, especially faith on the part of the 'healer'. He believes, however, that it goes far beyond biblical teaching to present faith as an indispensable prerequisite for healing or to imply that people will invariably be healed if only their faith (or the faith of those ministering to them) is strong enough.

24. In contrast, some teach that faith is spelt R-I-S-K. Charles Kraft refers to this in relation to the question: What if I pray for someone and it doesn't work? He presents it as an encouragement to Christians to be prepared to risk the embarrassment that their prayers for healing may not be 'successful'; see C.H. Kraft, *Christianity with Power: Your Worldview and Your Experience of the Supernatural* (Ann Arbor: Vine, 1989), p. 75. It seems to me that this kind of risk may often be self-inflicted; there are cases where it exists only because of a dogmatic 'naming and claiming' approach to ministry. 'Believe it, achieve it, receive it' is not a helpful catchcry. I am concerned that those who equate faith with risk in this way may inadvertently be encouraging people to take the 'risk' of relying exclusively on prayer (believing this to be evidence of their faith), instead of seeking medical help as well. This approach may also pave the way for people to 'risk' ridicule by claiming that a miracle has occurred despite clear evidence to the contrary.

25. Peter Ralphs, commenting on John 4:46–54, suggests that the Evangelist is addressing 'the situation where people with a superficial faith wish to participate in the healing activity associated with the early Christian community. They may come with a very imperfect understanding of Jesus, wanting only that someone they love and who is in danger be helped and healed. The

superficiality of their faith must be addressed but it is not to exclude them from the help that may be given. Participation in the life imparted by the risen Christ is a matter of grace not of human qualifications. Even a superficial faith can be encouraged in the hope that it will move onto a deeper level'; P.A.R. Ralphs, personal communication.

26. See P.G. Hiebert in 'Healing and the Kingdom' in Coggins and Hiebert, p. 143.

27. See Rom. 8:1, 33–34; 1 Jn. 2:1; Is. 53:12.

28. 1 Timothy 2:5 stresses that the mediator is 'the man Christ Jesus'.

29. It has been suggested that the powerlessness the disciples experienced when attempting to heal a boy possessed with a dumb spirit arose from their self-reliance, exemplified by their lack of prayer (Mk. 9:17–18). Prayer is the confession of weakness – of faith in, and willingness to depend on, the power of God!

30. The Greek word for the Spirit used in John 14:16, *paraklētos*, means one who comes to our side to help, strengthen and counsel.

31. J.R.W. Stott, *Men Made New* (London: Inter-Varsity Fellowship, 1966), p. 98.

32. The Spirit came as the result of the intercession of Christ and, no doubt, because of his death and resurrection, which removed the sin-barrier to the Spirit's outpouring.

33. While some interpret this passage as a reference to speaking in tongues, the text itself does not say this. Romans 8:26 is about the Spirit of God praying for us, not our spirit praying (cf. 1 Cor. 14:14); it applies to all Christians, not only those with the gift of speaking in tongues. See also Chapter 4, Note 20.

34. R. Haldane, *Exposition of the Epistle to the Romans* (London: Banner of Truth Trust, 1958), p. 387.

35. From the hymn 'O thou by whom we come to God' written by James Montgomery (1771–1854).

36. This is the literal meaning of the Greek expression in Romans 8:26, which is translated variously, e.g. 'groans that cannot be expressed' *NIV*; 'sighs too deep for words' *RSV*; 'inarticulate groans' *REB*.

37. Rom. 8:23; see *Healing and reconciliation* in Chapter 2. For possible examples in Scripture of groaning in prayer, see 1 Sam. 1:7,13; Ps. 77:1–3; Is. 38:14; Lk. 22:62; 2 Cor. 12:7–10.

38. Jesus assures us, 'The Father himself loves you' (Jn. 16:27), and John writes: 'Consider how great is the love which the Father has bestowed on us in calling us his children!' (1 Jn. 3:1 *REB*). That is why Jesus makes the promise, 'My Father will give you whatever you ask in my name' (Jn. 16:23).

Chapter 9

Why Are Some Not Healed?

Many Christians throughout the world will identify with the following poignant account of one church's struggle to come to terms with the loss of a valued member:

> We were sure God had promised healing; we thought that meant the cancer would not come back. But it did. We prayed for healing. We called the elders of the church to pray. We anointed with oil. We laid on hands. There were prayer vigils. There was fasting. We did everything that we could. We prayed every way we knew. Yet the dreaded disease brought about exactly the sort of physical and mental deterioration that the doctors had predicted. They suggested it would take between three and nine months . . . It took five. Where was God? Where was his promise of healing? What about his promise that the prayer of faith would make the sick person well?[1]

Any involvement in a healing ministry, whether formal or informal, will lead to the discovery that not everyone is healed. Many Christians are reluctant to accept this as a reality.

In Scripture we read of several New Testament believers who were not healed.[2] Paul's irritating 'thorn in the flesh' was not removed (2 Cor. 12:7–9). And when Epaphraditus, Paul's companion in ministry, became ill the disease was apparently permitted to run its course bringing him close to death (Phil. 2:25–30). Paul also advised Timothy (1 Tim. 5:23) to take a little wine for his stomach and frequent ailments (literally, weaknesses), a commonly accepted medical practice of the time, and he left Trophimus ill at Miletus (2 Tim. 4:20). Surely, if miraculous healing had been God's purpose for Trophimus at that time, there was no more gifted healer than Paul. God's provision of the gift of healing (1 Cor. 12:30) did not, it seems, guarantee that all would be healed. Clearly, Christian faith and experience are not a 'vaccine' against disease or disaster, and healing is not always God's present answer to illness. Thus, in life and in Scripture itself, we cannot escape the fact that there are people, including faithful Christians, who do not receive miraculous healing in response to prayer.

As we pray for the sick we discover a wide range of results. Some people are dramatically, miraculously and completely cured; others notice varying degrees of improvement – major or minor, instant or gradual. Some are helped only temporarily; others are not healed physically at all. Understandably, we ask: *Why are some not healed?* Theologically, this is a difficult and faith-stretching question, one that cannot be answered fully in this life. Those who are ill usually find it more helpful to consider the question: *Why am I not being healed?* As they do so, they may discover ways in which they are unwittingly contributing to their problems and be encouraged to explore avenues of healing previously overlooked.

THE PRESENCE OF MYSTERY

The way in which God governs his universe and cares for his children during this present 'time between the times' is full of mystery. He cures or relieves the suffering of some, while allowing others to experience ongoing illness with the offer of grace to help them cope – a special endurance that can bring glory to his name and advance his kingdom. In our ministry of healing, in our coming to terms with sickness and in all our theologising about it, we must acknowledge this mystery.

God is not arbitrary or erratic (Jas. 1:17). He is always purposeful even though we do not always understand what he is doing. Generally, we do not know why he heals in one instance and not in another. Even when, from Scripture or a prophetic word, we seem to gain insight into some of his reasons, his ways are always above our ways and his thoughts are always beyond ours (Is. 55:8f; Rom. 11:33). He is, as Christ revealed, a loving Father who wants to be in intimate relationship with us, but we do not know him in the depth that he knows us. To deny the presence of mystery in the way he works is to attempt to strip him of his divinity.

We can take great comfort, however, in knowing that the mysterious sovereign God of the universe has revealed himself in Jesus Christ. His action and decisions will always be consistent with the loving character he has shown to us in Jesus. Thus when we speak of mystery (what is concealed from us), we must also speak of revelation (what has been revealed to us in Christ). There is never any contradiction between the two. Many things remain full of mystery. Often we will not understand God's response to our prayers for healing. But he has revealed enough of himself to enable us to trust him, even when we do not understand what he is doing.

THE REALITY OF THE FALL

Scripture teaches us that the universe is, like a woman in labour, waiting in great pain and longing for the birth of the new age of perfection to come, when it will be freed from the shackles of decay (Rom. 8:20–22). The whole of creation, despite its appearance of order, has been affected by the ravages of sin and judgment and is groaning for release. Christians and non-Christians alike must share in the effects of the fall until Christ returns. Our bodies are wasting away (2 Cor. 4:16). We are vulnerable to accidents and sickness, age increasingly limits our powers (Ecc. 12) and eventually we die. The chaos and suffering we experience are an intrusion into God's perfect creation, part of the reality of the fall, which no one can escape.

Any theology that fails to face up to the reality of the fall (however we may understand this concept) is unbiblical[3] and cannot deal with the problems of evil and suffering. Healing in this fallen world is, at best, only temporary. It is also only partial, even when we might consider that a particular illness has been completely cured. Paul says that we groan inwardly as we await the redemption of our bodies (Rom. 8:23). Our salvation, which includes the renewal of our bodies, is in this sense not complete. Bodily perfection (ultimate healing and perfect health) is not ours in this life; it awaits the coming age (1 Cor. 15).

Thus we see that God has provided us with some general answers to our question: *Why are some not healed?* Sickness and death are an inevitable part of our fallenness and the 'incompleteness' of our salvation in this present time. We know that they are contrary to God's original and ultimate purpose. We know that in the kingdom of Jesus they were overcome and will be fully overcome in the future. In our present condition, however, we cannot know all things. But this supreme reality we do know: 'God is love'. Here is a truth written in blood and sealed by death. Because of the cross, in the midst of mystery, we can trust this sovereign God of love whether we are healed or not, as we await the ultimate healing of the age to come.

Clearly, to a certain extent, suffering is unavoidable in this fallen world. It is possible, however, to prolong suffering by behaving in ways that hinder the process of healing. Something can, and should, be done to avoid this unnecessary suffering.[4] In the following sections I describe attitudes and behaviours that may be detrimental to the healing process. I firmly believe that teaching about such barriers to healing (and how to deal with them in appropriate ways) is an important aspect of helping those who are ill receive all the healing God has for them in this life. Doing our best to deal with all that is unhelpful in our lives, however, does not guarantee that complete healing will automatically follow. We must be clear about that. On the other hand, even when we fail to 'do our best', God remains free to heal despite such barriers. He is sovereign in this, as in all things.

LACK OF LOVE

Of all the hindrances to healing, lack of love for God and others is the most insidious and widespread.

Being self-centred, not Christ-centred

Jesus said, 'You are my friends if you do what I command' (Jn. 15:14). Love for God in Christ is demonstrated by obedience. Conversely, disobedience, which is sin, represents lack of love for him. Persistent, wilful and unaddressed disobedience is a stumbling block in our journey towards wholeness and is therefore likely to impede the healing process. In the Christian, it is a sign of a life that is not fully Christ-centred, a sign of someone who is still trying to run his or her own life. Although surrendered to Christ at the time of conversion, there is no real desire to honour him as Lord in all things. Such a person is 'neither hot nor cold' (Rev. 3:16). Sadly, many Christians live in this unhealthy state. Indeed, as part of our fallen nature, we all do to a certain extent. It is a condition that can lead to a rapid deterioration that involves the whole person. The tendency is to cover up, to deny what is happening, to play games, to rationalise the problem away. We carry on, struggling to present a 'good Christian' image to ourselves and others. This leads only to further sinful behaviour and creates even more barriers to both healing and wholeness.

Living like this prevents us realising our full potential in Christ. Instead of a sincere faith there is an insincere faith, a bad conscience and an impure heart (in breach of 1 Tim. 1:5). Along with the fruit and gifts of the Spirit in our lives, there are 'Spirit barriers' such as resentment, fear of failure, envy, bitterness, etc. These not only impede the healing work of the Spirit in us, they also prevent our spiritual gifts from reaching their full potential. They may arise as a reaction to our current circumstances. In particular, some who become seriously ill may find it difficult to go on following and obeying Christ wholeheartedly because of ongoing resentment and anger against God for allowing their suffering. But 'Spirit barriers' may also be the aftermath of hurtful experiences in the past.

There are two ways of overcoming these barriers. Firstly, we need to repent in the light of God's grace, to be turned around and renewed. This is the most important step. Secondly, we need to deal with self-defeating attitudes, emotional scars and hurtful memories and this may mean seeking professional assistance (see *Emotional wholeness* in Chapter 7). For the Christian, overcoming barriers to healing is an ongoing process. While accepting that we will never be completely whole or perfect in this life, we should be willing to do all we can to deal with these barriers to health and wholeness. We need continually to be asking the Spirit of God to search our hearts and know us, to show us if there is any wicked way in us and to lead us in the way everlasting (Ps. 139:24 *RSV*).

Unconfessed sin, with its resulting guilt, may underlie all kinds of physical and emotional illness and represent a serious barrier to healing. For example, a person suffering from high blood pressure or anxiety may need confession and repentance before they can receive all the healing God has for them. In acknowledging this, however, we must be careful not to overemphasise the link between sin and sickness by teaching (or even giving the impression) that lack of healing is always a sign of some unconfessed sin. Such teaching imposes a never-ending sense of guilt on the sufferer, causing untold anguish. It may also encourage an unhealthy introspection or self-obsession, which can in itself be a barrier to healing (see below).

Lack of love for others

Lack of love for God is inevitably reflected in lack of love for others. I am convinced that the latter is a major barrier to receiving all the healing God has for us. We all know how soul-destroying, and body-destroying, bitterness can be. In Scripture, Jesus shows us that lack of forgiveness is a total barrier to salvation and wholeness (Mt. 6:15; 18:35; Mk. 11:25; Lk. 11:4). Wounded relationships, in biblical terms, are more serious than physical illness (Jas. 5:16). In my experience, resentment is a very significant barrier to healing. Thus learning to forgive and being willing to seek reconciliation whenever possible and appropriate can be important aspects of removing barriers to healing (see *Healthy relationships* in Chapter 7).

Interestingly, loving service seems to be very beneficial to health and healing.[5] Generally, the real barrier to our loving and serving others in a healthy way is selfishness, rather than hatred. In biblical terms, anyone who is completely self-absorbed is a very sick person, even if physically he or she appears to be in perfect health. The most important quality in someone who is becoming whole, in a biblical sense, is love: love that is demonstrated in loving service. Being able to love does not guarantee perfect physical health, of course. Many 'loving servants' have been allowed to endure sickness. Generally, however, ministering to others is very therapeutic. Conversely, self-absorption often appears to produce or exacerbate illness and hinder recovery.

One of the first things I encourage seriously or 'terminally' ill people to do is to find a way of serving others. Such a ministry provides encouragement, inspires hope and gives purpose to life. A sense of uselessness often accompanies the grief of finding oneself terminally ill. Serving others is a wonderful antidote. Although a desire for healing should not be our primary motivation, we will inevitably be blessed as we unselfishly give to others (Acts 20:35). On the other hand, ignoring the needs of others may prevent us from receiving all kinds of blessings from God, including healing.

Thankfully, we do not have to wait until our love for God and others is perfected before we are able to receive his healing. Indeed, one of the first expressions of our love for the Father is the confession of our unworthiness and lack of love. The loving Father forgives because he loves, and showers his blessing on us. We need to love the Father more, to worship and adore him with trusting hearts, overwhelmed with gratitude for his grace. Then we will more readily love his children all around us. I find it significant that Jesus taught us to pray, '*Our* Father in heaven', not '*My* Father in heaven'; there is both a horizontal and a vertical dimension to relating to the Father. Recognising this will help us to receive all the healing he has for us.

LACK OF FAITH

This barrier to healing receives great emphasis in many healing ministries. I feel that, due to simplistic teaching and lack of spiritual wisdom, it is often overemphasised. All too easily the impression can be given that lack of faith is the only reason that people are not healed. Great damage can be done by teaching or implying that God always heals, here and now, in response to faith. When healing does not come, the sufferer has even more to contend with. Their illness may well be aggravated by disappointment, despair and a sense of guilt and failure about the apparent inadequacy of their faith.[6]

As discussed in the previous chapter, there is no biblical warrant for teaching that everyone can be healed provided enough faith is exhibited. Nor is there any basis for teaching that lack of healing implies lack of faith. It seems that God in his grace will often heal people who have no faith.[7] We know, of course, that many unbelievers are healed through medical science which God, in his grace, provides (like rain) for believers and unbelievers alike (Mt. 5:45). This is sometimes true also of miraculous healing. God's intervention does not even depend on whether the person subsequently becomes a believer. His provision of healing is sheer grace.[8] We must never forget that *the gospel we proclaim as we exercise a healing ministry is not primarily a gospel of faith. It is a gospel of grace.*

While lack of healing in response to prayer is not always a sign of lack of faith and while God sometimes heals where there is no faith, it is nevertheless true that lack of faith must be regarded as a possible barrier to healing. Faith is important. It is essential in receiving salvation; it is usually important in receiving healing. When Jesus visited his own country where they knew him well he was unable to do many mighty works because of the people's lack of faith (Mt. 13:58). Lack of faith on the part of the healer can also be a problem (as in Mt. 17:20). Always it is the quality, not quantity, of faith that matters to God. Having faith means simply trusting in our heavenly Father, whose love for us has been revealed in Christ.

LOSS OF HOPE

Without hope we can exist but we cannot truly live. Hope is especially important for those who are ill, both present hope and future hope.[9] Present hope relates to all the things that give meaning and purpose to life in the here and now. Future hope is hope for the life to come, the utter confidence that one is ready to enter into it when the time arrives. The biblical notion of hope no doubt includes both aspects of hope: fullness of life and purpose in the present as well as a readiness for the age to come. The hope that God offers us is 'an anchor for the soul, firm and secure' (Heb. 6:19).

Loss of hope brings depression and despair and causes a lack of motivation for seeking healing. It can interfere with the healing process very quickly and tragically. On the other hand, genuine hope can be of great benefit, encouraging healing and improving quality of life, the latter being especially important for the terminally ill. Few other forces have so much impact. Hope must be genuine, however. Longing to be cured can easily trap us into clutching at false hope, hope that is out of touch with reality. In the end this will mean only despair. I know of many people who have been led into false hope of cure by unbiblical teaching that healing is available to all who have faith, making them, as we have seen, easy prey to guilt and despair. This experience is likely to have a negative rather than a positive effect on health. Alternatively, people may be led into false hope by exaggerated claims about the effectiveness of particular 'healers', diets or products. A proper biblical theology of healing, however, that focuses on the steadfast love of God and the gospel of Jesus Christ produces genuine hope, which maximises the healing process.

INSUFFICIENT PRAYER

Many people neglect to pray sufficiently for healing (or fail to pray at all) because they do not expect God to intervene miraculously. Others may pray infrequently and ineffectively because they have difficulty owning their own helplessness. They are crippled by the need to appear self-reliant in every situation.

A prayerless life that is characterised by self-reliance rather than God-reliance will be a powerless life. Similarly, a healing ministry lacking in prayer will be a powerless ministry.[10] Prayer is essential in preparing for and exercising a healing ministry (Jas. 5:14ff). Those who are sick should also be encouraged to pray for themselves. Not being healed may simply be the result of not praying. James warns us: 'You do not have, because you do not ask God' (Jas. 4:2). Failure to persevere in prayer – on the part of the sick person, the church or both – may also limit the amount of healing received.[11]

I have always felt the need in my own healing ministry to encourage the church to continue to pray fervently for those who have sought healing at a service. While illness continues, we keep on interceding; when there has been miraculous or dramatic healing, we offer prayers of gratitude and praise. I have been particularly conscious of the sustained prayer of the Church as many Christians and congregations continue to uphold my wife and myself. The cancer has been held in check, my general health sustained and I have been given special grace to cope. I believe that all this has come through the ministry of prayer.

Many people stop praying too soon because they do not understand that healing in response to prayer, even 'miraculous' healing, does not always happen immediately. Healing may come gradually and progressively over a long period as we continue to pray. Alternatively, it may be delayed for a time, but God's delay is not necessarily his denial. No doubt, until God makes it clear to us that healing is not according to his good purpose for us, we ought to continue to seek all the healing he has for us from every authentic source. And this includes continuing to pray while we await God's 'ripe' (Gk. *kairos*) time for healing.[12] This is a good principle to adopt in relation to every prayer request, not just our prayers for healing.

As prayer is an essential channel of healing grace, anything that prevents us from praying persistently and effectively can be a barrier to healing. We need to be on the lookout for such things: lack of love for others (see above) is one example. Broken fellowship with one's marriage partner is another (1 Pet. 3:7); however, I tend to think that Christians who are struggling in a difficult marriage may be more in need of encouragement to pray than a reminder of this potential problem with their prayer life.

Francis MacNutt, a Roman Catholic priest involved in the healing ministry, suggests that sometimes people are not healed because they fail to pray specifically. He believes this is particularly important in the case of prayer for emotional healing and I tend to agree with him.[13] It often does seem to be important to get to the root cause. It may be that a person is seeking healing for some physical or emotional illness, when the root cause is a moral problem or a trauma buried in the past. This may require appropriate prayer and counselling. We should be careful, however, not to overemphasise this point. We do not want to launch people on an endless round of introspection or counselling, when perhaps what they really need to do is accept their condition and the grace God offers to bear it. But whether grace is needed for healing or for endurance, this grace will often come to us through prayer.

God seems to be calling the Church in our day to renew its commitment to intercessory prayer. While this call is for all Christians, God also seems to be raising up many people whose *key* gift and ministry is intercession. This gift and ministry is no doubt of vital significance in the healing ministry. Without it the Church and its members cannot hope to receive all the healing God has for them. Nor can we fulfil our ministry of preaching and healing in the non-Christian world.

IGNORING POSSIBLE AVENUES OF HEALING

In the previous chapter we considered the many different ways in which God provides healing. Failing to recognise the whole range of healing resources available to us is obviously another way in which we can contribute to our illness or lack of healing. Praying for healing remains central, however. God's response may be to heal miraculously. But often, in the process of granting healing, he points us to some helpful action that we can take.

Rejecting medical science

As we have already seen, turning to medical science for help is not inconsistent with having faith in God's power to heal. God often uses medical intervention to answer the prayer of faith. Thus medical science plays a role in the healing ministry. To misunderstand this is to neglect a vast resource of God-given healing. This is not to say that medical science has the last word. It is important that we acknowledge God's control over the process. Even before we seek medical assistance we should pray; while seeking it we should pray; as we follow the advice we are given we should pray; and (ideally) as we take our medication or receive treatment we should offer a prayer of thanksgiving!

Christian doctors will be the first to admit that God who is in control of the way in which an illness proceeds, not medical science. Acknowledging God's sovereignty in this way helps us avoid idolising doctors for their skills. The latter attitude can in itself be a barrier to healing if it causes us to neglect prayer or other health-promoting strategies. We may also place undue stress on the skilled but fallible human beings who are our doctors if we expect them to be miracle workers.

Faulty diagnosis is another potential problem. Tragically, this can keep a person in pain and ill-health for years. It is up to us to take responsibility for our health and seek further medical advice if we suspect that the diagnosis of our condition is incorrect. The issue of correct diagnosis has a special significance in the context of the healing ministry of the church. The medical diagnosis may be correct, but there may be a root problem in some other area of the person's life (a 'moral' illness) that needs to be faced and dealt with before healing can take place (see above).

Other factors

Overwork, conflict, a hurried lifestyle and anxiety wreak havoc on the human psyche and body, not to speak of the damage done to one's spirit. All are barriers to healing. Conversely, an ordered, unhurried restful lifestyle is health-maximising. Life, especially for the Christian, cannot be lived totally without suffering or stress (see 2 Cor. 11:23ff, esp. v. 28) but we should be doing our best to minimise and manage it. There are ways in which we can avoid creating it for ourselves and others. Christians are called to live trustfully one day at a time (Mt. 6:34), to be peacemakers living as far as possible in peace with each other and their neighbours (Mt. 5:9; Heb. 12:14). They have inner resources for reducing stress and encouraging health and healing, which they need to appropriate.

Ironically, an all-consuming emphasis on praying for miraculous healing can in itself become a barrier to healing if it causes us to overlook other possible avenues of healing, for example, the importance of a healthy lifestyle. Those involved as leaders in the healing ministry, because of their position of influence, have a particular responsibility to advocate and also to *embody* a healthy lifestyle. A balanced concern for health, with attention to factors such as diet, rest, recreation and exercise, should be part of our Christian ethos. This is an important source of divine healing and to neglect it is to ignore biblical teaching and to 'tempt' God (cf. Mt. 4:7 *RSV*).

AN UNHEALTHY ENVIRONMENT

Some people may live and work in environments that are detrimental to their health. For example, people whose work has involved exposure to asbestos are succumbing to a killer lung disease, mesothelioma; lead in some paint residues and petrol fumes may be causing brain damage in children; air pollution is a worldwide problem in urban areas. For some years I lived in Port Kembla, NSW, where there was constant fallout from the huge industrial complexes in the area. When we lived near Los Angeles in Southern California, mountains only a few miles from our apartment were obscured by smog, which settled over the whole region. Such environmental hazards are significant barriers to health and healing that confront whole societies. We cannot expect people affected by such environmental barriers to receive all the healing God has for them. Christians need to work with government authorities and other people of good-will to minimise the health threats that come with over-industrialisation.

One of my special concerns is the ill-health of aboriginal Australians, which is due, in part at least, to changes in their environment and lifestyle associated with colonisation and westernisation. Poor health is also the norm in many regions of the so-called underdeveloped world. Here the underlying cause and also the greatest barrier to healing is undoubtedly poverty, which is often the by-product of warfare or injustice. Wide-scale education programmes of simple health care and nutrition could save the lives of millions, generally improving health and increasing life expectancy in many nations. But much more is needed. A more equitable distribution of resources could vastly reduce poverty and hunger, increase medical resources and lead to significant improvements in levels of community health.

The key to major health reform, to removing this major barrier to healing for many people, is to be found in the proclamation of the transforming gospel of Jesus Christ. This gospel motivates renewed concern for one's neighbour and the sharing of resources, which includes the provision of relief for the sick and hungry, and gives grace to sustain those who work towards change.

ACCEPTING SICKNESS TOO READILY

Many people, in my opinion, accept their illnesses too readily. Paul eventually had to come to the point where he could restfully accept his thorn in the flesh, but he did not accept it without a struggle. In fact, as already noted, he showed a healthy resistance to it, praying 'three times' that it be taken from him. Accepting sickness too readily may limit healing by preventing us from exploring all available avenues for curing or alleviating our condition. Many earnest Christians, misunderstand God's purpose for them, take an overpessimistic attitude and unnecessarily endure pain or illness thinking that it is their lifetime 'thorn in the flesh'. Others, having decided to face up to the worst possible outcome as a strategy for coming to terms with ongoing illness or disability, simply neglect to go on praying for healing. The following attitudes may also discourage people from praying for healing.

Seeing sickness as atoning for sin

Some people (perhaps unconsciously) feel that by suffering they are in some way atoning for their sins. Guilt causes them to hang on to their illness. If they bear their sufferings well, maybe God will have mercy on them. Indeed, he may even be obligated to them. They think that as they suffer they store up merit for themselves. Francis MacNutt argues that this happens particularly in his Catholic tradition,[14] but I do not believe that it is confined to this group.

Such an attitude is in direct conflict with New Testament teaching. In an age that declares 'there is no such thing as a free lunch', the hardest truth for humankind to accept is that salvation and forgiveness of sin come through grace alone (Rom. 3:24; Eph. 2:8.). Like all God's blessings, they are his free gifts. Neither suffering, nor good works, can ever earn God's grace or make atonement for the sins that keep us from him. Payment of this debt comes only through the cross of Christ.

Seeing sickness as good not evil

There are others who, although they do not see suffering as atoning for their sins or as meriting God's blessing, nevertheless see it as intrinsically 'good'. They therefore have little motivation to seek healing through prayer or other means. They rightly see that suffering can often assist growth in character and lead towards maturity (Rom. 5:3–5; Jas. 1:2–4) and therefore believe they should submissively welcome it as something good sent by God. They do not understand that, although the sovereign good Father is able to bring good out of sickness and suffering, these things in themselves are evil.[15]

When the kingdom of God arrived in the person of Jesus, the Messiah, he showed his hostility to sickness by healing those who were ill. Sickness will one day cease to be part of the human experience. Meanwhile, like other signs of this fallen age, it is to be resisted (see *Healing and reconciliation* in Chapter 2). Although on occasions the loving Father may permit suffering to remain for his good purpose, it is only temporary and is as nothing when compared with the (sickness-free) glory that will be revealed to us (Rom. 8:18).

In general, we ought to pray to our loving heavenly Father, who sent his Son to be the world's Saviour and Great Physician, in confidence that he hates sickness. He is actively opposed to it, as to all evil, he sees fit to deliver his children from it in this life (in so far as this is consistent with his altogether good purposes) and he is preparing them for the ultimate wholeness of the life to come. Just as the sovereign Father was able to work through the evil event of the cross for the world's salvation, so he is able to bring blessing out of evil sickness.[16] And sometimes he leaves his children with sickness or disability for a short time (which, on an eternal scale, may be for the rest of their earthly lives) in order to bless them abundantly. Many have found that great blessings have come out of their illnesses or disabilities. As they have prayed for healing, God has made it lovingly plain to them that healing is not his purpose for them at this time. To everyone he has promised his all-sufficient grace, which provides strength in weakness, and the knowledge that all things work together for good to those who love God (2 Cor. 12:9; Rom. 8:28).

Joni Eareckson Tada, now well-known as a singer and artist, had to work through these truths. When she became a quadriplegic through a diving accident in her teens, she was challenged by many in the healing movement to claim healing. She earnestly sought healing, but it did not come.[17] Now her life is a clear testimony to the ongoing grace of God at work within her. Her joy, warmth and vitality and her work in helping others with disabilities are used to bring blessing to many, many people throughout the world. David Watson was another whose prayers for healing from cancer were not answered in this life. He offers the following interesting perspective on this issue:

If we have any conception of the greatness of God, we should refrain from pressing the question *Why?* however understandable that might be . . . The questions are endless if we ask why? Instead we should ask the question What? 'What are you saying to me, God? What are you doing in my life? What response do you want me to make?' With that question we can expect an answer.[18]

We have seen that the question of non-healing during this period between the first and second comings of Christ is full of mystery. We do well to acknowledge in humility our ignorance of God's ways. We do well, also, to admit that, although we have listed many factors that may be barriers to healing, we do not always know what the problem is in any specific case; indeed, there may not be a problem at all in any of the areas mentioned. We must therefore be careful not to overemphasise the concept of barriers to healing as this could, in itself, create an additional barrier. Who among us would be healed if we had to remove all barriers – in effect, to become perfect – before we could receive healing? Healing, like all of God's gifts, is ultimately dependent on grace alone, not on our readiness for it. God's grace is always abundant and omnipotent. It has an uncanny knack of breaking through barriers and bringing about what we cannot do on our own and what we can never earn.

Let us ask God's grace and wisdom, for ourselves and for others, as we seek to discover barriers to healing that need to be removed. We can then rest in that wisdom and all-sufficient grace to heal or to sustain us. God has given us enough truth to enable us to believe even when we are not healed. The cross and the resurrection guarantee both God's love and his ultimate triumph. That is more than enough, for now and forever.

Notes

1. T. Geddert, 'We prayed for healing . . . but she died', in J.R. Coggins and P.G. Hiebert (Eds) *Wonders and the Word: An Examination of Issues Raised by John Wimber and the Vineyard Movement* (Winnipeg: Kindred, 1989), p. 85.
2. See J. Wilkinson, *Health and Healing: Studies in New Testament Principles and Practice* (Edinburgh: Handsel, 1980), pp. 110,112,135.
3. For teaching about the fall see, for example, Gen. 3; Rom. 1:18–32, 5:12–21; 1 Cor. 15:21–22; also *Healing and Reconciliation* in Chapter 2.
4. While the Spirit of Christ promises the power to lift ordinary human suffering into a participation in the sufferings of the Saviour, the Bible does not teach us to take pleasure in pain: 'Christian suffering is not sanctified neurosis'; see L.B. Smedes (Ed.), *Ministry and the Miraculous: A Case Study at Fuller Theological*

Seminary (Pasadena: Fuller, 1987), p. 53.

5. It should also be an important consequence of health and healing. Health and healing are not rights, nor ends in themselves. They are given so that with gratitude we may serve others in the name of the Giver. In most developed countries, great progress has been made in the provision of medical services in recent years and people are becoming increasingly pre-occupied with health for its own sake. It is easy to get caught up in this thinking. The Christian's response to healing should be loving service: gratefully using the extra years or strength granted to us in service to Christ and others, in his name. It seems that Hezekiah overlooked this principle. After being healed and receiving a gift of fifteen further years of life he became proud and self-centred (Is. 38, 39). His healed years were, in fact, rather tragic. How much better they would have been if they had been spent in gratefully giving his time and talents to those around him.

6. Emphasising the need for faith on the part of the healer(s) and the church as well as the sufferer, as is sometimes done, does not alleviate this problem.

7. See Note 22, Chapter 8.

8. See Lk. 17:11–19, for example. Only one of the ten lepers healed by Jesus returned to thank him and was commended for his 'saving faith'; the lack of gratitude in the others is presumably a sign that they were lacking in such faith.

9. This issue is also addressed in R.J. Hillman with C. Chamberlain, *There is Hope: For Those Who are Ill and Those Who Care for Them* (Sydney: ANZEA, 1992).

10. In Mark's Gospel, the failure of the disciples to heal the demon-possessed epileptic boy is attributed to both lack of faith and lack of prayer; see Mk. 9:19,23,24,29. This passage also suggests that it is not quantity of faith that counts but the humble prayerful admission: 'I believe; help my unbelief' (v. 24).

11. Many Scriptures point to the need to keep on praying. See, for example, Matthew 7:7 in which the Greek present tense means 'ask and keep on asking'; Lk. 18:1; and 1 Samuel 12:23, in which Samuel says to Israel: 'Far be it from me that I should sin against the Lord by ceasing to pray for you' (*RSV*). Our persistence should be a natural outcome of our belief in God's ability to redeem the situation.

12. There are two Greek words for time: *chronos*, which means chronological time, and *kairos*, which means opportune time, the right time for doing something.

13. F. MacNutt, *Healing* (Altamonte Springs: Creation House, 1988), p. 258.

14. Sickness may also be overvalued as 'redemptive', as a way of imitating Christ and sharing in his mission of redeeming humanity through suffering. To people who hold this view, asking for healing may seem like cowardice. See MacNutt, pp. 78–80,257.

15. *See Sickness and the fall* in Chapter 2. Note that there are others who correctly recognise sickness as evil, but go on to deny that evil sickness is ever permitted by the good Father. This too, is a great error and leads to tragic consequences,

such as placing the 'blame' for illness on the sufferer whom it is assumed must somehow be living outside God's will.

16. Paul's life provides us with two good examples of this: it was illness that led Paul to take the gospel to the Galatians (Gal. 4:13–14) and, as we have already noted, it was through sickness that the humbling power and grace of Christ came to him (2 Cor. 12:7-10).

17. See J. Eareckson and Steve Estes, *A Step Further* (Melbourne: S. John Bacon, 1981).

18. D. Watson, *Fear No Evil: A Personal Struggle with Cancer* (London: Hodder and Stoughton, 1984), p. 129. Note that Watson is speaking theologically here. As I have already indicated, there can be great benefit in asking Why? in the context of seeking to become aware of any ways in which we may be contributing unnecessarily to our own ill-health.

Chapter 10

A Gospel-centred Healing Ministry

Throughout the world there are many Christians who believe that miraculous healings and other signs and wonders are important means of demonstrating to unbelievers the reality of God's presence and power. For them the healing ministry is an essential weapon in the spiritual war against evil; 'power' healing and 'power' evangelism go hand in hand. Underlying this style of ministry seems to be the conviction that demonstrations of God's power encourage people to believe in him – to join the winning team or get with the strength. The 'signs and wonders' model for the healing ministry, popularised by John Wimber in recent years, is now being adopted in increasing numbers of churches, often as part of 'charismatic renewal'. While I am pleased to see such ministries enthusiastically bearing witness to the power of the Holy Spirit and his miraculous gifts, I also have a deep concern. In many churches where miraculous healing has become a focus, there does not seem to be a proper emphasis on the gospel, which is the very foundation of Christian belief and the key to holy living. Such churches have lost their balance.

I believe that the healing ministry will not fully realise its God-given purpose unless this imbalance is corrected. The dynamic biblical gospel must be its heart, its power, its message. For maximum effectiveness, the healing ministry needs both gospel and Spirit. It is only then that we will experience the renewing work of the Spirit in all his power.

MAINTAINING A GOSPEL EMPHASIS

If we are to keep the ministry of healing and the renewing work of the Spirit in our day in proper perspective, we need to go to the very core of the gospel: the cross and resurrection of Christ (1 Cor. 15:3,4). We need constantly to remember that Easter, which signifies Christ's death and resurrection, comes before Pentecost, the time when the Spirit's power was poured out on all believers. Without Easter, the events of Pentecost would never have happened. Our model for the healing ministry must reflect this.

Insights from the Old Testament

A recent series of talks on Elijah provided me with the following insight. The speaker contrasted the prophet's powerful experience of God on Mount Carmel, in his confrontation with the priests of Baal, with the gentleness of his subsequent encounter with God while hiding in a cave in fear for his life (cf. 1 Kgs. 18:16–39; 19:9–15). On the first occasion, God used fire to confirm his presence and power.[1] On the second, Elijah did not experience God in the mighty wind that tore the mountain apart and shattered the rocks, or in the earthquake and fire that followed. Instead, God revealed his presence in a gentle whisper. So the story of Elijah teaches us that sometimes God comes to us in great power – in that instance, to confront the forces of evil – and sometimes he comes to us gently in our weakness. God's presence and his miraculous interventions in our lives are not necessarily accompanied by overt displays of his power, that is, by signs and wonders. Nor do they require a display of power or strength on our part: ' "Not by might nor by power, but by my Spirit", says the Lord Almighty' (Zech. 4:6).

The power of the cross

The Spirit comes to us by the way of the cross. Paul contrasts the true power of the cross with its apparent futility and insignificance in the eyes of the world:

> Jews demand miraculous signs and Greeks look for wisdom, but we preach Christ crucified: a stumbling block to Jews and foolishness to Gentiles, but to those whom God has called, both Jews and Greeks, Christ the power of God and the wisdom of God. (1 Cor. 1:22–24)

The cross, then, is the symbol of both weakness and power. But we must begin with weakness. It is as we take up our cross daily that we experience the power of God's Spirit. It is as we identify with him in his death that we experience the power of his resurrection. It is in dying that we are raised to eternal life. It is in humble service that we first experience the fullness of the Spirit. With Paul we must acknowledge that, as for the crucified Christ, power is perfected in weakness; when we are weak, then we are strong (2 Cor. 12:10). So we do not begin with signs and wonders as the Jews thought (1 Cor. 1:22). We begin with the sign of weakness: the cross. We minister in the way of the cross – in humility and meekness, in servanthood, not letting our left hand know what our right hand is doing, in weakness and suffering for the world. We go forward knowing that it is not by power but by the Spirit alone that we carry out our ministry of reconciliation and healing.

Elijah had to learn that God was with him at all times, not only on Mount Carmel when he was confronting the forces of evil in the power of Yahweh. For Christians, God is always present by his Spirit in the daily struggles of life. He is present in the ordinary times, not only in extraordinary signs. And he is just as able to hear and respond to our prayers for healing whether they are whispered in solitude or shouted in the presence of a large congregation eagerly 'believing for' a miracle.

The power of the resurrection

It is only by way of the cross that we come to the empty tomb and to Pentecost itself: the cross is truly the crux of the gospel. The resurrection and gift of the Spirit are the Father's double 'yes' to the offering of his Son. Thus the power of the resurrection and of Pentecost arises out of the weakness of the cross. There is no other way.[2] If we are to truly minister in power, we must not short-circuit this line to genuine Spirit power. The whole foundation of the Christian faith rests upon the fact that the historical Jesus was raised from the dead. We need to have our inward eyes open to see the vastness of the resources available to those who have faith. The Father's mighty strength was pre-eminently seen at work when he raised Christ from the dead and enthroned him above all other authorities and powers (Eph. 1:18–23).

It is this resurrection power that comes to us through the Spirit. This power – which begins in weakness, the weakness of the cross – is operating throughout the book of Acts as the early church suffers and ministers in great power. Whether in prison (Acts 16), in preaching (Acts 2) or in power ministry (Acts 3), the Spirit who was present in the cross and resurrection continues his reconciling work. On the day of Pentecost, Peter proclaims that Jesus has been raised to life by God: 'Exalted to the right hand of God, he has received from the Father the promised Holy Spirit and has poured out what you now see and hear' (Acts 2:32–33). Thus Peter made it clear that all the remarkable events of that day flowed from Christ himself.

It is my strong belief that if we follow this gospel emphasis – on cross and resurrection – we will, in the long run, see more healing and more genuine miracles. When needing to validate to the Corinthians the authenticity of his ministry, Paul appeals at length to his sufferings and weaknesses (his floggings, imprisonments, shipwrecks, etc) as signs that he is an apostle (2 Cor. 11–12:10) sharing in the sufferings of the crucified Lord. Only then does he refer, briefly, to 'things that mark an apostle' – signs, wonders and miracles – which he performed among them 'with great perseverance' (2 Cor. 12:12). The emphasis seems to be more on the perseverance than the miracles themselves. Thus, he did not focus on miraculous signs or 'power' ministry, although clearly he was used very effectively as an agent of God's supernatural grace.

It pleases the Father, then, for us to follow in the way of his Son, the way of the cross. As we do, the Father delights to vindicate his children: to raise them up, to pour forth his Spirit, to restore the sick and heal the broken hearted, to exercise the same power by which he raised up his Son! This kind of spirituality, centred in the cross and the resurrection, opens up to us the fullness of God's Spirit and all his gifts and whatever healing he may choose to give. In the end no praise goes to us. All glory goes to God. For it is 'not by might nor by power, but by my [ever present, all-sovereign] Spirit', says the Lord.

The relationship between Easter and Pentecost

In Scripture, Luke's account of Christ's death and resurrection moves on into Acts. Easter stands at the threshold of Pentecost. A gospel-centred model for the healing ministry will be mindful of this relationship between Easter and Pentecost. Easter produces Pentecost. Jesus said: 'Unless I go away the Counsellor [the Holy Spirit] will not come to you; but if I go, I will send him to you' (Jn. 16:7; see also Jn. 7:37ff).

Pentecost, ushered in by the cross and resurrection, is itself a unique event. It begins a new age, the gospel age, which is the age of the Spirit. It is the birthday of the Church.

In Old Testament days, the Spirit came on particular people for particular purposes. In this new era, the Spirit is poured forth on the whole Church. The day of fulfilment arrives on the first Pentecost of the Christian calendar (Acts 2:1).[3] This prolific gift, poured out in unreserved and abundant measure, comes clearly as a result of Christ's death and resurrection (Acts 2:23–35). It is for all people who acknowledge Christ as Lord: 'Your sons and daughters will prophesy, your young men will see visions, your old men will dream dreams' (Acts 2:17). Men and women, young and old are included. The message is repeated: 'Even on my servants, both men and women, I will pour out my Spirit in those days [no limited revelation, Pentecost is a flood tide], and they will prophesy' and the result is that 'everyone who calls on the name of the Lord will be saved' (Acts 2:18,21).

The lavish gift of the Spirit is offered to all who respond to the gospel. 'Repent and be baptized, *every one* of you, in the name of Jesus Christ for the forgiveness of your sins. And you will receive *the gift of the Holy Spirit*. The promise is for you and your children and for all who are far off – for *all* whom the Lord our God will call' (Acts 2:38–39; italics added). The focus of the Day of Pentecost is not the extraordinary events that were taking place but a message, a sermon centred on a crucified risen Lord (v. 41). By the proclamation of that gospel message the Spirit of God swept three thousand people into the kingdom. All of them received the Spirit, his abundant baptism (Acts 1:5), which is clearly the fulfilment of John the baptist's prophecy: 'He will baptise you with the Holy Spirit and with fire' (Lk. 3:16). In the ongoing account of the work of the Spirit (in Acts), the Church is enabled by the Spirit to proclaim the gospel of the crucified risen Lord. That is their main task, although this proclamation is often accompanied by 'wonders and miraculous signs' (Acts 2:43; 3:7).

It is to this gospel priority and life in the Spirit that we are called today. We must give priority to the gospel of the crucified and risen Lord. All of us should seek to be open to the fullness of our heritage in Christ, the abundant gift of the Spirit. With the models of the cross and resurrection before us, we should minister both in weakness and in great power.

THE GOSPEL FOCUS OF THE EARLY CHURCH

To return to an earlier theme, many throughout the Church now believe that an emphasis on signs and wonders is an aid to evangelism. This generally means giving priority to praying for the sick and highlighting miraculous healing. In such ministries the gospel is presented in the context of miracles (or power healing). In a gospel-centred model, however, healing (including miracles and gifts of healing) will be presented in the context of the central biblical message summed up in the concept of the gospel. Careful study of the New Testament records of the early church suggests that a model that is gospel-centred is more appropriate than one that focuses on signs and wonders.[4] We find that the gospel permeates every aspect of the life of the early church and every ministry.

In my daily reading of Scripture, I recently came across two passages in the book of Acts that struck me as highly relevant to this issue. Acts 5, at first glance, appears to be an outstanding example of 'signs and wonders' ministry. On reading it I am reminded of the response of one agnostic to this account: 'What has happened to you Christians? Where has all this wonder and power gone?' The chapter begins with the dramatic death, through judgment, of Ananias and Sapphira. We are told that 'great fear seized all who heard what had happened' (v. 5) and that 'great fear seized the whole church and all who heard about these events' (v. 11). Immediately 'the apostles performed many miraculous signs and wonders among the people' (v. 12). Presumably this fear would make people reluctant to join the fellowship, but despite this 'more and more men and women believed in the Lord and were added to their number' (v. 14). The sick were brought into the streets. Even Peter's shadow falling on them was thought to bring healing (v. 15). As crowds from the towns around Jerusalem brought their sick and demon-possessed 'all of them were healed' (v. 16). What amazing examples of power healing and power evangelism! The chapter continues with another miracle. When the apostles were jailed an angel opened the prison doors and led them out (v. 19).

A closer look at this chapter, however, reveals that the emphasis is not on power healing or power ministry. Like the rest of Acts and the whole of the Bible, its focus is the gospel. The apostles are sent (v. 20) to tell the people 'the full *message* of this new life'. Then we read of them *teaching* the people (v. 25) and it is teaching in the name of Jesus to which the Jewish leaders' object (vv. 28,29). The true gospel emphasis of the chapter is found in verses 30–31; the God of their fathers has raised the crucified Saviour from the dead, leading to repentance and forgiveness. It is the name of Jesus (another way of describing the gospel) that is central (vv. 40,41).

It is true that here in Acts, as always, the gospel message is proclaimed in word and deed. The apostles' teaching about the crucified and risen Lord is accompanied and confirmed by the deeds of the Holy Spirit, such as healings. But the main focus is on the gospel itself (that is, on the crucified Lord), not on the miracles.

Although the following chapter, Acts 6, reports a completely different incident, a similar theme runs throughout. Some of the poor widows in the church were in need (v. 1). It was essential that this important social justice issue be dealt with immediately and thoroughly. The primary task of the apostles, however, was the ministry of the word of God (that is, the gospel) and not the waiting on tables (v. 2). Only as they were able to give themselves to prayer, without distraction, would they be able to fulfil this gospel ministry (v. 4). When priority was given to the gospel, and when the problem of social justice was dealt with by gifted Spirit-empowered people 'the word of God (the gospel) spread' and the number of disciples increased rapidly (v. 7). When gospel priorities are maintained, *every* valid ministry has its full impact, including the healing ministry and social service.[5]

In Hebrews we read: 'This salvation, which was first announced by the Lord, was confirmed to us by those who heard him. God also testified to it by signs, wonders and various miracles, and gifts of the Holy Spirit distributed according to his will' (Heb. 2:3,4). These manifestations, including miraculous healing, are a testimony to the gospel of salvation. The biblical link between gospel and Spirit and the centrality of the gospel in the healing ministry of the early church are again evident.

ARE SIGNS AND WONDERS IMPORTANT AS AIDS TO FAITH?

Many present day biblical scholars, after extensive research, see no justification in assigning a *primary* role to signs and wonders as aids to faith. Early theologians such as Origen, Calvin and Luther, who firmly believed in the miracles of the Bible, were also 'well aware of the fact that Christian faith is not based on the stupendous alone. Satan too could perform wonders'.[6]

Art Glasser, while acknowledging that the miracles reported in the Gospels did contribute to Jesus' fame, believes that their real purpose was to announce the coming of the Messiah and deny the authority of Satan over creation.[7] He notes that, once Jesus' messiahship is confessed, there is increasing emphasis on suffering rather than miracle. The command to participate in a miraculous ministry (Mt. 10:8) gives way to participating in suffering.[8] After Jesus' death and resurrection, the disciples do perform miracles (as recorded in Acts) but he sees these as 'revelatory signs of the messianic movement of the resurrected Christ'.

In the epistles there appears to be a shift in emphasis, Glasser notes. Although 'signs and wonders' are part of the ongoing witness of the Church (Rom. 15:19; 2 Cor. 12:12; Gal. 3:5), speaking gifts (of the Word) are valued more highly than miraculous gifts (1 Cor. 12:27–31). In Pauline churches, forgiveness takes precedence over miraculous healing. The former is guaranteed in a way the latter is not. Interestingly, Paul makes no reference to the miraculous in Jesus' ministry and, in writing about himself, dwells on his sufferings rather than ecstatic experiences (2 Cor. 11:22–12:21, cf. 12:1–4). He also challenges preoccupation with the charismatic and calls us to enlarge our understanding of the Church's total ministry. Jesus, the great miracle worker, is meeting primary needs in Paul's churches. The ministry happening there is much more than a 'signs and wonders' ministry. Glasser comments:

> There is also no mention of special healing meetings or of healing activities to soften up people so they will believe the gospel. Does this mean that in the early church healing largely took place within the caring Christian community and was not related to anything approximating any so-called 'power evangelism'?[9]

John Wilkinson, a medical practitioner and theologian, in his detailed study of New Testament healing points out that the emphasis in the gospels is on preaching and teaching rather than healing.[10] Healing is carried out in the context of preaching and teaching rather than the other way round. In Acts there is even less emphasis on healing than in the gospels and in the epistles it receives only a passing mention.[11] When healing does occur opportunity is taken to witness. Wilkinson concludes, however, that throughout the New Testament miracles are not presented as primary means of reaching people with the gospel or even part of the strategy for evangelism. In similar vein, Paul Hiebert writes, 'The fact is that few who were healed became disciples'.[12] He sees focusing on the signs themselves rather than the message they convey as a common mistake (Jn. 6:26; Lk. 23:8–9). Confusing the sign with the reality is another potential problem. 'Those who do this', he says, 'are like the man on his way to San Francisco who saw a sign pointing the way and camped under it, thinking he had arrived.'[13]

Peter Ralphs's detailed study of healings in the New Testament led him to the following conclusions.[14] As represented in the Gospels, Jesus did not always indicate his reasons for healing. When he did, however, they all related in some way to the fact that he ushered in God's age of salvation. He did not use healing as a way of attracting a crowd or to compel belief in himself, and only on rare occasions is it clear that it was a prelude to 'spiritual renewal' in the person healed. This, Ralphs suggests, should sound a warning against putting too much store on healing as a proof of the gospel or as a way of introducing people to faith in Jesus. This warning is reinforced when we realise that, while some people reacted positively to the healings of Jesus, others responded quite negatively. In any case, when miracles do lead to faith, it may be an inadequate, superficial faith (see, for example, Jn. 2:23–25).[15]

Any approach to ministry that tends to overemphasise miraculous healing can, in fact, be detrimental to effective evangelism,[16] as the following story from the mission field illustrates:

A visiting evangelist proclaimed the gospel with truth and clarity. At the end of his message he said, 'If there is anyone sick here today, Jesus has promised to heal you. Come forward and receive your healing.' People came forward, but no one was healed. The next year, when the same evangelist came to town, people were overheard saying, 'Don't listen to this fellow. Last year he promised that everyone would be healed and nobody was.'[17]

Summarising the place of signs and wonders in world evangelism, the writer continues:

Sometimes God allows the miraculous to take place so the rest of the community can see that the new teaching about Christ is indeed something of divine origin. God alone decides if and when signs are useful to encourage faith. Signs, wonders and miracles can be used as a temporary means to enhance faith. But that which is lasting and builds faith is the preaching of God's Holy Word [see Rom. 10:17].[18]

Both power healing and power ministry should be present to the maximum in the life of the Church today; however, as Hiebert points out, we need a *biblical* understanding of power. There is danger in equating power with miracles. The widespread notion of power as an active force demonstrating itself in power encounters intended to overcome (satanic) opposition is a worldly concept: 'Godly power is always rooted in love, not pride; redemption, not conquest; and concern for the other, not the self. It is humble, not proud, and inviting, not rejecting. Its symbol is the cross, not the sword. That is why to the world it is seen as weakness (1 Cor. 1:23–27).'[19] Orchestrating demonstrations of power in the worldly sense does not seem to be an appropriate strategy for leading people to truth and salvation.

Christians should be exercising God's power, never the power of the flesh. The power of the cross comes as we take up our cross daily and it comes from Christ alone. It is marked by non-authoritarian leadership: leadership that is never imposed, only recognised. It is authenticated by the Word and the Spirit, not by showmanship, forceful oratory or public displays of 'miracles'. It humbly seeks only the glory of God and is marked by an overwhelming sense of human weakness.

THE NEED FOR DIVERSITY IN MINISTRY

We have already noted that there are different approaches that can be used in praying for healing. Similarly, there are various legitimate ways of ministering to those who are ill. My recent reading of Peter Ralphs's thesis on healings in the New Testament brought this point home to me very clearly. I have drawn extensively on his insights in developing this section.[20] Ralphs notes that the writers of the Gospels approached their reporting of the healings of Jesus in different ways. He suggests that they did so because the problem of sickness needed to be addressed in various ways for the benefit of the early Christian community. There are lessons for today in this. We need to be open to a variety of ways of carrying out the ministry of healing. We need to be sensitive to the needs of the individual, the congregation and the particular occasion.

The 'faith' approach

Here the emphasis is on the need for faith. We find examples of this in Scripture. For example, in Matthew's account of the healing of Jairus' daughter (Mt. 9:18–26), the ruler's request to Jesus to save his daughter is a strong affirmation of faith in his power to do so: '. . . come and put your hand on her, and she will live' (v. 18).[21]

Intertwined with this story is the account of the woman with a haemorrhage, who was healed when she touched Jesus' garment.[22] In the latter, there is also an emphasis on the faith of the person being healed. Her confidence in Jesus' power to heal her is impressive, even if she did mistakenly see it in quasi-magical terms: 'If I only touch his cloak, I will be healed' (v. 21). It is especially remarkable, given the longstanding nature of her complaint and the fact that many physicians had been unable to help her. Jesus tells her later: 'Your faith has healed you'(v. 22). What did he mean by that? Ralphs suggests that Jesus is commending her for acknowledging him as the One who had the power to deal with her condition. Without that kind of faith she would not have approached him with her unspoken request for healing.[23] Graciously, he responds by immediately curing her physical ailment.[24]

These two interconnected stories, especially as recounted by Matthew, can be seen as exemplifying:

> . . . an approach within the early Christian community whereby faith could make great demands on the risen Lord Jesus Christ with the expectation that they would be fulfilled . . . there is an invitation to Christians to approach their powerful Lord with definite petitions for his help in times of illness and with firm assurance that help will be received. There is no hint that the situation might arise where faith's demands are not fulfilled nor is any attempt made at a resolution to such a situation . . . Such an emphasis may have been needed in the Christian community when there were those who had a low expectation about healing from the risen Christ and they needed to be challenged to have more faith.[25]

I see parallels here with an approach that is widespread in present day healing ministries that have been influenced by the traditions of the Pentecostal and Charismatic movements.

The cautious approach

In Luke's account of the story of Jairus' daughter (Lk. 8:41–56) there is no request to heal. We read that the father 'fell at Jesus' feet, pleading with him to come to his house' (v. 41). He simply requested that Jesus come in response to the girl's need, without any specific demand of him and without any presupposition about the outcome. Similarly, Luke omits any demand on the part of the woman with the haemorrhage (vv. 44,47).

Ralphs suggests that the supplicants in these stories, as told by Luke, can be seen as representatives of members of the Christian community, praying in the risen Lord's presence for someone they loved. They simply brought their circumstances before him and left him to act as he willed. In the case of the woman, healing came immediately but there was some delay before Jairus' daughter was restored.[26] Ralphs comments:

> Luke shows his reticence to allow the suppliant to request a miracle from Jesus . . . Thus Luke represents an approach quite different from that of Matthew, where faith can request a miracle with confident expectation and where there is no consciousness of any tension should the miracle not occur. Luke is only too aware of the tension resulting from some being healed and others not being healed . . . [He] presents a cautious approach to healing where no demands are made; rather he encourages grieving Christians not only to hope in the resurrection of the dead at the Parousia but also to share now in the joy associated with the eschatological kingdom brought by Jesus.[27]

The challenging (Christ-centred) approach

This is illustrated by Jesus' dealings with Martha following the death of her brother Lazarus (Jn. 11).[28] Martha greets Jesus with an affirmation of her belief in his power over death ('Lord, if you had been here, my brother would not have died') and her confidence in his ability to act appropriately in the situation (vv. 21,22). On this occasion, he chooses to enter into theological discussion and in doing so helps her (and, no doubt, the early Christian community as well)[29] to move beyond a general belief 'in the resurrection at the last day' (v. 24), which was widespread in Judaism at that time, to a Christ-centred understanding:

> Jesus said to her, 'I am the resurrection and the life. He who believes in me will live, even though he dies; and whoever lives and believes in me will never die'. (Jn. 11:25f)

Resurrection, he teaches, is entirely dependent on him. It is both a future hope and a present reality for believers – eternal life begins here and now. It therefore has significance not only for the dead, but also for the living. Again we see the 'now and not yet' tension of the coming of the kingdom of God and the centrality of Christ's role in God's redemptive plan (see Chapter 2).

Jesus goes on to challenge Martha by asking, 'Do you believe this?' Her reply is profound in its implications: 'You are the Christ, the Son of

God' (vv. 26f). In the face of death, the appropriate response for Martha (as for many Christians) is to reaffirm belief in the very nature of Jesus. It is to this point that he gently guides her.

The comforting approach

Later in the story of Lazarus we find Jesus ministering in a completely different way (Jn. 11:32–35). Seeing Mary's grief, he joins with her in weeping for their beloved friend and brother.[30] Thus, while his encounter with her sister Martha is largely theological, his interaction with Mary is entirely pastoral. In this we see a reminder that in our ministry of healing we need to be sensitive to the times when this is the most helpful approach. There are times when we need to recognise the pain of the sufferer and in genuine sympathy 'weep with those who weep' (Rom. 12:15 *RSV*).

These are just a few examples of ways in which we may minister to those who are ill. When we acknowledge God's sovereignty, mystery and grace; when we centre our healing ministry in the redemptive work of Christ; when we are flexible, teachable and open to the Spirit; then we will experience great freedom. We will find a great diversity of approaches. We will be equipped to meet the whole range of situations we encounter in our ministry.

The point of reference for every ministry of the Church is the cross, the source of all its power. Thus the healing ministry must not be seen as an end in itself. Nor should it be seen primarily as a means of providing opportunities for 'signs and wonders' to occur so that people may come to faith. The healing ministry, and every other ministry, must be approached and presented in the central theme of Scripture: the gospel itself. We must not settle for anything less than this or anything else. It is only as we view all our ministry through the clear window of Christ's incarnation, death and resurrection power that we will see where it truly belongs in the life and witness of the Church.

Notes

1. God also revealed himself to Moses and the children of Israel in fire or earthquake on occasions (Ex. 3:2; 19:16–19).
2. Accordingly, Paul writes: 'I want to know Christ and the power of his resurrection and the fellowship of sharing in his sufferings, becoming like him in his death, and so, somehow, to attain to the resurrection from the dead' (Phil.

  3:10–11).

3. Colin Brown sees a reminder of the mystery of the Trinity in this event: '. . . the Holy Spirit did not suddenly swing into action at Pentecost, taking over from where Jesus left off. After Pentecost the Spirit is the Spirit of Christ; before Pentecost Christ is the Christ of the Spirit of the Lord'; see C. Brown, *Miracles and the Critical Mind* (Grand Rapids: Eerdmans; Exeter: Paternoster, 1984), p. 310.

4. John Wimber presented some of his reasons for favouring a 'signs and wonders' style of ministry in his book *Power Healing* (London: Hodder and Stoughton, 1986); see pp. 60f. Referring to such ministry as a 'gospel advancer', he tells how he was strongly influenced towards this belief by Third World students at Fuller Theological Seminary. They reported finding it much easier to pray for people's healing than tell them about Christ, and easier to tell them about Christ after they had been healed. 'Scripture verifies this', he says. 'Notice how Christ frequently first healed the sick then proclaimed the gospel of the kingdom of God.' Elsewhere he writes: 'When first-century Christians came to a new town, signs and wonders followed . . . Signs and wonders resulted in dramatic church growth. They were the catalyst for evangelism'; see J. Wimber with K. Springer, *Power Evangelism: Signs and Wonders Today* (London: Hodder and Stoughton, 1985), pp. 107,117.

5. If those in 'signs and wonders' healing ministries need to take note of the gospel emphasis in Acts 5, social activists need to heed what is taught in Acts 6.

6. Brown, pp. 18,14. Brown also presents the arguments of Karl Barth, another who 'denies that the miracles [of the Bible] were mechanically effective instruments to produce faith'; see p. 246. Of those who hold a different view, Brown comments: 'Sometimes Christian apologists have spoken as if they could first establish the objective facticity of miracles and then proceed to demonstrate their connections with God. Miracles are then seen as some kind of objective authentication of the apologist's belief-system. This procedure is a dubious one, fraught with difficulties; it is certainly questionable whether anyone in the Bible thought of miracles in this way'; see p. 283.

7. For a more extensive treatment of the arguments presented in this and the following paragraph see Art Glasser in J.R. Coggins and P.G. Hiebert (Eds), *Wonders and the Word: An Examination of Issues Raised by John Wimber and the Vineyard Movement* (Winnipeg: Kindred, 1989), pp. 100–104.

8. 'The Great Commission, apart from the spurious ending of Mark (16:9–20), contains no suggestion that the miraculous will be normative in the performance of their worldwide mission'; see Glasser, p. 101.

9. Glasser, p. 104.

10. J. Wilkinson, *Health and Healing: Studies in New Testament Principles and Practice* (Edinburgh: Handsel, 1980). In Mark and Matthew, respectively, 50% and 75% of the text is given over to teaching while only 20% and 9% is about healing, and Jesus' final commission to his disciples, as recorded in Matthew, omits any specific reference to healing (Mt. 28:18–20); see Wilkinson,

pp. 39,84.

11. Only 4.5% of the text of Acts relates to healing; Wilkinson, p. 85. In the epistles, reference is made to natural processes in healing but not to healing by supernatural means; presumably, there was a lessened interest in this (p. 103f). There are, however, references in these letters to gifts of healing(s) (1 Cor. 12) and to the healing ministry of elders and congregation (James 5). In the latter case, the emphasis is on the place of prayer in healing rather than on spiritual gifts. James also presents healing as more than physical. It is part of the redemption of the whole person, part of the normal work of the Christian and based within the Christian community (pp. 150,155ff).

12. P.G. Hiebert in Coggins and Hiebert, p. 126.

13. Hiebert, pp. 132,133.

14. Appendix II represents a summary of some of this research.

15. Nevertheless, God may at times use a miracle to lead someone who is open to the truth to come to deeper faith. For example, Michael Cassidy of African Enterprise was changed when he saw a seven-year-old boy with deformed legs, who had never walked, take off his braces and run at a healing service. 'There and then', he says, 'I came to believe not just academically but deeply and truly that God still heals today'; M. Cassidy, *Bursting the Wineskins* (London: Hodder and Stoughton, 1983), pp. 43f.

16. It can also be detrimental to health (see the warning about generating false hope in *Loss of Hope*, Chapter 9).

17. H. Brant, in a paper entitled 'Toward an SIM Position on Power Encounter', p. 19; see Note 2 in Chapter 5 for detailed citation.

18. Brant, pp. 18f.

19. Hiebert, p. 134; see also pp. 125f.

20. See P. Ralphs, doctoral dissertation, esp. Chapters 6–7. Full citation is given in Appendix II, which also documents many different ways in which Jesus carried out his healings (see The means of healing).

21. Ralphs notes that in Matthew 9:18 the request is that she be raised to life, whereas in the parallel account in Mark 5:22–43 the request is to save her from dying. Matthew's version thus accentuates the power of Jesus over death at the outset and magnifies the faith of the ruler. See Ralphs, p. 245. There is also a strong emphasis on faith in James 5.

22. Mt. 9:20–22. See also Mk. 5:25–34; Lk. 8:43–48.

23. Ralphs comments: 'The fact that Jesus is presented as authoritatively pronouncing that she has been healed through faith implies that her faith is only instrumental; the effective cause of her healing remains in Jesus himself'; see Ralphs, p. 259. All three Gospel accounts ascribe an important role to the woman's faith. In the accounts of both Mark and Luke, we see that Jesus by his persistence brings her from the position of seeking his healing in a somewhat furtive way to the position of obeisance and confession before him and, according to Luke, a public declaration of the immediate healing she had received from him. In this way he is leading her away from an imperfect faith in the

    magical power of his clothes to faith in and a relationship with himself; see pp. 256–257.

24. And more than this: she went her way 'in peace' (Mk. 5:33; Lk. 8:48). Ralphs argues from Scripture that the description of the woman's healing and Jesus' dismissal indicate that 'her physical healing should be seen as a participation in the eschatological peace and as a sign of salvation in the larger sense'; see Ralphs, p. 260.

25. Ralphs, pp. 284–285,352.

26. Ralphs sees this as having significance in the context of the whole of Luke's Gospel, with its broad emphasis on the Parousia and its delay – the 'now and not yet' of the kingdom; see Ralphs, pp. 287ff.

27. See Ralphs, pp. 291,295f. See also pp. 290f.

28. Many important theological issues are raised in this encounter; see Ralphs, pp. 310–320.

29. Ralphs, pp. 339f.

30. Ralphs points out that the use of the Gk. *dakruō* specifically to describe Jesus' weeping (v. 35), rather than *klaiō* (as in v. 33, for example), indicates that he did not give way to unrestrained weeping as did the others who mourned without hope; see Ralphs, p. 324.

Chapter 11

Practicalities and Pastoral Concerns

How can we establish and maintain effective gospel-centred healing ministries that are firmly grounded in biblical theology? I have thought deeply about this issue over the years. In this chapter I present some of the conclusions I have arrived at as I have studied the Scriptures, ministered to the sick and learned to live with 'non-curable' disease. This chapter is not my attempt to provide the ultimate formula for conducting a healing ministry. That would be inconsistent with all I have said so far about the need for diversity and openness to the Holy Spirit's leading as we minister. I simply offer an assortment of general comments for your consideration, in the hope that you will find them useful as you develop your own particular style of ministry in the context of your own church and denomination.

KEEPING THE HEALING MINISTRY IN PERSPECTIVE

Scripture teaches that the present signs of the kingdom are expressed through a whole range of ministries: proclaiming good news to the poor, healing the broken hearted, delivering the captives, giving sight to the blind, liberating the oppressed, casting out demons, healing the sick, raising the dead, and so on (see *The nature of the kingdom* in Chapter 2). However we interpret these phrases, it is reasonable to suppose that at least some of these signs will become evident as individual Christians and the

Church as a whole live God-glorifying, Christ-centred lives in obedience to Scripture and the Spirit's promptings. It is easy to be 'selectively obedient', however, and this can create problems for the Church.[1] One group wants to give itself totally to expressing the social signs (interpreted literally, for example, serving the poor or liberating the oppressed) while another gives itself entirely to the more personal (often miraculous) signs like healing and exorcism. We must acknowledge the place of both kinds of ministry if we are to achieve biblical balance.

It is not good for a church to give its attention solely to issues of social justice or to the healing ministry. All Christians need to be concerned about what is happening throughout the world, in a general sense – concerned about oppressed peoples, wherever they are, and about the poor in our own society. Indeed, since the greatest cause of sickness in the world is poverty, helping to alleviate poverty is in itself a ministry of healing. At the same time, we need to be open to the 'miraculous' signs and to appropriate theologically sound ministries of healing within our congregations.

Because of the variety of gifts, there will always be a degree of specialisation in ministry. For example, those with healing gifts should be encouraged to give greater priority to the healing ministry than to other aspects of ministry.[2] Similarly, those who have the special gift Paul calls 'service' – a special facility in serving the needy that goes far beyond normal Christian caring – would generally do well to focus on avenues of ministry that allow this gift to be expressed.

Ideally, the healing ministry should be an integral part of the normal life of every church. Ministers and elders do not need to delay taking this initiative until a gift of healing emerges among them. They can be assured that Christ who is the Head of the Church will work with them, since they have been appointed to this ministry (Jas. 5:14). If healing gifts become evident, the healing ministry should never focus on gifted individuals[3] or in any other way distract from the glory of God. A low key approach should be adopted, one that avoids deliberate sensationalism. At the same time those who are gifted need to beware the smugness of false humility. Whatever we do must be motivated only by a passion for the glory of God. In recognising that the healing ministry is an integral part of preaching the gospel (which we are to proclaim in word and deed), we must never allow it to divert attention from the priority of preaching the forgiveness of sins.

We need to remember that healing is only one of the ministries to which the Church is called, not the only one, nor even the most important. Each church and each individual must find an appropriate balance in ministry. Recognising the importance of this, Michael Cassidy writes:

> If I think back over the years to the people, churches or ministries which have struck me as most truly Christian and most vitally attractive, the quality which always surfaces for me as an explanation is that of balance. They bring into harmonious unity and equilibrium the many-faceted concerns of our Lord, and like a prism or rainbow of many colours they radiate beauty and wholeness. They shine forth as the real thing. And one looks at such people and says: 'I like what I see!' Or one tastes such a church and says: 'To worship and serve here is beautiful.' In fact one is tasting salt which has not lost its savour. And salt makes one thirsty – thirsty for the Water of Life and for the kind of life and witness and heart from which flow rivers of living water to a parched world.[4]

THE SAFEGUARD OF SOUND BIBLICAL TEACHING

Continuous exposure to sound biblical teaching is essential for the spiritual and emotional welfare of those who seek healing and for sustaining healthy growth in the church itself.[5] Such teaching should reach to every member of the congregation and permeate every aspect of congregational life. This will ensure that the healing ministry of the church is kept in perspective.

Gospel-centred teaching

In the preaching of the Word a distinction is often made between proclamation and teaching. Proclamation (Gk. *kērugma* is generally understood to involve proclaiming the essence of the apostolic message,[6] what God has done through Christ's death and resurrection. In contrast, teaching (Gk. *didachē*) is ethical instruction that reveals the implication of this message for Christian character and conduct. The need to proclaim the biblical gospel to the non-Christian world is widely accepted; however, I believe it is of the utmost importance that *all* our preaching, including our teaching, be centred in and undergirded by the gospel message of the kerygma. At the same time our preaching and teaching need to be fresh and vital, addressing the issues of the moment in the life of the church and individual. This represents a great challenge to the presenter. It requires creativity and sensitivity to the specific needs of the audience at a level that can only be achieved through the grace of God and the inspiration of his Spirit.

Teaching in the Church degenerates into moralism and legalism unless it is founded on the gospel of God's grace towards us. Thus both the proclamation and the teaching of the Church must present Christ, who is the gospel and the ultimate expression of this grace.[7] I have been pleased to see a renewed emphasis on biblical exposition in many churches in recent times. But I am concerned that, too often, this is done without placing the moral teaching of Scripture in its proper context, without relating it to the central biblical gospel. Every sermon proclaimed to the watching world and every sermon preached to the Church should major in and climax in and be undergirded by the gospel. The presence of the crucified and risen Christ and the good news of the gospel should illumine it.

As both kerygma and didache are proclaimed in the full power of the Spirit, the Church will be rescued from weak preaching, helpless moralism and from being motivated by guilt – from a form of religion without power. With preaching and teaching that remind us continually of God's grace towards us, we will maintain a healthier perception of ourselves and others. We will be reminded of his love for us and our utter dependence on him and we will be encouraged to respond with joyful, grateful service. The Church will be renewed, revived and reformed by the Spirit and his gospel of grace so that every ministry becomes increasingly effective.

Clearly, any preaching or teaching about healing must also be grounded in the gospel. It must focus on the forgiveness and reconciliation that comes through the death and resurrection of Christ and through his indwelling Spirit. If it is to be effective in assisting people to find true wholeness, the healing ministry cannot stand independently of the proclamation of the gospel.

About the Holy Spirit and his gifts

Scripture teaches that from the very moment of conversion we receive the gift (or the person) of the Holy Spirit. As 'new creatures in Christ', we will each discover a special gift, or several gifts, of the Spirit given to equip us for ministry that will build up the body of Christ and ultimately bring glory to God. A proper understanding of the Holy Spirit and his gifts[8] helps us stay focused on the gospel. Describing the Spirit as a 'hidden floodlight shining on the Saviour', James Packer points out:[9]

> Spiritual gifts must be defined in terms of Christ, as actualized powers of expressing, celebrating, displaying and so communicating Christ in one way or another . . . our exercise of spiritual gifts is nothing more nor less than Christ himself ministering through his body to his body, to the Father, and to all mankind . . . Ability to speak or act in a particular way – performing ability, as we may call it – is only a charisma [gift] if and as God uses it to edify . . . We need to draw a clear distinction between man's capacity to perform and God's prerogative to bless, for it is God's use of our abilities rather than the abilities themselves that constitute charismata.[9]

Packer also reminds us that gifts should not be treated as proof that we are pleasing God, or as guaranteeing salvation, adding that:

> All through the New Testament, when God's work in human lives is spoken of, the ethical has priority over the charismatic. Christlikeness (not in gifts, but in love, humility, submission to the providence of God, and sensitiveness to the claims of people) is seen as what really matters.[10]

Understanding spiritual gifts and realising that we are really one body made up of many parts (1 Cor. 12:12) opens up vast human resources for ministry often overlooked by the Church. There is no threat to the roles of ministers of the Word or elders in this. Their functions emerge more clearly defined and crucial, while at the same time considerable burdens are lifted from their shoulders.

Sound teaching about the Holy Spirit and his gifts needs to be part of the ongoing gospel message proclaimed in all churches. Wherever the preacher denies the miraculous working of the Spirit today, that church and those people will be impoverished. On the other hand, over-enthusiastic preaching about the Holy Spirit, while correctly acknowledging his ongoing activity, can be just as detrimental if it is not theologically sound. For example, divisive 'elitism' becomes a real danger when it is taught that only some Christians have the Holy Spirit – a 'special' blessing, evidenced by their ability to perform certain apparently miraculous feats – while others do not.[11] It can also be damaging to teach (or create the impression) that each Christian can expect to exercise continually a whole variety of gifts, including miraculous gifts.[12] An extension of this thinking is the teaching that *all* Christians are gifted to heal miraculously.[13] It seems to me that the key problem with such teaching is a failure to make a clear distinction between general and special gifts (see Chapter 4). In a sense, every Christian does have a general role in the healing ministry (or a *general* gift of healing) but every Christian does not have an ongoing *special gift* of healing.[14]

A misunderstanding of biblical teaching about the Holy Spirit and his gifts can easily lead to an imbalance in ministry that affects both individual and church. Inadequate teaching that denies the intervention of the Spirit in the daily life of the Christian keeps entire congregations in a kind of bondage. Having accepted Christ as Lord their salvation is assured, but they are severely limited in their ability to serve God with the whole of their beings. They are missing out on the joy and freedom of truly living in the power of his Spirit, day by day, moment by moment.

On the other hand, inadequate teaching that encourages congregations to live in high expectation of exhibiting the various 'miraculous' gifts on demand (or virtually on demand) may result in an overemphasis on the healing ministry. Other important aspects of the life of the church, including its effective proclamation of the gospel, may be neglected as a result. In addition, a church may miss out on much growth and blessing by failing to recognise other ways in which the Spirit is at work. Thus the true giftedness of many of its members may go unnoticed.

About present and future hope

Sound, biblical teaching offers both present and future hope. The former gives meaning and purpose to life on this earth. It includes the hope of gaining at least some degree of healing or relief from illness or pain and the knowledge that grace will be provided to enable us to endure in difficult circumstances. Future hope, which relates to the life to come, prepares us to face death confidently when the time arrives. We all need both kinds of hope. Sooner or later health breaks down and eventually we will all die.

Many involved in the healing ministry engender false hope by incorrectly teaching that healing is assured in this life for all who have faith. Others convey this impression quite unintentionally by overemphasising the possibility of healing. In such a context, lack of healing almost inevitably produces a sense of failure, frustration and despair, causing untold hurt. Both those who need healing and their loved ones may be profoundly affected. As already noted, the reality is that we see a whole range of results in the healing ministry. Some people are 'completely' healed (that is, in human terms), others receive some healing, but many are not healed at all in the physical sense. The message from the pulpit should be clear and consistent: while God does graciously grant healing to some in this life, in various ways, there is no blanket guarantee of healing for all. Perfect healing belongs only to the age to come.

There may not always be healing, but there should always be hope. In fact, as we have seen, loss of hope can represent a serious barrier to healing. We should be encouraging those who are ill to be open to all the healing that is available to them in this life, from every legitimate source, but our primary focus should always be on the ultimate hope of the life to come. Accurately proclaiming the gospel message is vital to the healing ministry because it encourages both kinds of hope. Because the kingdom of God has come in Christ, we may be granted some healing now. And his death and resurrection mean that we can look forward to living with him for ever in perfect wholeness.

About suffering and evil

Donald Carson, reflecting on the problems of suffering and evil, wisely emphasises the need for putting in place a solid foundation of biblical teaching before hard times come. Seeing his book as 'preventative medicine', he writes:

> One of the major causes of devastating grief and confusion among Christians is that our expectations are false. We do not give the subject of evil and suffering the thought it deserves until we ourselves are confronted with tragedy. If by that point our beliefs – not well thought out but deeply ingrained – are largely out of step with the God who has disclosed himself in the Bible and supremely in Jesus, then the pain from the personal tragedy may be multiplied many times over as we begin to question the very foundations of our faith.[15]

There may be false expectations about what God is like, what God does, what place suffering has in the world. This may raise questions that range from *Why me?* to *Why are you punishing me?* and on to even bleaker thoughts: 'Maybe you aren't a God of love. Maybe you are capricious. Maybe you aren't fair, let alone holy. Maybe you aren't there.'[16]

We need preaching and teaching that will educate whole congregations so that they are well equipped to find comfort and answers to their questions should they experience serious illness or tragedy:

> It is important to stress the Christian's location – between the fall and the new heaven and the new earth, enjoying the "downpayment" of the Spirit

but by no means free of death and decay . . . where self-seeking, self-gratifying forms of Western Christianity predominate, it is essential to lay out these truths, loudly and often.[17]

Attempts to administer good theological 'medicine' such as this during the time of suffering, however, are not likely to be very successful or helpful. Compassionate pastoral support, which involves empathic listening rather than advice,[18] is far more likely to be beneficial at such a time.

PASTORAL CONSIDERATIONS

Providing our churches with ongoing biblical teaching is a very important way of promoting the well-being of both church and individual. In this section, I offer comments on a variety of issues that relate to other aspects of pastoral care. Some are about one to one ministry. Others are about being pastorally sensitive as we offer the ministry of healing to the congregation as a whole. Some apply in both these spheres.

Ministering to the whole person

The healing ministry of the Church, and the local church in particular, should be comprehensive. That is to say, the multiple needs of those who are ill should be addressed. Because we are whole persons, our ministry should have as its goal a movement towards integration and wholeness in the individual (as should all true Christian ministry), not just physical healing. In relation to illness or injury, it is important to be aware of the many ways in which God provides healing and to encourage those who are ill to explore them (see Chapter 7). Each individual needs to integrate the vast array of healing resources God provides in a wholesome, balanced way.

To lead or be part of a truly comprehensive healing ministry, we do not have to be experts in every relevant field, for example, medicine, psychology and theology. But we do need to be humble enough to own our limitations. If we acknowledge we cannot spell, we can always use a dictionary or ask for help. Similarly, as we minister, we must be prepared to acknowledge our need to call on and co-operate with professionals, as required. In addition, whether or not we have a medical degree, we should be sensitive to the person's medical condition and prepared to offer genuine and appropriate support before, during and after treatment. This should include encouraging them to seek the best medical help available if they have not already done so.

One factor that often seems to be overlooked in the healing ministry is the benefit to be gained by adopting a healthy lifestyle. I believe the ministry of healing should include encouraging people to take practical steps to improve their health through a whole variety of lifestyle modifications. I also believe that those in the healing ministry ought to embody this aspect of their message by adopting a lifestyle that is consistent with maximum fitness and health.

Respecting the dignity of the individual

Often the healing ministry is carried out in a very public way, with an invitation to come forward for prayer. I prefer a quieter approach, one that does not encourage spiritual 'voyeurism' in the congregation. I also prefer the healing ministry to be part of normal services in the local church rather than the focus of special healing services or seminars. At the end of any service, people in the congregation who are ill or otherwise in need of prayer and counselling may be invited to remain to receive the ministry of the elders.[19] With their right to privacy respected, some will feel more free to ask for prayer for deeper concerns, not just physical ailments. Such an approach also encourages more in-depth ministry within the context of caring personal relationships.[20]

On the other hand, there are times when ministry in which the whole congregation participates may be helpful.[21] For example, if someone who is well-known in the church is very ill, it may be appropriate for all concerned to gather in prayer for them with the elders. Sometimes when the congregation is large, I ask people to indicate their need for prayer quietly, by standing or raising their hand, just before the service ends and while all heads are bowed in prayer. After offering a general prayer for them, I invite them to remain for counselling by the elders and specific prayer with laying on of hands.

There are, of course, many different ways in which the dignity of the individual can be respected and protected when prayer is requested. Sadly this does not always happen in the healing ministry. For example, I know of one large public meeting where those receiving prayer were subjected to the glare of lights and the intrusive eye of TV cameras, presumably in the hope of recording a spectacular cure or some other exciting manifestation. This is a distortion of the healing ministry: it is miracle-centred, not

Christ-centred.

Encouraging realistic expectations

It is realistic to teach that God can and does heal miraculously. It is out of touch with reality, however, to suggest or teach that such healing is available to everyone in this life. We must be sensitive to the fact that people who come to us for ministry will fall into two broad categories: those whom God is wanting to heal and those whom (for his own good reasons) he is not going to heal. Many in ministry do not provide adequately for the latter group. Often it is not made clear enough that it is not God's purpose to heal *everyone* in this life. Even when this truth is explicitly stated during a healing service, people may still find it difficult to be content if God does not heal them at that time because such a sense of expectancy has been created in other ways. Furthermore, leaders who believe healing depends on being absolutely positive God is going to heal are at high risk of neglecting the needs of those who are not healed. Focusing on this group introduces a negative note and may therefore seem counterproductive.

The healing ministry requires deep understanding of the needs of the whole person. We need to take into account the fact that it can be difficult for people who are desperately ill to remain objective. Understandably, they will tend to hear what they are longing to hear. Messages that seem to reinforce their hope of cure will be much more readily received and retained than those that do not.[22] They are thus easy prey to false hope, which too often leads to guilt, despair and disillusionment if healing does not come.

In many healing services an inappropriately high level of anticipation that healing will take place is encouraged. For many, 'power' healing means, literally, *healing* people in the name of Jesus, not simply *praying* for them in the name of Jesus. It means having enough 'faith' to believe, or even command, that healing will occur.[23] Such practices can be very damaging to those who are not healed. They are robbed of the peace that could be theirs whether or not they are healed. The consequences can be particularly serious if, in the 'positive' (some would say overenthusiastic and uncritical) environment that prevails in many healing services, they have mistakenly become convinced that they have been cured.

I believe we should always and quite unambiguously tell those for whom we pray that God may respond in a whole variety of ways. We should be encouraging people to rest in God's sovereign love whatever measure of healing they receive and even when there is no apparent healing at all. It is not helpful to imply that healing depends on people psyching themselves up to believe they will healed or, alternatively, on someone receiving a clear 'word of knowledge' to that effect. If God so chooses, he is able to heal powerfully and completely if we present our requests to him simply and honestly, acknowledging our ignorance of what he is going to do. I like to say, 'May you receive all the healing God has for you now from every source and remain open to all that he has for you in the days to come', or words to that effect. If, as a church, we believe that we have been given prophetic insight, we may say, 'We believe that God is going to heal you, although in our humanness, we may be mistaken . . .' and then go on to pray for the healing of our brother or sister with confidence, sincerity and compassion.

People who are hesitant about the healing ministry in general seem to be open to the low-key, more reasoned approach to praying for healing I am suggesting here. I have found this to be so, without exception, in my ministry among churches of many denominations.

Awaiting God's ripe time

Having read this book and become aware of the many different factors that contribute to healing and non-healing, a natural human tendency might be to rush out and drop all this new knowledge on someone who is ill. But that would be counterproductive. Our ministry must be primarily a compassionate one, not advice or information centred. It must be a listening ministry. It involves empathy, weeping with those who weep, seeking to understand, being supportive and prayerful. Sometimes it means no more than a wordless hug or simply holding someone's hand. It means being content to sit quietly with those who are ill. If it is appropriate to give counsel at all, we should offer only as much as they are ready to receive without overtiring them.

We do not go about our ministry with a pre-assembled package of good advice and solid theology that we dump on everyone. We wait patiently until people are ready. A request for a visit may be a sign of this, but not always. We do not impose ourselves or take advantage of their illness as an opportunity for 'hitting them with the gospel'. We should try never to usurp the role of the Holy Spirit, always waiting on God's 'ripe' time for sharing his Word. Often it will mean sharing only a little at first. If this is appreciated, and as the Spirit of God works, we may be able gradually to say more, perhaps over many visits. Sometimes, when dealing with someone who is very ill, it may be months before it is appropriate to share the gospel or even talk about practical strategies for healing. This ministry requires living near to Christ, whose loving concern for each person's eternal welfare far surpasses ours, and praying constantly for wisdom.

Avoiding excessive emotionalism

This section is about group ministry rather than personal ministry. When people are gathered together and emotions are running high, unusual physical and psychological manifestations may sometimes be observed. These may include shaking, weeping, tingling sensations, feeling hot or cold or unable to move, or fainting. While God may sometimes choose to work in these dramatic ways in healing services or at other times, we should not set out to induce them. It does not take much to stir up a congregation or crowd to the point where unusual phenomena are very likely to occur, especially among suggestible people who have been conditioned to expect that such 'signs' will, or should, happen.

We must be careful that we do not employ, either consciously or unconsciously, techniques that play on people's emotions in ways that are unhelpful or even manipulative.[24] For example, with continuous repetition of choruses during prolonged sessions of worship or prayer, people may be encouraged to think that they are being stirred by the Spirit. In reality, for some individuals, an altered state of consciousness (dissociation) may be occurring. In this state people are more suggestible and less rational and display increased emotionality. This is a normal human response, to be expected in such an environment. Alternatively, what people are feeling may merely be the result of an adrenalin surge – also a very human response. Prolonged physical activity (such as dancing or leaping) which is sometimes part of worship sessions, raises the level of endorphins, euphoria-inducing 'drugs' that our own bodies produce. This is why some people become addicted to activities such as aerobics and jogging. They can just as readily become addicted to energetic worship work-outs![25]

The following are some of Packer's concerns about a style of ministry that encourages excessive emotionalism: 'Its warmth and liveliness attract highly emotional and disturbed people to its ranks, and many others find in its ritual emotionalism some relief from strains and pressures in other areas of their lives (marriage, work, finances, and so forth). But such sharing in group emotion is a self-indulgent escapist "trip" that must debilitate in the long run.'[26] When this happens, it is surely the leaders rather than the participants who must accept the greater responsibility.

Practices that have profound effects on the emotions are often used in ministry by people who do not understand the psychological implications of what they are doing. Susceptible people can lose intellectual control. Taken out of touch with reality into a state where they see everything as 'spiritual', they can be left in a very vulnerable and potentially unbalanced condition. This is a particularly serious concern because those who employ such practices are likely also to lack proper professional training in dealing with the consequences of heightening people's emotions and altering their state of consciousness.

When God's people gather together it is right that they feel free to express their emotion in appropriate ways. Many factors will determine just what is 'appropriate' in individual congregations, of course.[27] With a whole range of wonderful music available that allows us to praise God with our whole person, we do not have to abandon reason and surrender ourselves to our emotions or become high on adrenalin in order to 'exalt the Lord our God'. We can thank him 'with hearts and hands and voices' without going on an 'escapist trip'.[28] Our *primary* reason for gathering together must be to glorify God and hallow his name, not the expectation of a satisfying group experience or an emotional catharsis.

Casting out demons with caution

This is an activity that increasing numbers of Christians are coming to regard as a major aspect of the healing ministry. I have already expressed my concerns about overemphasising the risk of demon possession, especially when it is implied that subtle forms of 'demonisation' may come upon the unwary Christian who is less than perfect (see Chapter 5). How can we tell whether someone who comes to us for ministry is truly in need of exorcism? John Wimber suggests that the following may, in some instances, be indicators: contorted physical reactions, addictions, compulsions, bondage to specific emotions and sinful attitudes, chronic physical sickness, involvement in the occult and disturbed family history.[29] A list like this must be used with caution. Great confusion has arisen because some of these indicators have become widely accepted as conclusive evidence of 'demonisation', even though there are many other possible explanations for them, including psychological illness.[30] I am also concerned about the practice of judging people as *inevitably* demon-possessed on the basis of their personal or family history. We may cause untold damage if we adopt these attitudes.

Nevertheless, the Church does have a responsibility in relation to the ministry of exorcism, one that Christians of all traditions need to acknowledge. Certainly, we should recognise the great gravity of demon possession and the importance of exorcism and responsible counselling for those so afflicted. At the same time, we must do our best to ensure that the Church is never guilty of attributing demon possession to any individual when the problem lies elsewhere. What I am advocating is a responsible ministry of discernment and exorcism. No case should be overlooked and every case should be treated in the most responsible and competent manner. Involvement of Christians with appropriate spiritual giftings, specifically the gifts of exorcism and discernment, is an essential part of this ministry. In this context, it is crucial to remember that these will be given to relatively few Christians – 'we have different gifts, according to the grace given us' (Rom. 12:6).

The Church needs a balanced ministry of exorcism. It needs ongoing teaching that helps its members avoid the dangers of any kind of contact with the occult and New Age philosophy. It needs a ministry that is fully open to challenging the principalities and powers, without focusing on them unduly in a way that distracts from the pre-eminence of Christ. It also needs to teach individual responsibility for choosing to sin. Remember 'self-possession, not demon possession, is the greatest danger in our Western societies'.[31]

Serious pastoral problems are created by an overemphasis on demon possession. For new or immature Christians this is a source of great tyranny and anxiety, robbing them of assurance and joy. It is especially damaging when children become fearful that they may be demonised or, worse still, are accused of it. In medicine, 'iatrogenic disease' is the name given to any condition that results from the harmful intervention of a doctor. In the healing ministry there is no equivalent term, yet there is a parallel situation. Sadly, there are many Christians who now suffer from chronic anxiety and other serious psychological disturbances because of false teaching or counselling about demons or the intervention of a misguided 'exorcist'. The ministry of exorcism (or deliverance) is not to be embarked upon lightly.

Clearly, as a general rule, diagnosis of demonic influence and subsequent exorcism should not rest solely on the untested 'word' of an individual who claims to have discerned the presence of a spirit or demon.[32] Discernment and exorcism should be a ministry of the body of Christ, especially the mature leadership. Lewis Smedes, in his report of the deliberations of the Faculty at Fuller Theological Seminary, draws attention to the possible abuse of spiritual power, especially the tyranny that can be exercised by so-called discerners:

> All power is vulnerable to misuse, but never more than when it is spiritual power exercised over people whom someone discerns to have an evil spirit . . . While we are sensitive to life's mysterious vulnerability to destructive demonic forces, we are highly sensitive to the need for a high level of responsibility in any actual diagnosis of demons as the cause of physical illness, mental illness or moral turpitude. The need for controls is intensified a thousandfold when those who discern the demonic also claim the power to exorcise. It may be as important to protect people from the exorcists as to protect them from demons.[33]

He suggests the following: since the gift of discernment does not confer infallibility, it should be subject to the evaluation of wise, informed, responsible church members; informed consent must be obtained before exorcism; the exorcists themselves must be spiritually mature, wise, informed, responsible members of the church; those who are trained and skilled in diagnosis and therapy should be consulted; exorcism should not be done in secret; and careful, confidential records should be kept.

As we minister, we need to be sensitive to the many factors that contribute to illness and aware that, in most cases, these will be physical, spiritual, emotional, moral or relational, rather than demonic. We also need to remember that we may never know the reason for a particular ongoing illness in this life (see Chapter 9).

Caring for those not healed

Our ministry must be particularly compassionate to those who, despite receiving prayer for healing, are not healed. We must beware of increasing their burden. We must not leave them feeling that they are failures, lacking in faith or harbouring unconfessed sin. This may mean providing ongoing pastoral care. The church should continue to pray for them, praying for their healing unless there is a clear indication to the contrary (see *Prayer that is appropriate* in Chapter 8). In the latter case, ongoing prayer is still needed, prayer for strength and grace to cope with the difficult days ahead. As we await God's answer to our prayers, it is particularly important to remember that miraculous healing is not necessarily all-or-nothing. We need to be on the lookout for any genuine signs of improvement or remission, encouraging those to whom we minister to be grateful for any measure of healing they receive.

As we minister to those who are seriously ill, we will find that many are hesitant about accepting drastic treatments such as chemotherapy or surgery. They seem to do so much damage and often they do not provide a cure, but only prolong suffering. In facing this issue myself, I have come to see it this way. God is accustomed to radical solutions. In the cross of Christ we see an incredibly radical solution to the problem of evil humankind. Physical sickness is an evil. Sometimes God's radical solution to this evil is to heal miraculously, but there are times when he uses some other radical form of treatment, perhaps chemotherapy or surgery. I believe that, in our ministry, we should encourage people to be open to such treatments if it seems likely they will contribute to cure, remission or improved quality of life. Each patient needs to be fully informed of their situation so that they have a sense of personal involvement in the decision-making process, whether the choice is to accept treatment or to refuse it. In the latter case, understanding that their earthly life is probably drawing to a close (barring a miracle), they can give themselves wholeheartedly to spending quality time with family and friends and preparing to be with God in eternity. This is the position in which I now find myself.

Those in ministry must face the fact that some people in the 'not healed' category will eventually die of their illness. Thus pastoral care of the dying is an important aspect of the healing ministry. Our theology must encompass suffering and death, not see them as failure. We need to appreciate the grace of 'godly' dying, in which our passing is marked by a God-given serenity, anticipation and hope. In recent years I have had the privilege of walking the road with many cancer patients during their last weeks. I have always tried to help them open themselves to all the healing God has for them in this life, while focusing their main attention on the great hope of the life to come. Some have received dramatic healing, many have died, but almost all have experienced the remarkable hope and peace that comes to those who, through Christ, put their trust in the loving heavenly Father.

Many books about the healing ministry include stories of people being raised from the dead in answer to prayer. I do not wish to deny the possibility that God may choose to use people to bring about this miracle today, just as he seems to have done in the past (1 Kgs. 17:22; 2 Kgs. 4:32–35; Acts 9:40, 20:9f). Nevertheless, I am concerned about overenthusiastic reporting of claims of 'raisings from the dead', which may focus too much attention on this aspect of ministry and create false expectations. It is possible that many of the incidents reported may have been resuscitations. Significantly perhaps, many of the stories come from countries that lack sophisticated medical facilities. How did untrained observers know that the person really was dead? Was their condition such that a doctor in a modern hospital would have been willing to terminate life support systems or approve organ transplantation?

While recognising that God is miraculously at work in all the healing we receive, we must acknowledge that 'miraculous healings' are relatively rare events. We must also acknowledge that the miracle of resurrection from the dead is the ultimate of all such miracles. It is also the rarest.

In the rare event that praying for the raising of the dead seems appropriate, the greatest possible pastoral care must be exercised. It should happen only with the consensus of the leadership of the church and with the minimum of publicity. Those ministering may believe that a prophetic word (or what appears to be a prophetic word) has been received. But they may be mistaken, and if they are, they may cause unspeakable damage to the relatives and to Christian witness in the community. While some may see this attitude as lacking in faith, I would see it as an expression of wisdom and compassion and no barrier to God's power to bring about such a miracle, if that is his intention.

If those who adopt a 'name it and claim it' approach were to become zealous in this area of ministry, it could have devastating pastoral consequences and bring the gospel, the Church and God's name into great disrepute.[34] The need at all times is for those in the healing ministry to recognise that the fullness of the kingdom is future and that sickness and death, as well as sin, are characteristics of the present age.

Facing the facts

I recommend that patients ask their doctors to keep them fully informed of their medical condition.[35] At the same time I encourage them to recognise that such diagnosis is not the last word, thus ensuring that they remain open to all the healing God has for them. I am convinced that facing reality by acknowledging the full seriousness of an illness need not be detrimental to praying effectively for healing. I also see it as more glorifying to God than rejecting a doctor's attempts to give a scientifically accurate assessment of the disease. It is not only the patient who needs prayer and the grace of God to help them face reality when the prognosis is poor. Those in ministry may also have difficulty in this area, especially when the person who is ill is very dear to them. It can be hard to acknowledge that someone's condition is deteriorating. Their suffering distresses us and the possibility that their death is imminent reminds us of our own mortality.

Eagerness to claim victory for the kingdom is another factor that can push us towards overestimating the measure of healing received. Yet, to truly honour God, it is essential that we keep in touch with reality when claiming that prayers for healing have been answered. Lewis Smedes calls for 'modesty and reserve in the face of understandable temptation to herald too soon the wonders of healing'. He makes a clear distinction between credulity, which 'rises from deep desire that something be true' and credibility, which 'is earned by reliable and trustworthy testing'.[36]

In all probability, because of our human tendency to see what we want to see, when expectations are high, many claims of miraculous healing will be nothing more than wishful thinking. Testimonies about healings are not self-validating.[37] Because of this, for the safety of those who receive prayer for healing, it is essential to involve the medical profession in confirming cures and determining whether or not treatment should be suspended. On the other hand, it is possible to overlook genuine miracles, for example, when healing comes gradually or relief is only partial or temporary.

Paul Hiebert suggests that Christian ministers should be willing to subject any report of miraculous healing to objective, rigorous, and scientifically responsible testing and ready to report their failures 'as well and as loudly' as their successes.[38] Similarly, I believe the healing ministry should allow room for balanced, scientific assessment of illness and recovery. I do not believe, however, that it is necessary to keep meticulous records and attempt to scientifically evaluate the response of every person for whom prayer is offered.[39] This seems to me an intellectual overreaction and a waste of resources. Gifted Christians tied up in such work could be much more gainfully employed for the kingdom in other ways. Our heavenly Father does not need our help to prove that he is there and capable of working miracles.

In any case, although changes in medical condition can often be verified, some would argue that miracles by their very nature are unprovable by scientific method. Should this really be a burning issue for the average Christian? Should our faith (or that of others) be so weak that it needs proof of a miracle to prop it up?[40] If we understand clearly that all healing comes from God, surely it does not matter whether he has responded to our prayer by granting miraculous 'supernatural' healing or not. What really matters is that the patient has been helped physically, emotionally or spiritually and that God's name has been glorified.[41]

Set free from the need to claim that all or most healing received in response to prayer is miraculous, from having to discriminate between the so-called natural and supernatural, we can gratefully receive God's healing from every legitimate source.[42] How liberating it is to be able to say we do not know whether God has intervened miraculously to grant healing in a particular instance. Sometimes we may feel fairly confident that he has; at other times we cannot be so sure. I do not see this as a problem. God does not ask or need us to analyse the way in which he answers our prayers for healing. Wholehearted adoration and gratitude for his gracious provision for us seems a more appropriate response, whatever form the healing takes.

By now it should be clear that I am deeply concerned about practices and teaching that are part of the healing ministry in many places. I have felt it necessary to express these concerns in the interests of helping the Church achieve a more effective, pastorally sensitive ministry of healing; however, I do not want my comments to be a discouragement to anyone involved in or contemplating such a ministry. On the contrary, I long to see a God-glorifying, comprehensive and balanced ministry of healing at the heart of the life of every church, as part of its wider pastoral ministry.[43] Note that the balance I am advocating will not result in a lukewarm, powerless healing ministry. Quite the reverse. It means having a multifaceted ministry that is fully open to the present-day working of the Spirit, yet also trying to do justice to every aspect of biblical teaching. I pray that God will bless you and make you a source of great blessing, as you minister in his name in the many creative ways he will reveal to you through his Spirit.

Notes

1. I was introduced to this concept by Peter Wagner while at Fuller; see C.P. Wagner, *Church Growth and the Whole Gospel: A Biblical Mandate* (San Francisco: Harper & Row, 1981), pp. 19ff. He suggests (p. 16) there are two broad categories of signs: social signs that apply to a general class of people (e.g. proclaiming good news to the poor, liberating the oppressed) and personal signs or signs applied to individuals (e.g. restoring sight to the blind). He favours a spiritual rather than a literal interpretation of the social signs.
2. Those with gifts that are complementary to gifts of healing – for example, gifts of intercession, exhortation, pastoring – may also contribute to the healing ministry.
3. Paul Hiebert suggests that in individualistic, culturally-diverse societies such as North America there is a strong tendency for Christians to focus on personalities and exalt leaders and, in the context of the healing ministry, to attribute healings to their faith. It is to these 'significant' people that they take the sick for special prayer when others fail. This is not a helpful model; healing belongs to the congregation. See P.G. Hiebert in J.R. Coggins and P.G. Hiebert (Eds), *Wonders and the Word: An Examination of Issues Raised by John Wimber and the Vineyard Movement* (Winnipeg: Kindred, 1989), p. 148.
4. M. Cassidy, *The Passing Summer: A South African Pilgrimage in the Politics of Love* (London: Hodder and Stoughton, 1989), p. 260.
5. Paul Hiebert points out that sound, biblical teaching helps new believers move from a focus on themselves and their immediate needs to a concern for others and to deeper things of faith – such as discipleship, holiness, witnessing and suffering for the sake of the gospel. He urges all mature Christians to be examples and teachers, noting that 'Paul himself was an example of this. When a movement of ecstasy swept through the church in Corinth, causing some members to exalt speaking in tongues, healing and other visible manifestations of God's work, Paul took a strong stand, seeking to maintain order and unity in the church . . . He did not reject the spiritually young for their excesses and their pursuit of the spectacular. Rather, he instructed them in love and firmness to work as one body and to guard lest their behavior bring offense to the gospel in the world around them. And he showed them the higher way of Christian maturity – of love and mutual submission'; see Hiebert, pp. 150f.
6. The apostolic message has been defined as 'a proclamation of the death, resurrection, and exaltation of Jesus that led to an evaluation of His person as both Lord and Christ, confronted man with the necessity of repentance, and promised the forgiveness of sins'; see R.H. Mounce, *The Essential Nature of New*

Testament Preaching (Grand Rapids: Eerdmans, 1960), p. 84. I believe we should add to this statement, '. . . and the gift of his Spirit'. These essential elements are to be found in virtually every sermon preached in the book of Acts. It is clear that talking about the kerygma amounts to the same thing as talking about the gospel, albeit from a different perspective; the former emphasises the essential content of the apostolic message, the latter 'good news'. Note that in Romans 16:25 'gospel' and 'the proclamation (kerygma) of Jesus Christ' are virtually equivalent terms: 'Now to him who is able to establish you by my gospel and the proclamation of Jesus Christ . . .'

7. Christian life-style is developed out of the proclamation and influence of the central gospel of Christ. God establishes (Gk. *stērizō*, to make fast, fix, set; from *stērigx*, a prop) his people by the gospel and the proclamation of Jesus Christ (Rom. 16:25).

8. By 'proper' I mean biblically-sound. I have already offered comments on some aspects of this topic (see Chapter 4); see also R.J. Hillman, *27 Spiritual Gifts* (Melbourne: JBCE, 1986).

9. J.I. Packer, *Keep in Step with the Spirit* (Leicester: Inter-Varsity Press, 1984), pp. 66,83ff. He adds: 'Glossolalia and power to relieve bodily malfunctions by laying on hands might, for instance, be found – in fact, I think, are found – outside the church as well as inside it; and within it these are not necessarily spiritual gifts to all who have them' (p. 85).

10. Packer, p. 32.

11. Packer, p. 191.

12. I find John Wimber's teaching particularly confused and unhelpful in this respect; see J. Wimber with K. Springer, *Power Healing* (London: Hodder and Stoughton, 1986), pp. 199–207. For example, Wimber describes it as 'erroneous' to teach that all Christians possess only one or two gifts (which they need to discover) and are limited to functioning only in those gifts, expressing his concern at 'the implication that only a few are called to ministries like divine healing' (p. 200). Yet elsewhere he acknowledges that 'few Christians will be called or drawn by God to the ministry and office of healing' (p. 202) and that most of the time 'Christians exercise [only] one or two [specific] gifts' (p. 201). Confusingly, he also says that gifts of healing often come to Christians as special anointings for specific tasks (p. 202). Taken as a whole, his teaching tends to create the impression that all Christians should live in high expectation of being 'gifted' to perform miracles of healing (or to receive a 'word of knowledge', etc.). He clearly reinforces the latter notion in a more recent book, in which he writes: 'They [spiritual gifts] come and they go, like fragrant flowers that open and close. In fact, they can come and go in milliseconds. One time a certain gift goes to one person, at another time it goes to another person. At any given time a person could minister in prophecy, in tongues, in healing, or in some other form of blessing for the good of others', see J. Wimber with K. Springer, *The Dynamics of Spiritual Growth* (London: Hodder and Stoughton, 1990), pp. 151f. Another unhelpful aspect of Wimber's teaching is his suggestion that the

whole of 1 Corinthians 11:17–14:40 should be interpreted in terms of gifts given corporately to the body, rather than the individual. He bases this on an unconvincing interpretation of the Gk. *diaireseis* (1 Cor. 12:4) as indicating 'both a variety of spiritual gifts and a diversity of their assignments'; see Wimber, *Power Healing*, p. 201. (I certainly do not agree with him if he is suggesting that 1 Corinthians 12:29–30 does not apply to individual members of the body in an ongoing way.) I believe that Wimber also paves the way for an unhelpful overemphasis on the gift of speaking in tongues in the healing ministry when, having argued that speaking in tongues is not necessary, he adds 'yet, though I acknowledge this, everyone I have met who is effective in healing prayer speaks in tongues' (p. 217).

13. See, for example, C.H. Kraft, *Christianity with Power: Your Worldview and Your Experience of the Supernatural* (Ann Arbor: Vine, 1989), pp. 136f. He writes: 'I'm not saying that I don't believe in "gifting." But as I see it, Jesus commanded us all to do two things: to communicate the gospel and to heal (Lk. 9:2; 10:9; Mt. 10:7,8). Thus the point of "gifting" with regard to these two tasks is to discover just which aspects of evangelism and healing we are most gifted in . . . It is not, then, that some are gifted to heal while others are not. Rather, all are given this power and authority, and then commanded to minister in this area.' This is clearly inconsistent with the teaching on gifts in 1 Corinthians 12:9. Note also that the passages in Luke and Matthew cited by Kraft are references to Jesus' sending out of specific groups of disciples within the context of his Palestinian ministry.

14. See *Special and general gifts* in Chapter 4. While those who have been given a special gift of healing or particular role in the healing ministry (e.g. the elders of the church) will generally have more frequent opportunities to serve in this way, sometimes our God in his wisdom may choose to use an unexpected person or group as his agent of healing. We live under the sovereignty of the Spirit. He may use any humble servant, even one who has no special healing gift. He may even effect healing without any human agent, a fact that should remind us of God's grace in allowing us to be his partners in this ministry.

15. D.A. Carson, *How Long, O Lord: Reflections on Suffering and Evil* (Grand Rapids: Baker Book House, 1990), p. 9; see also pp. 247–252.

16. Carson, p. 10.

17. Carson, p. 250.

18. Referral to a suitably qualified counsellor may also be appropriate at times; see Note 21 in Chapter 7.

19. Elders, whether or not they have a gift of healing, will also be involved in visiting the sick, in praying with them and laying hands on them. As leaders of the church they are representatives of the whole congregation. Other members of the congregation, especially those who have gifts of healing, should also be invited to participate in this ministry.

20. These benefits of adopting a 'small ministry team' approach to healing, instead of holding large healing services, are noted in an appendix by George W.

Eckart included in C.P. Wagner, *How to Have a Healing Ministry Without Making Your Church Sick* (Eastbourne: Monarch, 1988), p. 263. Eckart also points out that a team approach will generally be more helpful than individual ministry, because a group has at its disposal a greater variety of spiritual gifts and experiences. I commend this appendix to you as it contains many insightful answers to common questions about the healing ministry. These could well be taken as the basis for a written philosophy of the healing ministry of any church.

21. [Robert Hillman's report of a service held on Sunday 18 March 1990 (at which he received prayer for healing) is included in Appendix III. It is not presented as a formula to be followed, but simply because it illustrates many of the principles discussed in this book.]

22. When I visited Wimber's church in California some years ago it happened to be on the day that he chose for the first time to talk about his friend David Watson, who had died from cancer. The differing recollections of these two men about events that occurred during Watson's illness highlight the importance of being clear in our ministry. When we are dealing with issues that affect people very deeply, grief and longing for healing, our own or another's, can easily influence perceptions and lead to misunderstandings. During Watson's illness, Wimber flew to England to pray and lay hands on him. During that visit, Watson came to believe that Wimber was telling him (or prophesying) that God was going to heal him (see D. Watson, *Fear No Evil: A Personal Struggle with Cancer* (London: Hodder and Stoughton, 1984), pp. 56–57; also p. 99). On the other hand, Wimber was adamant that he made no such claim (see Wimber, *Power Healing*, pp. 13–19). What really happened? Was Wimber over-comforting or over-positive because of his own need to feel reassured that his friend would be healed? Were his messages ambiguous, perhaps? Or did Watson's own longing for healing colour his interpretation of what was said? Only God knows the answers to these questions. What is clear, however, is that these two well-meaning, genuine Christian leaders perceived their shared experience in quite different ways. One heard a promise of healing here and now, the other thought he offered only a promise of healing in the hereafter.

23. I am very concerned about the practice of commanding or claiming healing. This is not the language of grace. God is Creator, we are his creation – nothing is ours by right! We see this in its most extreme form in triumphalist theology, with its failure to acknowledge that the final victory of the kingdom awaits the coming age. Some say they are merely 'standing on the promises of God' when they claim healing. The danger in this is that, if healing does not come, people are left feeling as though Satan has won, presumably because they did not have enough faith to 'stand' firm on God's promises. Unlike Scripture itself (see 1 Cor. 15:54–57; 2 Cor. 12:9–10, for example), this theology and style of ministry fails to produce a sense of triumph when there is no physical healing or the person dies. John Wimber, who has had a profound influence on many in the healing ministry today, advocates a healing environment where the Holy Spirit is present and people are full of faith in God for healing. It is a key 'value' in his

integrated model of healing. He also emphasises the need to believe that Jesus not only can but will 'do it now'; see Wimber, *Power Healing*, pp. 185f. Elsewhere, he is reported as saying that he 'wants people to know that God can heal and wants to heal and therefore to ask expectantly'; see article by Phillip D. Jensen in *The Briefing*, Issue 45/46, 1990, p. 5. Although I do not identify with the generally negative tone of the article in which the latter report appeared, I tend to agree with its author's conclusion: 'Like a politician, John Wimber is not promising unequivocally that each person will be healed. But it would seem that his mixture of generalization and overconfidence results in all but the wary being misled.'

24. We must also be careful to avoid manipulating people by using a sensational, hype-ridden, secular style of promotion and advertising for the healing ministry.

25. Merely singing choruses without feeding the mind can be very shallow unless accompanied by teaching of Scripture. This problem is aggravated if the words which accompany the music are superficial or unhelpful theologically. Selwyn Hughes believes that 'one of the reasons the Welsh Revival [of 1904] fizzled out – it only lasted about a year – was because there was not enough Bible teaching or counselling to help people with their problems. They would meet with a lot of repetitive singing or praying but no real coming to grips with people's problems. As a result many got discouraged and left'; from an interview with Daniel Batt reported in 'The Three R's of Selwyn Hughes' in *On Being*, April 1991, p. 5.

26. Packer, p. 192.

27. Levi Keidel, in a chapter entitled 'The Role of Emotions in Christian Faith', contrasts the authentic role of emotion in Hebrew and certain Zairian worship with the extremes of some forms of revivalism. He comments: '. . . feelings or emotions in themselves should play no role in validating the rightness or wrongness of one's Christian faith . . . a problem comes when emotions alone are used as the criteria for deciding what is right or wrong, when emotions themselves become my final authority . . . True Christians have always claimed to live not under the lordship of emotions but under the lordship of Christ'; see L. Keidel in Coggins and Hiebert, p. 51.

28. See 'Exalt the Lord our God', a contemporary song based on Psalm 99:5, by Rick Ridings in *Scripture in Song*, Vol. 2 (Auckland: Scripture in Song, 1981) and the hymn 'Now thank we all our God' by Martin Rinkart (1586–1649) tr. Catherine Winkworth (1827–78).

29. Wimber, *Power Healing*, pp. 136f.

30. In emotionally overstimulating environments that encourage people to abandon their objectivity and open themselves to subjective impressions, many will have unusual experiences, such as physical manifestations, 'visions' or behaviour that seems to be out of their control. Emotionally-damaged individuals – and most of us have some emotional 'hang-ups' – are particularly susceptible. Such phenomena may also be symptoms of a number of psychological and

psychiatric disorders.

31. Hiebert, p. 141.
32. In a detailed study of healings and associated phenomena at the Wimber conference in Harrogate in 1986, participants' claims that a spirit of anger (or affliction, resentment, insomnia, asthma, etc.) was the source of a particular sufferer's problem seem to have been accepted as evidence that exorcism or 'deliverance' was required. These claims generally rested on a 'word of knowledge' received by one or more of the participants; see D.C. Lewis, *Healing: Fiction, Fantasy or Fact?* (London: Hodder and Stoughton, 1989), pp. 118–128. Not surprisingly, the proportion of people who believed they experienced some benefit from deliverance ministry was relatively high (p. 125).
33. L.B. Smedes (Ed.), *Ministry and the Miraculous: A Case Study at Fuller Theological Seminary* (Pasadena: Fuller, 1987), pp. 72,74; see also *Discernment and wisdom* and *Testing the gifts* in Chapter 4.
34. I am aware of an occasion when a Christian went into a large public hospital in Sydney and insisted on praying (without success) over someone who had died. This incident brought immediate and widespread ridicule of Christianity throughout the hospital.
35. There are some in the healing ministry who believe it is unhelpful for doctors to give patients detailed information about their condition, such as the statistical likelihood of recurring disease; see, for example, Wimber, *Power Healing*, p. 212.
36. See Smedes, p. 59. Smedes also suggests that even when it seems that a credible miracle has occurred we must be careful to keep it in perspective: 'There is a difference between someone's glad report that he or she was miraculously healed and an understanding that God was at work redemptively in what happened. If we do not keep the difference in focus, we may reduce the miraculous to the same level of value as the magic of the shaman'; pp. 59f.
37. Hiebert, p. 142. In offering this caution, he writes: 'Within two weeks of the testimonies being given [testimonies of healings at a Wimber course at Fuller] and before they appeared in print, my wife and I visited one person who had to be taken to the hospital and talked to another who no longer felt well'.
38. Hiebert, p. 142.
39. This would be an extremely difficult and time-consuming task, requiring considerable expertise in scientific methodology. Some have attempted a 'scientific' approach, but I have not yet seen an analysis of the results of a healing ministry that would pass rigorous scientific review. This is not to say that none exists. I have not attempted to research such literature exhaustively, as I do not really see a need for this kind of validation of miracles.
40. Jesus refers to people of his day as a 'wicked generation' that asks for a miraculous sign (Lk. 11:29); however, note that God does sometimes grant a miracle to lead someone to deeper faith (see Note 15 in Chapter 10).
41. In the study of healings mentioned above (see Note 32), it is arguable whether even one case of miraculous healing or deliverance from demonic influence was

established with the degree of certainty that would make it scientifically credible; others may interpret the results differently, of course. However, I see it as more noteworthy that many people seemed to benefit from the experience, reporting some improvement in their health and/or their emotional or spiritual well-being. This outcome is to be expected when we come to our loving Father in prayer, telling him our needs and humbly waiting on him. There will not necessarily be a barrage of spectacular miracles.

42. In rare cases, this may even include psychosomatic relief and/or placebo effects. However, such apparent 'healing' can also cause serious problems if it leads people incorrectly to assume that they have been miraculously cured and can therefore reduce or discontinue essential medications or other ongoing treatment; see, for example, the case of a diabetic reported in Lewis, p. 36.

43. Pastoral ministry, which includes ministry to the needy and lost, should be part of every church's ministry together with evangelism. 'As humans, we need the spiritual healing that comes from being loved even more than we need physical well-being'; see Hiebert, pp. 149f.

Chapter 12

Healing, Revival and Renewal

Revival and renewal are themes very close to my heart. Almost since the day of my conversion over forty years ago, I have had an intense longing to see a great spiritual awakening across my own nation. Over time this vision has grown to include a longing for a worldwide movement of God's Spirit, a movement that will bring revival and renewal to the Church and liberating faith to the many still outside it. This has been a major focus of my prayers, ministry and study over many years. The healing ministry of the Church needs to be seen in this wider context: in relation to a contemporary movement of the Holy Spirit that will bring renewal, revival and awakening.

I will explain what I mean by some of these terms because I realise they are open to various interpretations. I use the term *renewal* in a general sense to include all renewing work of the Holy Spirit within the Church. This is a process that has been going on since the gift of the Spirit was first given at Pentecost. *Revival* is renewal happening on a grand scale, a monumental movement of God's Spirit in the Church that results in a dramatic revival of its life and witness, and *awakening* is the coming to faith of unbelievers that accompanies revival. *Reform* means any significant, positive change in the life and thought of the Church.[1] The latter may precede renewal or revival but is often a practical outworking of these movements of the Spirit. Thus revival, renewal and reform refer to what the Spirit does in the Church; awakening refers to what he does in the world.

A clear message of this book is that God graciously uses us in ministry despite our weakness. Indeed, it is often when we recognise our weakness that he is able to work most effectively through us. Nevertheless, there is a sense in which Christians who are healthy – physically, emotionally, and especially spiritually – are able to minister more effectively to those around them. Consequently, we should be seeking, in a balanced way, to be as healthy as possible in all these areas. It is one way in which we are to resist the effects of the fall, that intrusion of sin and sickness into God's good creation. Similarly, as a Church we should be seeking to be as healthy as possible so that we can be more effective in ministering to the needs of those around us, especially in sharing with them the truth, love and hope of the gospel.

The Church is a living organism, the body of Christ. In revival God reaches out and touches this body, granting healing that is instantaneous and miraculous. Renewal and reform represent different kinds of healing. As a Church we need God's healing and we need to be open to every possible means he may use to bring it about. Sometimes healing comes through sensational, dramatic experiences, for the Church as for the individual, but God also heals in other ways.

REVIVAL: MIRACULOUS HEALING FOR THE CHURCH

Since the Spirit first came upon it in power at Pentecost, the Church has experienced many great revivals.[2] These are well documented in the writings of historian Edwin Orr.[3] In this section I will explore some of the characteristics of revival, patterns that are common to all such movements throughout history,[4] and consider ways in which revival may be encouraged and its long term effects maximised. The following are all features of genuine revival: prayer; strong biblical preaching and teaching; conviction of sin and a desire for holiness and justice, which begins in the Church and flows out into the community; and an enhancement of unity between Christians of different denominations.[5]

Revival is a term that has been used rather loosely over the years. My interest is in genuine revival that is clearly linked with the great revivals of Church history. It is a movement of the Holy Spirit of such extraordinary proportions that it is difficult for those of us who have not lived through such a time to comprehend its impact:

A true Holy Spirit revival is a remarkable increase in the spiritual life of a large number of God's people, accompanied by an awesome awareness of the presence of God, intensity of prayer and praise, a deep conviction of sin with a passionate longing for holiness and unusual effectiveness in evangelism, leading to the salvation of many unbelievers.[6]

When revival comes, churches are filled to overflowing, often every day of the week, with people praying long and fervently, praising God and hungering for his Word. Nominal Christians are revitalised and there may be hundreds or even thousands of conversions, affecting the social and business life of whole communities. This is how Edwin Orr describes the effects of the revival in the United States in the mid 1800s:

> The influence of the awakening was felt everywhere in the nation. It first captured the great cities, but it also spread through every town and village and country hamlet. It swamped schools and colleges. It affected all classes without respect to condition. A Divine influence seemed to pervade the land, and men's hearts were strangely warmed by a Power that was outpoured in unusual ways. There was no fanaticism. There was remarkable unanimity of approval among religious and secular observers alike, with scarcely a critical voice heard anywhere. It seemed to many that the fruits of Pentecost had been repeated a thousandfold. At any rate, the number of conversions reported soon reached the total of fifty thousand weekly, a figure borne out by the fact that church statistics show an average of ten thousand additions to the church membership for the period of two years.[7]

The church historian James Buchanan has described revival as 'the imparting of life to those who are dead, and the imparting of health to those who are dying'.[8] Like miraculous healing of illness, revival is a relatively rare event. While it will have significant long term consequences, revival is also generally short-lived, seldom lasting beyond a generation. It is as though the normal work of the Holy Spirit in the Church is intensified for a time, as though God is 'graciously giving his people all that they want for a while' – often before periods of great persecution or suffering.[9]

I have found great inspiration in reading of these significant periods in church history. This is the kind of genuine revival that I long to see repeated in my own country and elsewhere. Of course, no one can predict the specific form that such a revival may take:

> [We] cannot limit God to work in a particular revival in exactly the same way that he has done elsewhere; there will be common features to all revivals, but every revival is unique . . . in some, phenomena like healings,

faintings, visions and so on are fairly commonplace, whilst in many they are virtually unknown. All revivals are accompanied by deep emotion, but while some express it in loud and enthusiastic behaviour, others are quiet, controlled and even solemn. And so we could go on. It is dangerous to read one revival and assume all are like that.[10]

Revival is certainly not induced by encouraging the expression of particular phenomena or patterns of behaviour observed in previous revivals.

What, if anything, can we do to promote revival? Should the Church simply go about its normal business and leave it all to God? Or does revival come only when there is a heightened readiness on the part of the Church, or a particular church, to respond to his Spirit at some point in history? Clearly, when there is a revival it is always because of God's sovereignty. We cannot bring it on by our own efforts; the wind of the Spirit 'blows wherever it pleases' (Jn. 3:8). But the Church also needs to be available to the Spirit.

Some characteristics of revival

Widespread prayerfulness – an earnest, open-hearted waiting on God – has been identified as a consistent feature of revival; it both precedes and results from the coming of the Spirit.[11] Edwin Orr maintains that, historically, there is a link between revival and the gathering together of Christians from a number of denominations in fervent prayer. This concerted prayer is motivated by a recognition of their own and society's spiritual poverty, the desperate need of both Church and nation for revival and a longing for holiness. Also evident is a willingness to be open to the searching, convicting light of the Spirit of God, a willingness to be changed by him – whatever the cost. Referring to the period between 1792–1842 when there was widespread revival, Orr writes:

> The spiritual preparation for a worldwide awakening began in Great Britain seven years before the outpouring of the Spirit there. Believers of one denomination after the other, including the evangelical minorities in the Church of England and the Church of Scotland, devoted the first Monday evening of each month to pray for a revival of religion and an extension of Christ's kingdom overseas. This widespread union of prayer spread to the United States within ten years and to many other countries, and the concert of prayer remained the significant factor in the recurring revivals of religion and the extraordinary out-thrust of missions for a full fifty years, so commonplace it was taken for granted.[12]

My own country, Australia, is among the many that have experienced genuine revival following a period of intensive prayer. The beginnings of revival here can be traced back to mid-1857, when a conference of ministers resolved to 'pray for general revival and for themselves . . . promising to pray for each other and to promote Saturday evening meetings for prayer'. In the state of New South Wales, prayer meetings were held in almost every town; in Sydney some of these had huge attendances. 'It was not long before the rising tide of prayer produced a flooding of revivals throughout the Australian Colonies', Orr reports.[13]

When revival comes, the unity of purpose among Christians of different denominations, exemplified in their concerted prayers for revival, crosses traditional boundaries that are often thought of as almost impenetrable. For example, firmly held differences of theological viewpoint, although not necessarily resolved, can cease to be stumbling blocks to united fellowship and witness. It is as though, provided they are not inconsistent with the biblical gospel itself, these issues lose significance when Christ himself becomes all in all.[14]

A strong emphasis on biblical preaching and teaching is another characteristic of revival. Revival does not begin in places where the authority of the Word is denied, and if people who do deny Scripture are effectively influenced by revival it will change their attitude to it.[15] It is often through preaching that the Spirit touches people's hearts:

> Preaching in revival times is not always graceful or polished, or even eloquent, but it is always powerful . . . the sermons are real and felt by the congregations. In revival, congregations do not discuss [a person's] style or eloquence, in fact they do not even debate the content; they are moved to action. Revival preaching has a power and an authority that bring the Word of God like a hammer to the heart and conscience . . . As a result of this kind of living preaching, people love to hear the sermon . . . the sermon becomes central in the activity and worship of the church.[16]

Similarly, preaching was a central feature of the New Testament Church. For example, the Day of Pentecost culminated in a sermon focused on the crucified risen Lord which had a profound impact (Acts 2:22–41). The hearers were cut to the heart: 'What shall we do?' they cried. Three thousand people were swept into the kingdom that day. This pattern of preaching and response occurs repeatedly in times of revival.[17]

Another characteristic of genuine revival is a longing for holiness, which begins with an overwhelming conviction of sin.[18] It is as though, deeply touched by the Spirit, people become transparent: the masks and defences behind which they normally hide from God, themselves and others are stripped away. Sin is acknowledged unselfconsciously with deep contrition, and often with tears, forgiveness is requested and received, freely and without awkwardness – with resultant joy and praise. People become more obedient to the Spirit and sinful behaviour declines. These effects spread from church to community as unbelievers are 'awakened' through inspired preaching. Again, as in the New Testament Church, the spontaneous, everyday witness of individual Christians and the love they show for one another contribute to this awakening.

In genuine revival, the impact of the Holy Spirit on individual lives inevitably finds expression in social concern and a longing for justice, as illustrated in the following account of changes that occurred in the nineteenth century:

> Emancipation of slaves, protection of prisoners, care of the sick, improvement in working conditions, safe-guarding of women and children, and extension of popular education, prison reform, hospitals, asylums, orphanages, schools, high schools and colleges stemmed from the Revivals. The work of Wilberforce in Britain and the work of Fliedner in Germany were outstanding. The most evangelistic Methodists in England gave leadership to trade unions. In the United States, there were numerous good causes which were the object of evangelical benevolence. On the mission fields, wherever possible, missionaries became social activists in education, medicine and other fields.[19]

Revival-awakening is primarily a grass-roots movement – a movement of God's powerful Spirit among his people. Just as he moved among the miners and working class in the eighteenth century revival under John Wesley, so he may begin his contemporary revival among the most deprived of our lands. They may well become the channels of his grace to the remainder of the nation. Mindful that deep concern about sin and injustice in society is often a forerunner to revival, as well as an end result, I humbly suggest to my fellow Australians that our prayers for revival and our concern about injustice should begin with our own Aborigines. Perhaps our neglect of them is proving to be an enormous barrier to the healing of both Church and nation and robbing us of great blessing.[20] They may very well be the people chosen by God to be the channels of revival to the whole of our nation. I will leave readers from other countries to consider whether there may be a parallel in their own situation.

While genuine revivals are movements of the Spirit among the masses – first the Church and then the general population – visionary, competent, Spirit-directed leadership also seems to be an important factor.[21] We see an example of this in the ministry of John Wesley, who provided overall visionary leadership for the eighteenth century revival in Great Britain. He had strong gifting in both evangelism and administration. Thus people who came to faith through his preaching were wisely incorporated into the fellowship of believers under the ministry of lay preachers. These were well-trained by him in the gospel and other disciplines so that they too could be effective and competent leaders. Competent leadership is important not only during revival but also in the period that follows.

The secondary nature of signs and wonders

Although often encountered, 'signs and wonders' such as healings are not generally stressed in first-hand accounts of revival movements. Perhaps, other aspects of the Holy Spirit's work seem even more remarkable at the time.[22] During revival, when the glory of God is the sole focus of the Church and the movement of his Spirit is quickened, miracles of healing may well be more prevalent. (Note that revivals have often led to the establishment of hospitals and medical care for the sick and poor, which should also be seen as an aspect of the Spirit's healing work.) It would be a mistake, however, to assume that the growing preoccupation with healing and other signs and wonders in many churches today is a precursor to revival. Nor should we assume that a great healing movement will necessarily accompany revival when it occurs. Similarly, the inspired singing and hymn writing that are often associated with revival do not induce it, nor are they central to it. They are a natural overflow of the joy in forgiveness that is experienced.[23]

Physical manifestations (similar to those sometimes observed at 'healing services') may also occur during revival; again, they are not a major focus. Levi Keidel, reviewing several great revival movements spanning four centuries,[24] records that extreme forms of emotional expression and non-rational manifestations were noted in all of them in their early stages. These included seeing visions, weeping, shrieking, hysterical laughing, bodily jerking and fainting. Such phenomena are certainly not essential to revival.[25] Nor are they evidence that revival is taking place. When they do occur, they seem to be responses to an overwhelming sense of God's presence and deep conviction of sin. (Note that they have not generally been interpreted in terms of 'demonisation' or deliverance from demons.) Keidel suggests that there may be a tendency for the human psyche to respond automatically in such ways to the sudden impact of the Spirit, but concludes that ongoing manifestation of such signs has almost always proven counterproductive.[26] John Wesley came to realise that there was danger in attaching too much significance to them, as did other great leaders in revival such as Jonathan Edwards, George Whitefield and Charles Finney.[27] I believe we should place little credence in their presence. We should not encourage them or try to evoke them; nor should we deny their existence. If they occur they occur. The accompanying or subsequent fruit of the Spirit is our proof that they are truly of the Spirit.

RENEWAL: THE ONGOING WORK OF THE HOLY SPIRIT

In a sense, being 'filled by the Spirit' is meant to be an ongoing experience for every Christian. Thus the Church that we comprise is continually being renewed and refreshed by the Holy Spirit. Sometimes this renewal is a subtle, almost imperceptible process, a gradual healing. But many Christians, having received the gift of the Spirit at conversion, experience a time (or even several times) when they become 'filled' by the Spirit in a special way. When this happens there are often immediate and obvious changes that effect both individuals and churches.

Towards a broader understanding of renewal

What are the signs of renewal? Does it mean a new freedom in worship with uninhibited expression of emotion? Does it mean impassioned prayer, exuberant singing, dancing, speaking in tongues, visions, words of knowledge, healings and other miraculous signs? We hear of 'Charismatic renewal' happening within congregations of many denominations. This is often associated with a strong emphasis on miraculous healing. We hear of churches, all over the world, which place great emphasis on miraculous 'signs and wonders' and are experiencing effective evangelism and rapid church growth. Enthusiastic reporting of these ministries often gives the impression that this is present day revival.

It is true that there are some similarities between contemporary 're-newal movements' and revival. For example, there is often a new freedom to express emotion through joyful singing and in other ways, as there is in revival. There may be a general increase in 'signs and wonders' and in the expression of gifts of the Spirit. Physical phenomena may occur. As I have already pointed out, however, none of these is in itself evidence of revival. The focus in revival is on God himself, on individual and corporate sinfulness. Its hallmark is deep contrition and grateful acceptance of forgiveness through Christ's death and resurrection. Effective evangelism finds expression in a strong concern for social justice, with the emphasis on the gospel as the remedy for our human predicament in its totality. Significantly, revival generally brings unity, rather than division to the Church.[28]

To the extent that these attributes of revival are evident in any present day 'renewal' and associated healing ministry, we should rejoice and give thanks to God. But to the extent that there is a preoccupation with the miraculous, an emphasis on experiences of the Spirit (gifts, miracles and healing) in place of a God-focused understanding of the Spirit and a neglect of social responsibility, such movements fall short of genuine revival.[29] In some cases, they may not even represent genuine renewal. A common problem is that many of these ministries, while they wholeheartedly acknowledge the authority of Scripture and the power of the gospel, lack sound biblical teaching and preaching. It seems to me that inadequate understanding of biblical theology is a major cause of confusion and division within the Church today. Throughout this book I have tried to highlight and address what I have come to see as key problem areas. I have done so in the hope that this will help clear the confusion and lead to reconciliation in the future.

As many Christians will be painfully aware, so-called 'renewal' has often split congregations and resulted in churches severing ties with their parent denominations. Clearly, this is at variance with the unifying effect of genuine revival evident throughout history. I believe that, generally, such disunity is a consequence of false teaching and a sign of underlying spiritual problems. Conflict is almost inevitable when those who have received inadequate teaching about the Holy Spirit and his gifts and are overenthusiastically promoting a more 'charismatic' style of ministry encounter those who are doggedly, and just as inappropriately, denying that the Holy Spirit intervenes at all in day to day events. This is especially so when the encounter occurs within a single congregation. In such cases, change (in the adherents to the new teaching) and resistance to change (in other members of the church) both contribute to division.

Misunderstanding of biblical teaching causes major problems for both parties.[30] Sinful human nature undoubtedly plays a part as well! We need to remember that for those among whom 'Christ is all, and is in all' – in truth as well as theory – there is no 'Greek or Jew, circumcised or uncircumcised' (Col. 3:11). We may also say that for those among whom 'Christ is (truly) all, and is in all' there is no Charismatic or non-Charismatic, Evangelical or Liberal, Catholic or Protestant. Such classifications, which recognise and respect existing differences in heritage and opinion, should cease to be barriers to our oneness in Christ.

We must face the fact that the Church is, at present, experiencing difficulties as a result of 'renewal' movements. However, just as we should give thanks for any measure of physical healing we receive, whether or not we are cured, so we should recognise the ways in which God has used and is using these movements for the good of his Church. Clearly, they have led to a greater emphasis on the role of the Holy Spirit and encouraged a greater openness to his miraculous intervention.[31] Thus such movements have been the vehicle of true Spirit-inspired renewal. A degree of healing is coming to the Church through them. It may not be the dramatic healing that we see in revival, but it is healing nevertheless – one way in which the Spirit is at work today. Wherever we see such movements pointing people to the gospel and the work of the Spirit, let us acknowledge it with praise and gratitude as we continue to pray for greater wholeness.

Church history will doubtless affirm the positive influence of the twentieth century Pentecostal and Charismatic movements in encouraging openness to the Holy Spirit, but it is very clear that the miraculous working of the Spirit of God is not – and never has been – confined to any one particular denomination or division of the Church. He has certainly been at work outside these two recognised movements in this century. Indeed, who can say whether he has been working more powerfully outside than within them. I believe that a significant movement of the Spirit is taking place in the hearts of Christians right now. I also believe that it is not necessary, or even helpful, to think of this as associated exclusively with the Pentecostal or Charismatic movements. I see this general stirring of the Spirit as motivating increasing numbers of Christians outside these traditions to become more 'charismatic' in a *biblical* sense: more aware of the Holy Spirit as a personal indwelling presence and more aware of the need to live daily in the Spirit's power, with an openness to his gifts in all their diversity.[32,33] In the present spiritual climate, I believe it is crucial for

Christians generally to acknowledge that being involved in renewal or revival does not *necessarily* mean joining a Pentecostal church, being baptised in the Spirit, speaking in tongues or experiencing 'Charismatic renewal', although for some it may. God is not limited to these means of providing healing for his Church.

Our heavenly Father deals with his children personally, lovingly and creatively, in a diversity of ways suited to the needs of each individual, each church, each society. Understanding this, sets all Christians free to pray wholeheartedly for renewal, which may include revival. We need grace that will enable us to present our requests humbly before our God and Saviour, ready to be exposed to the searching light of the Spirit and willing to be obedient to his promptings. This is essential if we, individually and corporately, are to grow in Christlikeness, which is the essence of wholeness. Praying for renewal means stepping out into the unknown, trusting our heavenly Father to answer our prayers – in his 'ripe' time and in his best way.

Experiencing the fullness of the Spirit

Living in the fullness of the Spirit, or being 'Spirit-filled', involves total openness to the indwelling Christ. For both the individual and the Church, it means openness to doing whatever must be done to deal with sinfulness. It means openness to both the fruit and the gifts of the Spirit and also to the unity of the Spirit, which is expressed in harmony between all believers. It means openness to all aspects of the Spirit's power and to the truth of his Word, the *whole* counsel of God in the written Word of the Spirit. There is no separation of Spirit and Word.

Living in the fullness of the Spirit involves deep spirituality, prayerfulness, a constant meditation on the Scriptures, an eager participation in life, action and service, a deep, incarnational involvement in the world. If our primary focus is on Christ – on the incarnational principle of identifying with people, creation and events, both past and present – we will not lose contact with the reality of today or with historic Christianity.

Living in the fullness of the Spirit is not triumphalism. It does not mean striving to live as though the final age has already come. That is basically wrong eschatology. In the present age, healing (and prosperity) are not available to all Christians. Evil is not simply to be banished or rebuked in the powerful name of the Lord. Living in the Spirit is primarily about love, not power or miracles. It is more about fruit than gifts. It is not primarily about supernatural guidance – visions, prophesies or words of knowledge – but about authentic Christian living.

Implications for the healing ministry

The healing ministry is a natural outworking of authentically living in the fullness of the Spirit. It is for all churches, not only those that enter into Charismatic renewal. It should arise out of, and always be a part of, the proclamation and practical expression of the whole counsel of God. At its very heart is the gospel of God's grace towards humankind. Following the example of the New Testament, this ministry should be gospel-centred, comprehensive and compassionate, carried out in the power of the Spirit and for the glory of God alone. I long to see increasing numbers of churches becoming involved in this kind of healing ministry as the Spirit of God moves in our day bringing renewal to the whole Church.

The Pentecostal and Charismatic movements have traditionally placed great emphasis on healing. Thus many Christians, upon recognising the legitimacy of the healing ministry, have (quite unnecessarily, I believe) adopted styles of ministry that are generally associated with these movements. This trend is evident in books written by Evangelicals who have become deeply involved in the healing ministry.[34] Of greater concern to me is the fact that many have also adopted a whole range of erroneous teaching, from a variety of sources, and are now promulgating it. In particular, we find unbiblical notions about demons, often accompanied by a quasi-Dualistic interpretation of spiritual warfare, triumphalism with its unrealistic expectations, and a tendency to undervalue human reason and commonsense. As I have indicated throughout this book, these and other issues are causing serious problems in the contemporary healing movement.

Uneasy about teachings and practices that have become widely associated with the healing ministry this century, many Christians and churches avoid involvement, even those who accept that God does heal miraculously today. Becoming involved seems to mean accepting, as a package, a whole collection of radical ideas and practices. But the truth is that many of the items in various healing ministry 'packages' currently being advocated are not necessary for an effective healing ministry. For example, the 'package' that is being widely offered through the teachings of John

Wimber and the Vineyard movement contains a disturbing mixture of helpful and unhelpful items.[35] It is better to be selective than indiscriminately accept the lot.

While recommending caution, I nevertheless want to encourage all Christians, including my fellow Evangelicals, to become more open to the miraculous activity of the Holy Spirit and to the possibility of renewal. It is a great tragedy when Christians who emphasise the priority of the biblical gospel undervalue the healing ministry, especially if this also means that they are closed to God's miraculous intervention in other ways. How sad it is when those who begin well (at the cross) fail to appropriate the fullness of their heritage: the fullness of the resurrection and the fullness of the Spirit's power that stem from that cross (see *The relationship between Easter and Pentecost* in Chapter 10). In drawing upon all the resources available to us through God's omnipotent Spirit, we will experience in greater measure the abundant Christian life that Christ has promised us.

A biblical understanding of healing and the healing ministry cannot be achieved by considering only the work of the Holy Spirit and his miraculous gifts. The primary focus in this ministry, as in every other aspect of Christian life and ministry, must be on the living Christ and on the cross, the symbol of humility, servanthood and total dependence on God. In our weakness, the Holy Spirit will minister to us, and through us. Any form of 'renewal' that serves only to encourage or 'empower' people to pray for and expect miraculous healing cannot be regarded as a sound basis for the healing ministry.

REFORM: MAKING HEALTHY CHANGES

In his first letter to the Corinthians, Paul paints an absurd picture of a human body in which the various parts are at war with each other or trying to exist independently (1 Cor. 12:15–21). In real life, such a state of chaos would represent life-threatening illness. Within the Church today, we find fragmentation that is just as alarming. There are hostile, defensive, warring factions. In these terms the Church is sick, and it is suffering unnecessarily. We are called to suffer for the gospel; instead we often suffer through our own foolishness and waywardness. There is a great need today for the Church, as one body, to appropriate all the healing that God has for it. We have seen that many factors can work against the healing of the individual (see Chapter 9). There are also many ways in which the healing work of the Spirit within the Church, including revival and renewal, may be hindered.

When someone becomes ill, he or she can cooperate with God in the healing process by choosing to adopt appropriate attitudes and practices (see Chapter 7). Similarly, when as a Church we find ourselves ailing, we can take action to promote healing. What can we do? Many of the general principles already presented in the context of the healing of the individual have relevance to the healing of the Church. For example, the whole Church will benefit from prayer, the study of the Word and meaningful worship and fellowship. The whole Church will benefit from strategies that encourage emotionally healthy behaviour, good relationships and resolution of conflict, within and between congregations. The best 'medical' attention is also essential: we will need to draw on the best resources available, even if that means using the skills of a 'specialist' from another denomination. Across the denominations, it will mean biblical, doctrinal reform. Radical 'lifestyle' changes in other areas may also be needed.

As we seek healing in these ways we will need to be faithful to the plain truths of Scripture (see Appendix I). We will also need to acquire the ability to listen to each other and to differing points of view with a spirit of grace. Maintaining our balance will be important too. Christians have a great deal of trouble doing this. There are churches that are built around relationships, but very weak on doctrine; this produces very superficial Christianity. At the other extreme, there are churches strong on doctrine and weak on relationships; this invites legalism. Some churches over-stress evangelism, others social justice or spiritual gifts, and so on. A study of Church history will soon reveal that this is not a recent phenomenon. Like a drunken person trying to mount a horse, we get on one side and fall off the other.

As Christians, irrespective of denominational, doctrinal or theological traditions, we are called in the name of the gospel to work towards greater unity. To achieve this will mean raising issues about which we hold strong and divergent opinions, and we will need to deal with them sensitively and graciously. Yet we must dare to do this because it is as we honestly face up to historically difficult and divisive issues within the Church, with an openness to finding God's way forward, that we will grow in the unity of the Spirit.

Across the Church, there is a pressing need for reform in relation to teaching about the Holy Spirit and his gifts. This is a key issue not only for those involved in contemporary renewal movements but for all Christians. Weak or erroneous teaching in this area may in fact represent a major barrier to renewal and revival. We all need to be open to the Spirit and the whole range of gifts he provides, but we must beware of Satan's counterfeit 'miracles'. If he can trap us into believing that every apparently supernatural experience comes from God, he can do untold damage to the Church and the individual.[36] Authentic spiritual giftedness will be grounded in the gospel of the crucified and risen Christ and graced by the fruit of the Spirit.

In our enthusiasm for experiences of the Spirit and his gifts we must not neglect to proclaim the whole counsel of God, especially the gospel of the kerygma.[37] All preaching should be undergirded by the proclamation of the biblical gospel and inspired by the Spirit. How I long for everyone who is involved in the training of future ministers of the Word to embody the dynamic message of this gospel and present it in the power of the Spirit and in the context of biblical truth. In a general sense, the whole Church is called upon to be both evangelical and charismatic. It must acknowledge both gospel and Spirit, Easter and Pentecost, and keep them in proper perspective.

Our focus must be on Christ himself, not the Spirit. James Packer addresses this point:

> I remember walking to a church one winter evening to preach on the words "he shall glorify me", seeing the building floodlit as I turned a corner, and realizing that this was exactly the illustration my message needed . . . floodlights are so placed that you do not see them . . . It is as if the Spirit stands behind us, throwing light over our shoulder, on Jesus, who stands facing us. The Spirit's message to us is never, "Look at me; listen to me; come to me; get to know me", but always "Look at *him*, and see his glory; listen to *him*, and hear his word; go to *him*, and have life; get to know *him*, and taste his gift of joy and peace". . . the Holy Spirit glorifies Christ, according to Christ's own word . . . A person receives the Spirit by receiving Christ . . . the idea that one can have the Spirit and be "spiritual" apart from personal encounter with the risen Lord is a damaging error.[38]

We need inclusive ministry that affirms all gifts and, especially, all Christians. We need to abandon any approach to ministry that does not seek the unity of the people of God in truth and love and that leads to a defensive, exclusive spirit. To this end, I humbly call upon those who hold the view that every Christian, after conversion, needs to undergo a second experience of 'baptism in the Spirit' to reconsider their position. This teaching is inherently and unnecessarily divisive and many discerning Charismatics have already rejected it. As already discussed,[39] Scripture makes it clear that all Christians are given the gift of the Spirit at conversion. While subsequently some do experience specific 'fillings' of the Spirit, which produce significant and lasting benefits, these are experienced in a whole variety of ways. They may sometimes be accompanied by an unusual manifestation, such as speaking in tongues, but this does not always happen. I long for the day when Christians will be united in accepting the foundational teaching of Scripture on the work of the Holy Spirit in the believer's life. Only the gospel of the cross and resurrection of Christ surpasses it in importance. I also humbly challenge Christians of every denomination to recognise all genuine charismatic (and Charismatic) experiences, acknowledging that after conversion some do receive second, third (and even more) memorable touches of the Spirit.

As Christians our priority should be obedience to our Lord, who guides and enables us through both Word and Spirit. This should override denominational and theological differences. To a certain extent, following him will mean different things for different people. We are members of one body, but the body has many different parts. We need continually to ask for wisdom to enable us to discern what is essential to Christian life and ministry, what is legitimate but just a matter of personal preference, and where we are in error and need to change. In our humanness, none of us is beyond error. Every denomination, every school of theological thought has its strengths and its weaknesses and needs to be open to change under the guidance of the Spirit and in accordance with biblical truth. We would do well to take Paul's advice to the church in Colossae as a prophetic word to the Church of our day:

> Therefore, as God's chosen people, holy and dearly loved, clothe yourselves with compassion, kindness, humility, gentleness and patience. Bear with each other and forgive whatever grievances you may have against one another. Forgive as the Lord forgave you. And over all these virtues put on love, which binds them all together in perfect unity. Let the peace of Christ rule in your hearts, since as members of one body you were called to peace. And be thankful. Let the word of Christ dwell in you richly as you teach and admonish one another with all wisdom, and as you sing psalms, hymns and spiritual songs with gratitude in your hearts to God. And whatever you do, whether in word or deed, do it all in the name of the Lord Jesus,

giving thanks to God the Father through him.[40]

I would encourage you to participate in any spontaneous, united prayer for renewal or revival that may be inspired by the Spirit of God among the churches in your region. The kind of opinionated denominationalism that represents a barrier to united prayer is a sin for which we – in our denominational institutions, in our local churches and in our ourselves – need humbly to repent.

Holding the vision of a healthy Church

Perhaps one of the greatest barriers to healing in the Church is defeatism over past failures in our efforts toward unity. We need to acknowledge and throw off the cynicism, stubbornness and prejudice that cloud our vision and become teachable people. This will involve sacrifice and humility. It will mean a willingness to recognise that no one denomination or Christian organisation has all the answers. While acknowledging that both Church and individual will reach perfection only in the age to come, we need to affirm that God has in the past and can in the future revive his ailing Church. Just as appropriate prayerful visualisation of a positive outcome may assist physical healing, so it is helpful for us to hold in our hearts and minds the vision of a healthy Church – redeemed by Christ and open to the continuous transforming work of his Spirit. Can you imagine it?

It would be a Church that not only tolerated differences in expression of gifts and ministries but encouraged them and revelled in the creative way God had put them together – 'just as he wanted them to be' (1 Cor. 12:18). It would be a Church in which humility shone in every member from the established leadership to the newest convert – with weaknesses acknowledged, aid given and strengths affirmed. It would be a Church in which issues of disagreement were resolved by the give and take of a loving family, with each member's role recognised and valued. It would be a Church in which those weakest financially or socially would be cared for, not by the few, but by the Church as a whole. A Church without a fortress mentality, whose humility allowed for easy access to those outside its ranks. Moved by compassion, we who comprise the Church would indeed be a light in the darkness. This whole and hearty Church would be a compelling, loving servant to a needy world and represent a clearer image of the Christ it worships. Above all, it would understand its need of God.

And that is where our vision for change must begin. As the body of Christ, we need to repent and listen to God. We need to be reconciled, each 'member' to the other. And we must begin on our knees.[41] We have no hope of growing to our full stature as the people of God unless we begin by laying our hearts at his feet. If we can grasp our calling to servanthood and, as Christ commanded, regain the teachable spirit of a little child, we will begin to change. Then, open to the power of both gospel and Spirit, we as one body will receive all the healing God has for us in this present age and afford the world a glimpse of the glory of the age to come.

Notes

1. I am using the term 'reform' in the literal sense, that is, amendment of what is wrong. No specific reference to the Reformation or any particular model for church reform is intended.

2. See, for example, Brian H. Edwards, *Revival! A People Saturated with God* (Darlington: Evangelical Press, 1990), pp. 20,269ff; quotations in this chapter used by permission. As Edwards points out, detailed accounts of revival movements are available for only the last 200 years of church history, since diary-keeping became common practice. His book is written for the general reader in the hope that it will encourage all Christians to eagerly desire and pray for revival in our time. It is a helpful book in that it offers the non-academic reader a fascinating glimpse of the many times throughout its history when the Spirit has come powerfully upon the Church. (Please note that I do not endorse the author's occasional pronouncements against women in ministry.)

3. See, for example J. Edwin Orr, *The Eager Feet: Evangelical Awakenings, 1790–1830* (Chicago: Moody, 1975). Note that Orr uses the term 'Evangelical Awakening' to refer to both Christian revival and the associated coming to faith of those outside the Church. A world authority on religious revivals and awakenings and an influential member of faculty at Fuller Theological Seminary during my time there, Orr has written numerous books on this subject. I strongly recommend them, especially to readers seeking a thorough, scholarly treatment. [Also recommended is a keynote article by Stuart Piggin, which presents a biblical perspective on revival, published recently in *Encounter with God: Daily Notes* (London: Scripture Union, 1994), Jan–March 1995, pp. 53–64.]

4. Orr, *The Eager Feet*, p. vii.

5. Duncan Campbell, who was involved in revival in Scotland earlier this century, described it as a 'community saturated with God'. See Edwards, p. 26.

6. Edwards, p. 28. Like Brian Edwards, I include in this category only events that

involve large numbers of individuals. Edwin Orr's definition is broader: 'Such an awakening may change in a significant way an individual only; or it may affect a larger group of believers; or it may move a congregation, or the churches of a city or district, or the whole body of believers throughout a country or a continent; or indeed the larger body of believers throughout the world' (see Orr, *The Eager Feet*, p. vii). Note that: 'Revival, in the classic sense, does not occur in unevangelized or Bible-ignorant communities. In the so-called Christian countries, a renewal of Bible study and an interest in Bible doctrine has preceded the great awakenings, while on the mission fields, phenomenal revival has occurred only after a Christian community, however small, has been gathered. In a certain sense, evangelism must precede revival. There must be a gathered community to be revived . . .'; see J.E. Orr, *Evangelical Awakenings in Southern Asia* (Minneapolis: Bethany Fellowship, 1975), p. 64; this and all subsequent quotations used by permission.

7. J.E. Orr, *The Second Evangelical Awakening in America* (London: Marshall, Morgan and Scott, 1952), p. 33.

8. From Edwards, p. 26.

9. Edwards, pp. 222,230.

10. Edwards, pp. 93f; nevertheless, some common features of past revivals and events which preceded them can be identified (see above and next section).

11. Edwards, p. 78.

12. Orr, *The Eager Feet*, p. 191. A strong motivation for prayer was the awareness that, in the wake of the French Revolution, the faith of whole nations was being undermined. Orr writes, 'Voltaire made no idle boast when he said that Christianity would be forgotten within thirty years'. Elsewhere he writes: 'The Concert of Prayer for revival in the 1780s in Great Britain and in the 1790s in United States, and the renewed Concert of Prayer in both countries in 1815 and in several European realms besides, was clearly demonstrated to be the prime factor in motivating and equipping Christians for service in a worldwide movement which totally eclipsed the military might of the nations at the Battle of Waterloo. A century of comparative peace among nations made the great century of pioneer evangelization possible'; see Orr, *Evangelical Awakenings in Southern Asia*, p. 16. Later in that book, describing revival in India, he writes: 'The recognised antecedents of Revival were first united prayer, such as three hundred or more intercessors at the Moody Bible Institute in 1899, and the prayer for world-wide revival on the part of a band of ministers and laymen meeting each Saturday afternoon for eleven years or so in Melbourne, and the movement of the Keswick Convention in 1902 where 5000 Christians resolved to form home prayer circles for world-wide blessing, and praying bands all over India; the second was the revival of Bible study in many missions, and the third was the faith, obedience and self-sacrifice on the part of many Indians'; see p. 110.

13. See J.E. Orr, *Evangelical Awakenings in the South Seas* (Minneapolis: Bethany Fellowship, 1976), pp. 50,51; this and following quotations used by permission.

Significant church growth resulted. For example, Methodist statistics show an active membership of five thousand in 1852, but in 1867 the number exceeded twenty thousand, an increase of 300% in fifteen years; see p. 58. Orr concludes: 'It is fair, therefore, to treat the seven years from 1858 to 1865 in Australia as seven years of plenty, paralleling the seven years of blessing experienced in many other parts of the world . . . From 1858 till 1888, the spirit of prayer continued, perhaps dwindling with the passing of a generation . . . Although the tide did not far recede, it came in again in the next generation, for 1889 ushered in a period of ardent prayer for revival, followed by another quarter century of advancement of the evangelical cause'; see pp. 58,63.

14. Orr reports that the revival in America of 1858 'affected impartially the two great divisions of Evangelicalism . . . the two systems of interpretation were not reconciled. Rather they were blended. There was little friction between Calvinist[s] and Arminians anywhere . . . although the Revivalists prayed like Calvinists, they worked like Arminians for the salvation of souls'; Orr, *The Second Evangelical Awakening in America*, p. 146. Sadly, this is not always the case. Orr also notes, 'the Calvinist–Arminian controversy had been extremely bitter following the First Evangelical Revival'. Revival does not mean instant sinless perfection, just as miraculous healing does not mean instant perfect health. We will experience perfection in both these areas only in the age to come (see *Healing and the kingdom* in Chapter 2).

15. Edwards, p. 104. Edwin Orr notes that a renewal of Bible study and an interest in Bible doctrine preceded the great awakenings; see Orr, *Evangelical Awakenings in Southern Asia*, p. 64 (see quote in Note 6 above).

16. Edwards, pp. 102f,105.

17. See Orr, *The Eager Feet*, p. viii. Note that although miraculous signs were evident on that day, they were not the primary focus.

18. Brian Edwards comments: 'It must be admitted that when revival comes, those who have longed most for it may suffer most conviction in it. Revival always touches the conscience of those who long to serve him most'; see Edwards, p. 114.

19. Orr, *The Eager Feet*, pp. 198–199; he is referring to revivals that took place between 1792 and 1842.

20. Some years ago, I was given the task of leading a school of theology in connection with a Synod at which the first Aboriginal moderator of the Uniting Church in Australia, Rev Djiniyini Gondarra, was installed. Djiniyini and his wife had been the leading figures in the revival that had broken out some eight years or so earlier on Elcho Island and which had spread to many Aboriginal communities throughout Australia. I was deeply moved by the presence of the Aboriginal leaders at the Synod and by the news of a revival movement among them. This was clearly an answer to the prayers of many who, like me, had been praying long-term for the revival–renewal of the Church and the awakening of our nation. I had to confess to my Aboriginal brothers and sisters that it had never entered my mind that God would begin his work of revival among them,

the most down-trodden and ill-treated of our nation's citizens (like the poor of Matthew 5:3?). Yet I discerned that this was indeed happening.

Two other factors seemed to me to be significant in this movement of deep spirituality: the message of the gospel was being proclaimed in indigenous languages and there was a concern for justice. I was overwhelmed by a sense of appropriateness of this call for justice. I felt the strongest conviction that the nation of Australia could probably not receive God's full and richest blessings without specific repentance and that ongoing injustices were almost certainly barriers to the Spirit's gracious work of renewal and awakening. I pray for the spread and deepening of the revival among Aboriginal people which began at Elcho Island. I pray for the redemption of this race and for justice for its people. I also pray for its leaders (some by name) and for its theological college, Nungalinya, in the Northern Territory of Australia.

21. Edwin Orr writes: 'In the United States and in British North America, there were preparatory movements of revival in the 1780s that raised up leaders for the wider movement in the following decade'; see Orr, *The Eager Feet*, p. 194. His books contain numerous specific examples of the key role played by suitably gifted leaders prior to, during and following revival.

22. This suggestion is supported by the following report of an interview with two English missionaries about their time at Madiun in eastern Java: 'During the summer of 1972 about thirty of the young people were gathered for a week of intensive Bible teaching. During a time of testimony and prayer they were suddenly broken, and with crying and confession many grievances and grudges were put right. It was the beginning of a new work of God among the people . . . [Subsequently] the Spirit began to move among the whole congregation as he had among the young people. Evil attitudes and thoughts were confessed, cherished charms were thrown away, and Warcito, a blind lad, had his sight restored. Healing was not a significant part of this work but God moved in the lives of a few to restore them physically. Barriers seemed to fall away, and the church, normally a caring and loving people, though sensitive and easily offended, now experienced a depth of love and reality of faith unknown before. Rivalry disappeared and all evangelized as one. Over the next six months there was much evidence of the work of the Spirit spilling over into the community'; see Edwards, p. 265.

23. Edwards, pp. 137–143; Orr, *The Second Evangelical Awakening in America*, pp. 148–153.

24. See L. Keidel in J.R. Coggins and P.G. Hiebert (Eds), *Wonders and the Word: An Examination of Issues Raised by John Wimber and the Vineyard Movement* (Winnipeg: Kindred, 1989), pp. 49–50.

25. Edwin Orr writes: 'In 1798, the awakening [in the United States] became general. Congregations were crowded and conviction was deep, leading to numerous thoroughgoing conversions. Every state in New England was affected, and every evangelical denomination. There were no records of emotional extravagance, and none among the churches of the Middle Atlantic

States, where extraordinary revivals broke out . . . In the western parts of New York and Pennsylvania, there were more startling displays of excitement . . . In 1800, extraordinary revival began in Kentucky . . . there were extremes of conviction and response, such as trembling and shaking – described as 'the jerks' – weeping for sorrow and shouting for joy, fainting. Extravagances occurred among a comparative few, but were exaggerated by critics out of all proportion, so that twentieth century historians have stressed the odd performances and ignored the major thrust of the awakening in the United States'; Orr, *The Eager Feet*, p. 194.

26. Similarly, Brian Edwards writes: 'We have a small view of God if we do not expect that when a man or woman sees himself or herself in the light of God's holiness there will never be an intense reaction. What must be noted is that in revival such a terrible experience of conviction is always followed by as great a joy in forgiveness . . . [Such phenomena] are not present in every revival and they should never be prayed for as a sign of reality . . . the more people expect them, the more they will appear, but that proves nothing apart from the frailty of the human mind . . . phenomena in revival need not be feared because they are passing things and will soon be gone. It is the lasting fruit that really matters. If the church majors on the phenomena it will soon bring revival to an end'; see Edwards, pp. 203f.

27. See J. Schmidt in Coggins and Hiebert, p. 79, and Edwards, pp. 196ff.

28. While this is true in general, there may still be some misunderstandings and differences of opinion in times of revival. See, for example, Note 14 above.

29. See J.B. Toews in Coggins and Hiebert, p. 92, also A. Glasser, pp. 98ff.

30. See J. Schmidt in Coggins and Hiebert, pp. 78–84, for a helpful discussion of factors that contribute to the division that often arises when the leaders or members of a congregation become influenced by the Vineyard movement.

31. Art Glasser's comments about the Vineyard movement are pertinent here: 'It has unabashedly brought onto center-stage the realities of New Testament koinonia (fellowship), the activity of the Holy Spirit and the experience of direct contact with the living God through the redemptive death and victorious resurrection of Jesus Christ. Its sheer numbers of radically transformed people making common confession of Jesus Christ as Lord and Savior are most impressive'; see Glasser in Coggins and Hiebert, p. 99. In this chapter, Glasser also expresses deep concern about certain aspects of the movement.

32. Because the term 'charismatic' is so closely related to the Greek word for 'spiritual gifts' (charismata), it does seem appropriate to use it in this biblical sense, and it is not surprising that this usage is gaining acceptance. Great confusion will arise, however, if being 'charismatic' in this biblical sense is regarded as tantamount to adopting Charismatic or Pentecostal practice and teaching. In particular, it seems almost inevitable that using this word (with its multiplicity of meanings and many shades of interpretation) in multidenominational discussions will lead to confusion and misunderstandings, especially when highly emotive and potentially divisive issues are under consideration. Using

capitalisation to make the distinction, as I have done in this book, only helps in written communications and then only if the terms are carefully defined. Perhaps we need to find an alternative word for 'charismatic' when we mean Christians of all denominations who are open to the Spirit (including those in Charismatic churches) and reserve the term 'Charismatic' only for the particular stream of Christian thought and practice that is associated with the Charismatic movement. (It has been suggested that the Vineyard movement is in fact fostering a new Charismatic denomination; see D.M. Lewis in Coggins and Hiebert, p. 61.) Attention to semantics in this area may pave the way for healthy, non-defensive reassessments of theological differences of opinion – a difficult yet, I believe, important process if we are to achieve greater unity among all Christians.

33. In 1983, Peter Wagner recognised the trend I have described, calling it the 'third wave' of the Spirit. The first wave, he says, was the Pentecostal movement, which arose at the beginning of the century; the second, the Charismatic movement, which began in the fifties throughout major denominations; and the third, a new movement of God's Spirit among non-Charismatics, including many from the vast Evangelical wing of the Church; see C.P. Wagner, 'A Third Wave?' in *Pastoral Renewal*, 1983, Vol. 8, pp. 1–5 and *How to Have a Healing Ministry Without Making Your Church Sick* (Eastbourne: Monarch, 1988), pp. 15–63. He suggested that the latter group was in a sense becoming more 'charismatic', but without doing it in a 'charismatic way'. Evangelicals were acknowledging the present day activity of the Spirit and accepting biblical teaching on spiritual gifts (including gifts of healing), but without regarding 'baptism in the Spirit' as an essential post-conversion experience or placing much emphasis on speaking in tongues. When I first read this article I found it encouraging. I could identify with Wagner's 'third wave'; I too was 'charismatic' in that sense (see *The ongoing work of the Holy Spirit* in Chapter 1), although I remained part of the Evangelical wing of the Church. I have since come to realise, however, that while Wagner's article was insightful in certain respects, his 'three wave' model may not be entirely helpful. For example, it does tend to give the impression that the Holy Spirit was not active prior to the turn of the century and also suggests that, apart from the recent 'third wave', his activity has been confined to the Pentecostal and Charismatic movements. This concept may thus inadvertently cause offence to many Christians and, by adding to disunity, even hinder the moving of the Spirit and the development of balanced, maximally-effective healing ministries.

34. See, for example, C.P. Wagner, *How to Have a Healing Ministry* . . . and C.H. Kraft, *Christianity with Power: Your Worldview and Your Experience of the Supernatural* (Ann Arbor: Vine, 1989). Note, however, that Wagner and Kraft have not taken on board the distinctive Pentecostal–Charismatic doctrine of 'baptism in the Spirit' (see Wagner, pp. 24–27, Kraft, p. 166f). Some Charismatics, including John Wimber, have also rejected this teaching (see Note 3 in Chapter 4). Wagner and Kraft both seem to have been strongly influenced by John

Wimber's approach to the healing ministry.

35. See Note 5 in Chapter 5.

36. Satan can also use this lie to trap unbelievers who are genuinely seeking spiritual truth (and even Christians) into involvement in the New Age movement and various cults.

37. See *The power of the gospel* in Chapter 2; *Maintaining a gospel emphasis* in Chapter 10; *Gospel-centred teaching* in Chapter 11.

38. See J.I. Packer, *Keep in Step with the Spirit* (Leicester: Inter-Varsity Press, 1984), pp. 66,93; his text was from John 16:14. Packer believes that questions about the Holy Spirit that are not forms and facets of the basic question, 'How may I and all Christians – indeed all the world – come to know Jesus Christ and know him better?' should not be asked (pp. 91ff). A lack of gospel emphasis and biblical understanding together with an overemphasis on the role of the Holy Spirit places a congregation in grave danger. For example, I know of one church in which a very troubled girl had a 'vision' that led to her being accepted as a 'prophet'. The girl's influence was strong. There were many 'miraculous' signs, which were unquestioningly accepted as being of the Spirit. Eventually, some members of the congregation began to express the view that under her ministry people did not need to hear the gospel; they just went 'straight through to the Holy Spirit'. Clearly, it is heresy to teach that bypassing Easter and going directly to Pentecost is the ultimate way to come to God.

39. See *The gift of the Spirit* and *Speaking in tongues and interpretation* in Chapter 4.

40. Col. 3:12–17. As we obey this call to unity and peace, we must recognise that some degree of disunity may be an unavoidable part of the 'admonition' required to correct wrong teaching and attitudes. The Church must always gently and lovingly, but uncompromisingly, agree to disagree with individuals in its midst who are not willing to respond with obedience to God's call to holiness.

41. This is in accordance with the teaching of Scripture: 'If my people, who are called by my name, will humble themselves and pray and seek my face and turn from their wicked ways, then will I hear from heaven and will forgive their sin and will heal their land' (2 Chr. 7:14). We need to pray continually for the Church as a whole as well as for individual churches. Paul sets us a good example: 'I face daily the pressure of my concern for all the churches' (2 Cor. 11:28). The word Paul uses for 'concern' is Gk. *merimna*, the same word he uses in Philippians 4:6 when he says: 'Do not be anxious about anything . . .' Concern for the churches, however, is a beneficial kind of anxiety that finds its proper expression in prayer. At the beginning of virtually every letter of Paul he assures the church to which he is writing that he is praying for them (see Rom. 1:9f; Eph. 1:16ff; Phil. 1:9ff; Col. 1:9ff; 1 Thes. 1:2); note that thanksgiving and intercession for the churches always go together. Everyone needs prayer, but those who are in leadership roles, both clergy and laity, especially need to enlist the help of others who will pray for them fervently. They have a special need for the following reasons: they have more responsibility and accountability than

other Christians (Jas. 3:1); they have more temptation – the evil one is particularly active to bring them down; they are targets of spiritual warfare, e.g. Satanist and occult groups focus prayer against them; they have great influence on others; they are very visible and therefore targets of gossip and criticism. (The above list comes from a seminar entitled 'How to Have a Prayer Ministry' presented by C.P. Wagner in Sydney, Australia in May 1991). I also urge you to pray for the raising up of those who train the pastors of our churches in theology and ministry. Centres of theological education are frequently keys to maximising the effectiveness of renewal in Church and nation. How I long to see in my country – indeed in every country – an independent, interdenominational, evangelical postgraduate school of theology and ministry, equipping future leaders to minister in the fullness of the Spirit.

A Final Word

I have tested the ideas presented in this book in churches of different denominations all over Australia and found a great openness to them. I have noticed that congregations (and individuals) tend to lose their reservations about the healing ministry when they sense that it can be balanced. It does not have to make extravagant claims, nor lead to a total preoccupation with healing or the Holy Spirit to the neglect of the gospel of forgiveness through Christ. It does not have to be emotionally supercharged or focus on the human healer or spectacular miracles or unusual physical manifestations. Such practices detract from the glory of God. Congregations are also reassured when they realise that the healing ministry can, and should be, part of the ongoing life and ministry of the church, carried out with the full endorsement of its leadership.

In terms of maintaining balance it is helpful to remember that the healing ministry, while important, is only one among many ministries. Above all, our task is to proclaim the gospel of the crucified risen Lord, in both word and deed. When we do this we do not separate the dynamic power of the gospel from healing power, nor do we fall into the trap of identifying the healing ministry with the gospel. Christians of every denomination need to explore gospel-centred models for the healing ministry. There are many different legitimate approaches to ministry and many different resources for healing. Whatever our approach, a strong teaching ministry must accompany the healing ministry, as it did in the ministry of Jesus. Where biblical teaching is lacking, simplistic or flawed, the healing ministry is weakened and, pastorally, on dangerous ground.

It is my prayer that this book will encourage every church to participate in ministering to the needs of those who are ill in appropriate and effective ways. I also pray that this book will assist those who are ill to receive all the healing that God has for them, by highlighting the multiplicity of ways in which his healing may come. I acknowledge, however, that some may be called upon to witness to the power and grace of Christ through sickness. For some, taking up the cross and following him may involve living with serious illness or disability. Thus my greater prayer is a prayer for wholeness, that we may all be transformed more and more into the likeness of Jesus Christ himself.

I believe there is a yearning for wholeness and holiness in the hearts of Christians everywhere and a deep desire for an authentic movement of God's Holy Spirit that will bring unity across denominations. My fervent prayer is that this will happen in our time. I pray that a mighty God-glorifying movement of the Spirit will come, uniting God's people, filling them with his power and making them authentically Christian. Although such a movement will probably start at the grass roots, I believe it will need strong leadership if it is to have any long term impact. It will need leaders who are living in the fullness of the Spirit and whose focus is on the gospel and the truths revealed in Scripture.

I long for the Church to give itself to prayer for renewal and revival and a great awakening to faith among all nations. I long for it to give itself to service of the poor and oppressed, in the love and full power of the Spirit, and to give itself primarily to mission (in the fullest sense of the word), rather than just maintaining itself. I long for the Church to embody the integrity and morality of living in the fullness of the Spirit.

Let us be open to the depth and power of the Spirit working to bring the unity of truth and love to the Church of our day, so that every nation may be awakened to him. And let us do all we can to ensure that any contemporary wave of the Spirit in renewal or revival neither dissipates against a breakwater of conservatism nor leaves us in a turmoil because of divisive and unbiblical theology and spirituality.

We live at the intersection of the ages. The power of the kingdom that arrived in the coming of Christ is here; the pain of this fallen age is still with us every day. We have been liberated from the power of evil, in order to fight against that power. Victory in struggle, healing in sickness, strength in weakness are our lot. And here is paradox – the strength comes through the weakness, the resurrection comes from the cross. In our weakness God's strength is perfected; we are overwhelmed by grace. We are not bludgeoned into submission by adversity. We simply come to the end of our resources and realise at last that God's grace is sufficient. This is where we belong. This is the relationship for which we were created.

We press on towards the final age of ultimate peace and wholeness, opening our lives to the present powers of the kingdom, including healing, seeking first the kingdom of God and finding Christ himself to be our health and our life. We look forward to that great day when together we will be completely whole in him, when Christ will be all in all, to the glory of God.

> May the God who gives endurance and encouragement give you a spirit of unity among yourselves as you follow Christ Jesus, so that with one heart and mouth you may glorify the God and Father of our Lord Jesus Christ. Accept one another, then, just as Christ accepted you, in order to bring praise to God. (Rom. 15:5–7)

Appendix I

The Plain Truths of Scripture

We must look for the clear, plain message of each passage of Scripture, in its proper context.[1] And if we are to discover the plain meaning and message of Scripture (as revealed by the Holy Spirit), we must avoid reading it through the distorting glasses of rationalism, tradition or cultural influence. For example, coming to the Bible with a non-Christian preoccupation with the individual will blind us to the fullness of biblical truth. Western society, in contrast to Hebrew and Christian world views, is predominantly individualistic. Biblical faith focuses on community, the community of Israel and the community of the Church.

The Bible is basically a pastoral book and biblical truth is related to life. It is written for faith, not to satisfy curiosity or to provide a complex system of theology. Understanding Scripture is not entirely, or even mainly, a matter of intellectual understanding. Nevertheless, human reason when redeemed by Christ and purified by his Spirit, does have a role in receiving and applying the Word of God that is revealed in it.[2] Human reason should never be the primary or ultimate source of truth, however.

Christians often begin with a simplistic interpretation of a Bible passage, then make a series of logical deductions based upon that interpretation. In the process, human reason usurps the place of divine revelation. But we are often blinded to that fact. Each step seems so logical and irrefutable that we fail to see that the final conclusion is contrary to the clear meaning of other passages of Scripture. The tragedy is that often the meaning of the other passages eventually becomes contorted to fit into the theological framework that we have developed. We fall into the trap of assuming that this framework, because it was derived from a biblical text, is itself biblical. Thus we can become insulated from the plain meaning of Scripture by our natural desire to use our logic to resolve mystery.

This is how a human tradition builds up that can continue for generations. Each generation is blinded to the plain meaning of various passages of Scripture because of the inherited framework of theology through which they are continuously viewing it. The tragedy is that we may think we are teaching Scripture, when we are simply teaching an interpretation of Scripture imposed by the particular framework we have inherited or adopted.

When we are not content to remain within the boundaries of what God has revealed in his Word, when we add to or subtract from God's Word in the interest of making everything clear, we may remove mystery from biblical truth that is essential. To remove all mystery from our understanding of God and his ways of working is to strip God of his essential 'godness' (see Is 55:8, Rom. 11:33–34); Christian theology ceases to be Christian when it is stripped of mystery. (It even ceases to be *theo*logy for the subject is no longer God [Gk. *theos*] when mystery is absent.) In this life, we must rest content with the truth God has revealed and the mystery that will always remain.

This mystery contains no hidden threat to faith. God is never arbitrary in his decision or actions; he never acts without good reason. Often he does not reveal these reasons to us but we know that there is no shadow of turning with him (Jas. 1:17). He always acts in accordance with his character. In particular, nothing he does violates his nature as the God of love. He is always dependable, steadfast love (Ps. 103:8; 1 Jn. 4:8). We must never think that the truths that are hidden from us can in any way contradict or undermine those revealed to us. Faith can rest in the complete reliability and consistency of the God and Father of our Lord Jesus Christ.

We must take into account the 'whole counsel of God'. The difficult passages of Scripture must not be regarded as forbidden territory. We begin with the truths that are obvious, using careful principles of interpretation (exegesis), but we must also lay the teaching of such passages side by side with the teaching of other related, but more difficult, passages. The warnings of God in Scripture are just as real as his promises and must be taken seriously and given their full biblical force, not rationalised away by elaborate frameworks of theology. For example when the

Bible warns us about the danger of falling away (e.g. Heb. 6:4ff), we must not weaken the force of this passage. We must not adopt any framework of human theology (really philosophy) that will lead us to a simplistic 'once saved always saved' understanding, for example. On the other hand, the warnings of Scripture about the danger of spurning God's grace must be balanced by the promises about the adequacy of God's grace to keep us (Jn. 10:28–29). When Scripture presents counterbalanced truths such as these we must acknowledge *both*. We must lay them side by side, not with the harmony of logic, but with the contentment of faith.

In the final analysis, the truth and unity of the Bible is to be found in the gospel (or kerygma). Jesus Christ who is the gospel (see *What is the gospel?* in Chapter 2) brings together many diverse Scriptures, giving to Scripture its true unity and harmony (Lk. 24:27,44,46–47). This unity retains great mystery. But faith is content with mystery, when it is presented in the context of what was hidden but is now revealed to us in Christ (Col. 1:26–27). In other words, developing a theology that has no 'loose ends' in terms of human logic and understanding is not the way to unity. We need unity that is based on the gospel of Christ (Eph. 1:7–10).

Notes

1. When we speak of the plain meaning of Scripture we are referring to the author's intention. Although all interpretations are subjective, the reader, under the inspiration of the Spirit (Jn. 16:13) has various resources which will help him or her to comprehend the author's main meaning in a given passage. Scripture simply cannot be made to mean anything the reader wishes (Mt. 5:18; Lk. 1:1–4; Jn. 10:35; 21:24; Acts 17:11; 2 Tim. 3:16f; 2 Pet. 1:20f). The Spirit is able to make clear to the believing Christian and Church, when they are open to his inspiration, God's purpose and meaning in a given passage. Such an interpretation is not necessarily infallible but it has a certain objectivity, which can be compared with other interpretations made by the Church.

2. Biblical scholarship assists the church greatly in arriving at the meaning of a given passage in its original cultural and theological context. An extensive knowledge of biblical background helps to anchor the interpretations of the Church in some kind of objectivity, which is open to discussion, denial or confirmation. The original (plain) meaning of the text, while remaining full of mystery, is not altogether beyond the understanding of the careful believing Church which seeks the guidance of the Spirit of truth and the insights of its biblical scholars and teachers. See Alan M. Stibbs, *Understanding God's Word* (London, Inter-Varsity Fellowship, 1950) esp. pp. 12ff,17ff,255ff.

Appendix II

Healing in the Bible

Peter A.R. Ralphs

The Church today is rediscovering that the gospel is not only about the salvation of the soul. Increasing numbers of Christians are beginning to acknowledge that Jesus Christ heals men and women physically and psychologically as well as spiritually.

This fresh appreciation of healing is causing us to look more closely at the biblical records in order to understand more adequately what they have to say on the matter.[1] In doing so, it is not enough to look only at the Bible's examples of healing and its explicit statements about healing. For example, it may be tempting to build one's understanding of healing on the following passage:

> Is any one of you sick? He should call the elders of the church to pray over him and anoint him with oil in the name of the Lord. And the prayer offered in faith will make the sick person well; the Lord will raise him up. If he has sinned, he will be forgiven. Therefore confess your sins to each other and pray for each other so that you may be healed. The prayer of a righteous man is powerful and effective. (Jas. 5:14–16)

Or on a simple reading of the miraculous healings performed by Jesus and sayings about faith such as this:

> 'Have faith in God', Jesus answered. 'I tell you the truth, if anyone says to

this mountain, "Go, throw yourself into the sea", and does not doubt in his heart but believes what he says will happen, it will be done for him. Therefore I tell you, whatever you ask for in prayer, believe that you have received it, and it will be yours.' (Mk. 11:22–24)

Indeed, there are those who have adopted such an approach, especially some who have experienced a marvellous healing themselves or who know someone who has. Understandably they want others to have a similar experience, especially when it all seems so biblical.

However, biblical theology arises as much out of the overall biblical story of God's dealings with humankind as out of particular statements and examples. So we need to see how healing fits into this overall story in order to have an adequate biblical understanding of the matter.

HEALING IN THE OLD TESTAMENT

Because many of the antecedents for the New Testament lie in the Old Testament, we need firstly to look – in very general terms – at attitudes to sickness, health and healing in the Old Testament Scriptures, particularly those elements that will help us understand the healing ministry of Jesus.

In the Old Testament writings, physical sickness and healing are not clearly differentiated from other forms of affliction and relief. Sickness is seen as but one expression of affliction (the wider suffering of human life). Moreover, issues of health and sickness are not in the first place individual issues. While the plight of the individual is not ignored (e.g. Job; 2 Kgs. 5:1–19; 20:1–11), the concept of healing is closely linked with national restoration (e.g. Is. 58:8; Jer. 14:19; 30:17). It was within a context of group solidarity – the overall good of the Israelite nation – that a remedy for sickness was often sought. Sickness often had repercussions with regard to one's relationship with the rest of the community. This happened particularly when the sick person was considered as stricken by God and therefore shunned lest his guilt be shared or contamination result (e.g. Lev. 13).

The Israelite saw both health and sickness as deriving from Yahweh (Ex. 4:11; 15:26; Deut. 7:15; 32:39; 2 Kgs. 5:7; Job 5:18; 1 Sam. 10:19); he brings prosperity and creates disaster (Is. 45:7; cf. Amos 3:6). The dualistic approach of neighbouring peoples which attributed sickness and disaster to malicious gods and spirits was rejected by Israel,[2] and it is consistent with the Israelite's view of life controlled by Yahweh that there are no clear examples of exorcism in the Old Testament.[3] It is understandable, then, that the Israelite – both as part of the nation and as an individual – looked to Yahweh to heal and save in times of sickness and distress, a fact that is well illustrated by psalms of lament (e.g. Ps. 22; 38; 41; 69; 90). Thus prayer is the main means of healing in the Old Testament.

Unlike other ancient peoples, Israel lacked a group of specially appointed healers.[4] With rare exceptions, prophets and priests did not fulfil this function, nor were they called upon to be intercessors in time of sickness. The main responsibility of the latter was to act as 'medical examiners' who pronounced whether sufferers were fit to retain (or return to) their normal place in the community (Lev. 13). The absence of a healing profession, however, does not mean that Israel rejected the practice of folk medicine.[5] Simple treatments, which could be applied by anyone, were used as an adjunct to praying for healing.

In the Old Testament, various strands of thought about health and sickness coexist. A constantly recurring theme in the Old Testament (and also in Rabbinic literature such as the Talmud) is that health, prosperity and life are the rewards of obedience to God and his law, whereas sickness, misfortune and death are the direct result of disobedience and sin. Accordingly the path to healing lies in repentance and forgiveness. Sometimes the sin-induced sickness is seen as, directly or indirectly, having a positive value for the person in terms of his relationship with God. In contrast to this concept stands the story of Job, a 'blameless and upright man' who nevertheless suffered great affliction. Job does not know why he is suffering, but his relationship with Yahweh helps him accept his lot with humility and equanimity.

There are in the Old Testament a number of healings which might be described as 'extraordinary'.[6] Such healings are infrequent and tend to be concentrated around certain periods of Old Testament history marked by a life and death struggle for God's people. For example, many great Old Testament leaders – including Isaac, Jacob, Joseph and Samuel – were the offspring of women who were healed (extraordinarily) of barrenness.[7] Likewise, coinciding with the crucial time when the Israelites had to choose between Yahweh and Baal, we find a concentration of extraordinary healing events centred around the ministries of Elijah and Elisha.

A SURVEY OF THE HEALINGS OF JESUS

A close examination of the extraordinary healings performed by Jesus provides us with much valuable information to help us understand the place of healing in the New Testament and in the Christian gospel. His healings are variously described as deeds of power, works, signs or wonders, or as wonderful, remarkable or strange things. At the same time, it should be noted that generally 'the accounts pay little attention to the miraculous process as such; they concentrate on the encounter of Jesus with the whole man in his physical and spiritual needs'.[8]

According to the evidence of the Gospels, Jesus healed a wide variety of people. Sex, age, race,[9] social standing and religion made no difference: for example, he healed both a young Gentile girl and an aged Jewish woman (Mt. 15:22–28; Lk. 4:38–39); the son of a royal official and the socially disadvantaged (Jn. 4:46–54; Lk. 17:11–19). Thus he made it clear that the blessings of God's kingdom were available to all people. Moreover, Jesus was able to heal every type of illness he encountered.[10] He healed long-standing and congenital illness and restored a severed ear; he healed those who were demon-possessed, and even restored dead people to life (Lk. 4:33–35, 6:17–19; 7:11–17, 8:43–48; 22:50–51; Jn. 9). There was no illness beyond his ability to heal (Mt. 4:23–24; Mk. 1:32–34; Lk. 4:40–41).

At times Jesus is said to initiate the healing, as when he singled out from amongst the crowd in the synagogue the man with a shrivelled hand (Lk. 6:6–11). At other times, the sick person took the initiative and asked to be healed (see, for example, Mt. 9:27–31; Lk. 17:11–14) or touched him in the hope of healing (Lk. 6:19). Often, however, some other person acted on behalf of the one who was ill, as in the case of the demon-possessed boy who was brought by his father first to the disciples and then to Jesus for healing (Mk. 9:17–29). A careful reading of the Gospels thus reveals that Jesus did not adopt only one approach to initiating healing and reminds us that he always remained sovereign in the matter.

There is no suggestion that Jesus healed every sick person he encountered. Clearly on occasion he did heal all those present who were sick (see, for example, Lk. 6:17–19) but, apparently, on other occasions this was not so. For example, he chose to heal just one of 'a great number of disabled people' at the pool of Bethesda (Jn. 5:1–15). In fact, on one occasion (his encounter with a Canaanite woman who pleaded for him to heal her daughter), Jesus initially resisted healing at all (Mt. 15:21–28)! Once more we see the freedom of Jesus to act in a sovereign manner.

Motives for healing

In the Gospel records, there is no one motive common to all the healings. Indeed, a motive is rarely given. When reasons for healing are stated or implied, they include the following: in response to faith (Mk. 2:5); out of pity or compassion (Mt. 14:14); as a sign of the coming of the kingdom or of Jesus' authority to forgive sins (Mt. 12:28; Mk. 2:10–11); to show Jesus is the Messiah who fulfilled Old Testament prophecy (Mt. 11:2–5); to point to Jesus as the light of the world who gives spiritual insight or as the Resurrection and the Life who imparts these gifts to men and women (Jn. 9 and 11); to demonstrate the right use of the Sabbath as an opportunity to do good and to participate in God's acts of salvation (Lk. 14:1–6); to glorify Jesus or God and to show forth God's actions (Jn. 9:3; 11:4); so people would believe (Jn. 11:15).

The reasons Jesus healed are thus many and varied but they all relate in one way or another to the fact that God's age of salvation had come in Jesus. It is worth noting that apparently Jesus did not use healing as a way of attracting a crowd or to compel belief in himself (Mk. 7:33; 9:25).

The spiritual benefit of healing

Only in a handful of instances is it clear that 'spiritual renewal' took place in the person healed (Jn. 9:38). Sometimes it is even implied that no such renewal occurred, as in John 5:9–16 where the lame man healed at the pool of Bethesda becomes informer to the pharisaic Jews, resulting in persecution of Jesus. This warns us about putting too much store on healing as a 'proof' of the gospel or as a way of introducing people to faith in Jesus. The warning is reinforced when we realise that, while some people reacted positively to the healings of Jesus, others responded quite negatively.

There were those who, amazed by it all, began to wonder who Jesus was and even praised God for it (e.g. Lk. 4:36; Mt. 12:22–23; Lk. 5:26), and there were some who followed Jesus or came to faith in him (e.g. Lk. 8:1–2; Jn. 11:45). There were, however, those who refused to see the action of God in what Jesus was doing and decisively rejected him, seeking to kill him (e.g. Mt. 12:24; Lk. 6:11). It is noteworthy that Jesus did not wish his fame to be spread as a healer and that, when this did occur despite his instructions to the contrary, his mission was at times hindered (e.g. Mk. 1:43–45).

The means of healing

Although there are some points of contact between Jesus' healings and the practice of medicine of the time,[11] Jesus is not presented in the Gospels as just another physician.[12] The healings of Jesus are to be seen in the wider context of salvation-history. Indeed, there is an implied contrast between his approach and a physician's in the story of Mark 5:25–34. The physicians' diagnosis and medicaments cost the sick woman all she had but did not prevent a deterioration in her condition and further suffering. In contrast, relief was provided freely and immediately by Jesus when she simply reached out in faith and touched his clothes.

Jesus used various methods to heal. Normally he healed with a word of command (e.g. Mk. 2:9–11; Lk. 6:10), even at a distance (Mt. 8:13; Jn. 4:50). Rebuke is used at times, especially in the case of demon possession (Mk. 1:25; 9:25; but cf. Lk. 4:39). Sometimes he used means such as touch (Mk. 1:31; Lk. 4:40), although sometimes it is the sick who touch Jesus (Mk. 3:10; cf. Lk. 6:19) or his clothes (Mk. 5:27–28; 6:56).[13] On other occasions he used saliva or anointing with clay (e.g. Mk. 7:33; 8:23; Jn. 9:6)[14] and washing (Jn. 9:7). A combination of such methods was used at other times, such as word and touch (Mk. 1:41; Lk. 8:54). There is no record of Jesus himself using oil for anointing (as advocated in James 5:14), but the apostles are recorded as using it when sent out by Jesus (Mk. 6:13). Thus, there was no stereotyped method for healing as far as Jesus was concerned.

THE ROLE OF FAITH

We need to consider carefully the role of faith in the New Testament healings. The presence of faith on the part of the person being healed or some other person is sometimes explicitly mentioned (e.g. Lk. 8:48; Mt. 15:28) and was undoubtedly an important factor (e.g. Mt. 13:58). However, often there is no mention of faith, thus leaving it an open question. In at least one instance, the faith mentioned is weak (Mk. 9:24) or the only faith present is that of Jesus himself (e.g. Lk. 22:51, where the person healed was an antagonist of Jesus). The account of the healing of a lame man in John 5:1–15 reminds us that Jesus at times heals people who in no way look to him for it and quite apart from any faith on their part. The man cooperates only because the healing has forced him to get up and carry his bed, but shows no sign of knowing who Jesus is and has not even the most superficial faith even after the event. Jesus seeks him out to tell him of a deeper wholeness than his physical healing but it appears the man does not respond with faith.

The description of a failed attempt at healing by the disciples in Mark 9:14–29 seems to indicate that faith on the part of the 'healer' (expressed through prayer) may be a more decisive factor than faith on the part of the sick person or others involved (vv. 28–29). When Jesus says to the father of the demon-possessed boy whom the disciples could not heal, 'Everything is possible for him who believes' (v. 23), the father responds, 'Lord, I do believe' but asks Jesus to help his 'unbelief'. Some have taken this to mean that Jesus' ability to heal the demon-possessed boy somehow depended on the faith of the father. It seems more likely, however, that the effective faith Jesus is referring to is his own prayerful faith in God, not an increased level of faith that must be achieved by the doubting father (v. 24) before Jesus can, or will, heal his son. Throughout this story the power of Jesus (that is, his effective faith) is contrasted with the powerlessness (or lack of faith) of the disciples.

The implication of all this would seem to be that faith does have an important role to play in healing, especially faith on the part of the 'healer'; however, it goes far beyond biblical teaching to present faith as an indispensable prerequisite for healing or to imply that people will invariably be healed if only their faith (or the faith of those ministering to them) is strong enough. God in Jesus Christ always remains free and sovereign in this as in all his operations in the world.

THE NATURE OF THE HEALINGS

It is interesting to note that the vast majority, if not all, of the healings described in the Gospels (and elsewhere in the New Testament) were then and there events rather than gradual events spread out over a period of time (e.g. Mk. 1:40–42; Lk. 5:25; 8:44; 13:13; 18:43; Mt. 8:13; 15:28; Jn. 4:53). In almost every instance where it is not explicitly stated that the healing was instantaneous, it is very clearly implied that it happened then and there. In fact, there is no clear instance of a gradual healing. (In the 'two stage' healing described in Mark 8:22–26, in which the sight of the blind man is only partly restored initially, complete healing follows almost immediately.). The reason for this may be that an instantaneous healing more adequately demonstrated that the kingdom of God was present in a decisive way in Jesus. Of course, gradual healings experienced today may also be miraculous. When God grants healing, he is free to bring it about in any way he chooses.

HEALING IN THE NEW TESTAMENT CHURCH

The pattern of healing that we find in the Gospel accounts of the ministry of Jesus is also found in the ministry of the early Christians, especially the apostles, as reported in Acts. Indeed, there are a number of parallels between the miracles of Jesus and those of Peter and Paul. For example, Peter's healing of a paralysed man and raising of Tabitha to life both echo incidents in Jesus' ministry (Lk. 5:17–26; 8:40–56; cf. Acts 9:32–35; 36–42). In comparing the ministries of Jesus and Paul we find that both cast out demons (Lk. 4:33–37,41; 8:26–39; 11:20; Acts 10:38; cf. Acts 16:16–18), healed a lame man (Lk. 5:17–26; cf. Acts 14:8–10), healed many sick people (Lk. 4:40; 6:17–19; cf. Acts 28: 9); cured a fever which led to many sick people coming to be healed (Lk. 4:38–40; cf. Acts 28:7–9) and both possessed healing power which was imparted through physical contact (Lk. 5:17; 6:19; 8:46; cf. Acts 19:11–12).

That these parallels exist should not surprise us, as the ministry of the apostles is but the continuation of the ministry of the risen Lord Jesus Christ through them. They followed the model given to them by Jesus in his words (e.g. Lk. 9:1–2; 10:9) and in his own healing actions. That the Church at a later stage should concentrate solely on saving people's 'souls' and not be concerned about healing their bodies would have been a surprise to them and a departure from what they had learnt from Jesus. It would be wrong, however, to conclude therefore that healing always occurred in the life of the New Testament Church. We have to remember constantly that what we have in the Acts are highlights from the life and mission of the early Church.

The New Testament Letters fill out our information about the ups and downs of first century Christianity and, while they have little to say about healing, what they do say is instructive. It appears that the ability to heal people was associated with 'spiritual gifts' and was given to some

Christians but certainly not to all (1 Cor. 12:9,28,30). It seems that both Peter and Paul were specially gifted in this respect (e.g. Acts 3:6–8; 16:18). James 5:14–16 is an affirmation to the Church of the promise of God to heal in response to 'the prayer of faith'.[15] That this promise was not viewed as an infallible guarantee of healing in every instance, is shown by the experience of Timothy (1 Tim. 5:23), Trophimus (2 Tim. 4:20) and Paul himself (Gal. 4:13–15; 6:17; and probably 2 Cor. 12:7–10).[16] If healing was more or less automatic in response to faith, we are left with some intriguing questions. Why did Paul not tell Timothy to exercise faith to be healed rather than to use an accepted medicine for his stomach complaint? Why did Paul, who apparently had the gift of healing, not take the initiative and heal Trophimus rather than leave him behind sick at Miletus? Why did Paul himself continue in a state of ill-health throughout his ministry as he preached the gospel to the Galatians if healing was available to him then and there through faith?

To understand James 5:14–16 as an absolute promise of healing in every instance, is to interpret it apart from the rest of the New Testament. Indeed, so interpreted, one could presumably use this promise to postpone death indefinitely! It seems that there needs to be a balance in our faith between trusting God for healing and a realistic appreciation that healing may not occur in all instances.

THE FRAMEWORK OF NEW TESTAMENT HEALINGS

Jesus saw illness (even when it did not involve demon-possession as such) and death as attributable to Satan's oppression of men and women and part of his domain (e.g. Lk. 13:16; cf. Acts 10:38; e.g. Heb. 2:14). There is a strong biblical link between the overcoming of illness and death and the defeat of sin and Satan brought about by Jesus' death on the cross. The prophets of the Old Testament looked forward to this victory through the coming of the Messiah (see, for example, the allusions in Mt. 11:2–5 to such Old Testament passages as Is. 35:5–6, and in Lk. 4:18–19 to Is. 61:1–2). Through the Messiah, God would remove the disorder brought into the world through sin and restore order to it (as described in Is. 33:24, for example). Indeed, the few 'extraordinary' healings we read of in the Old Testament, associated with the ministries of Elijah and Elisha, may be seen as 'promises in action' of a restored world.

The healings of Jesus Christ and the early Church must be seen in this light. By his healings, Jesus announced in action that God was present in him restoring order to the world and to individual human lives. Sin, sickness and death were being defeated; however, this process of restoration will reach completion only when Christ returns in power and makes an end of all that is in opposition to God. The biblical records of healings by Jesus and his disciples need to be viewed within this eschatological framework, that is, in relation to biblical teaching on the 'last days' or 'end time' which began with the first coming of Jesus into the world and which will conclude with his second coming in glory.[17]

Notes

1. This topic is dealt with in greater depth in my doctoral thesis: P.A.R. Ralphs, *A New Testament Theology of Healing with Special Reference to Tension in Eschatology and the Issue of Healing and Non-Healing/Death in the Restoration-to-Life Stories of the Gospels and Acts*, Australian College of Theology, Sydney, 1992. Copies are available at the following colleges in Australia: Ridley College, The Avenue, Melbourne, VIC 3052; the United Theological College, 16 Masons Drive, North Parramatta NSW 2151; and the Bible College of Queensland, 1 Cross Street, Toowong, QLD 4066. In this appendix, I often use only one or a few representative Bible passages to illustrate a point, rather than cramming the text with every possible reference.

2. M.T. Kelsey, *Healing and Christianity* (New York: Harper & Row, 1976), p. 38.

3. The closest the Old Testament comes to an exorcism is 1 Samuel 16:14–23; however, the evil spirit that intermittently torments Saul is said to be from Yahweh, and the playing of the harp by David which brings relief is more like a primitive form of 'music therapy' than an exorcism.

4. Israel's firm belief in Yahweh as the giver of life and health, sickness and death, together with the close relationship between sickness and sin found throughout the Old Testament would both have served to discourage the emergence of a healing profession at that time. If sickness is regarded as the result of sin, then the proper response is to accept one's punishment and to turn to Yahweh in repentance rather than to a human healer. Several other factors may also have contributed. This issue is dealt with in greater detail in my thesis; see Note 1.

5. See, for example, 2 Kgs. 20:7; Is. 1:6; 38:21; Jer. 51:8; Ezek. 30:21; 34:4; Hos. 6:1.

6. To call these healings 'supernatural' would be to use a term inconsistent with the monistic philosophy of the Old Testament where any distinction between 'natural' and 'supernatural' is blurred. Yahweh alone is the source of healing, whether or not external remedies are applied.

7. See Gen. 18:11 and 21:1–3; Gen. 25:21; Gen. 30:22–24; 1 Sam. 1:1–20.

8. W. Mundle, O. Hofius and C. Brown, 'Miracle, Wonder, Sign' in C. Brown (Ed.), *The New International Dictionary of New Testament Theology*, Vol. 2

(Grand Rapids: Zondervan, 1976), p. 631.

9. It is to be acknowledged that Jesus concentrated his ministry on Jews, but occasionally he made an exception and ministered to non-Jewish people.

10. D.H. Trapnell rightly points out that the biblical descriptions of health, disease, healing and death are limited by certain factors: a) the purpose of Scripture is theological rather than medical; b) contemporary, medical and public knowledge allowed only simple descriptions of disease, confined to what could be seen or felt by an observer of the patient; and c) the same word was used to describe different diseases at different times and in different regions; see 'Health, Disease and Healing' in J.D. Douglas and others (Eds), *The Illustrated Bible Dictionary*, Vol. 2 (Leicester: Inter-Varsity Press, 1980), p. 616.

11. The medical term *sōzō* is used frequently in the Gospels (see, for example, Mt. 1:21; Mk. 5:23,34; Lk. 7:50; 8:36,48,50; 19:10); it has the double meaning 'heal' or 'save'.

12. Unlike a physician, Jesus had no need to diagnose the sufferer's ailment. He did question them, but with a different purpose: to call forth faith (Mk. 9:21–24), to invite them to articulate their intense desire/need (Mk. 10:51) or to encourage participation (Jn. 5: 6–8). Generally Jesus is shown as instinctively recognising the afflicted person's malady.

13. It has been suggested that the act of touching was a means of communicating healing power to the sick, but this interpretation faces the difficulty that Jesus often healed without touching the sufferer. The reference in Luke 6:19 to power going forth from Jesus means only that he was exercising his power to heal; it does not mean that some involuntary discharge was involved which led to diminution of power like a battery being drained of its charge.

14. There was a superficial similarity between techniques used by Jesus and primitive medical techniques of the day. Thus his use of spittle and clay (and the apostles' use of oil) may perhaps be regarded as an endorsement of the use of whatever medical means are available. In this sense, they may be seen as comparable to the 'poultice of figs' which the prophet Isaiah instructed King Hezekiah to use as part of God's plan for his healing (Is. 38:21). The occasional use of such means by Jesus, however, should be seen primarily as sacramental or symbolic rather than medical (or magical). The way in which Jesus employs these means and the whole context in which they occur put them on quite a different level.

15. Note that the sick person takes the initiative in calling the elders, who collectively have the authority to heal or among whom, it is assumed, will be found at least one with the gift of healing. The elders offer 'the prayer of faith', and confession of sin may be necessary.

16. Whether Paul's 'thorn in the flesh' was indeed a physical ailment is still debated. It has been pointed out that because his condition has been left undefined in this passage, all Christians who suffer affliction of any sort can identify with Paul in the experience of God's sufficient grace in weakness; see P.E. Hughes, *Paul's Second Epistle to the Corinthians* (Grand Rapids: Eerdmans,

1975), pp. 442f.

17. Eschatology (derived from the Greek *eschatos* meaning 'last') is the branch of theology that has to do with the study of the 'last things'. It would be a misunderstanding of biblical evidence to think that this refers only to events surrounding the second coming of Jesus at the end of time. From a biblical perspective, the 'last days' began when Jesus entered the world to reassert God's sovereign rule over all things ('the kingdom of God') and to commence his great rescue mission of humanity (e.g. Heb. 1:1–2). These 'last days' are the time of fulfilment of the promises of the Old Testament (e.g. Mk. 1:15; Acts 2:17) and will continue throughout history until Jesus returns (cf. Heb. 9:28). In the meantime we live between the time when the kingdom of God has come amongst us with its blessings and the time when it will be experienced in all its fullness. This creates a certain 'now and not yet' tension in the experience of the blessings of the kingdom, which include healing.

Appendix III

Excerpts from Robert Hillman's Journal

It was the author's suggestion that these records of his experiences be included, if he should die before the completion of this book, especially because of their relevance to the subject of prophesy.

21 November 1989
Today as I write this I am expecting to enter hospital for the commencement of extensive high risk treatment which will involve various radical processes over several months. All of this treatment involves a twenty-five per cent chance (or more) of death. However, it also involves a fifty per cent chance of cure. Until now 'no hope of cure' and 'non-curable' have been the terms used. [Robert Hillman entered hospital but was discharged the next day without treatment because of staff difficulties.] This morning my wife Jeanette turned to the Scripture Union reading for today. To her utter amazement it was 2 Kings 20:1–21, which describes Hezekiah's illness and the gift of fifteen years more of life . . . (It seemed amazingly providential. Is it a prophetic word for us?) . . . The thing that impressed us most was Hezekiah's failure following his healing. There is a chilling complacency about his attitude to future generations (vv. 17–19).

16 March 1990
Over the last few months I have continued to sense that God will cure me although from time to time, as I have suffered side effects from the chemotherapy, I have lost some conviction concerning this prophetic word. This word seemed to be confirmed again today [while reading Tim Geddert's chapter in *Wonders and the Word*, see Note 13 in Chapter 8]. For the past

eight years I have been opening my life daily to all the healing God has for me from every source from which he would give it. But I have not had the slightest idea as to whether or not God would cure me. I have received a great deal of healing; otherwise I would not still be alive. But I certainly have not been cured. During that time, God has not given me insight into his purposes or his timing . . .

At my conversion some forty years ago I dreamt of a great awakening across Australia and in some way being part of this . . . All my prayers, ministry and study have been directed toward this . . . and in the two awakenings associated with [Wesley and Calvin] I saw great movements of the Spirit of God that I had for many years dreamt about in terms of my own church and nation. For several years, under the Bob Hillman Foundation, I was released to participate in a wide-ranging teaching and renewal ministry. I now feel that through all this affliction God has been preparing me to return to this work – cured that I may give the rest of my life in gratitude, using 'the healed years' in the service of Christ and humanity.

Now I know that there are some traps to be avoided here. I may be deluded by wishful thinking and especially by the desire to avoid further traumatic chemotherapy. So we must pray an overriding prayer to any prophetic word: 'Your name be hallowed, your kingdom come, your will be done.' Nor do I want to be cured if, like Hezekiah, I am to make a mess of the healed years. I look for confirmation of my prophetic word . . .

◆　◆　◆

Robert Hillman then goes on to record the responses of several close friends with whom he shared this insight. Their experiences were not offered as inerrant revelation but in a spirit of humility:

I met with . . . [who] responded in a remarkable manner. He said that last Monday (5 March) he was praying before going to the Bible and had a sense of receiving a word from God, 'I will heal Bob'. This gave him a new confidence in his prayer. He felt it was O.K. to pray with boldness. This was the first time he had had this sense of permission. The next day he prayed again for me. The sense this time was, he said, 'It's already taken care of'. He sensed that it was not any longer necessary to pray the healing prayer . . .

Reporting other friends' experiences, Robert Hillman writes:

On retreat, and as he had been thinking and praying for me, God seemed to speak to [my friend] from John 11:4: 'But when Jesus heard it he said, "This illness is not unto death; it is for the glory of God, so that the Son of God may be glorified by means of it" '[*RSV*]. This seemed to me to be a remarkable confirmation of what had been revealed to me especially in its repeated emphasis on the glory of God. Later in this week I shared with two of the elders . . . One of them said that on about three occasions he had felt a similar conviction about my healing but had cast it aside.

This afternoon I visited . . . and she responded with a confirming experience from a recent prayer meeting. She said: 'I would love to tell you that I had a clear word of knowledge that you would be healed, but that would be misleading you. What I did experience was a strong sense that we should all be praying specifically for you to be completely healed, not just praying for relief of your symptoms.'

I spoke to a friend over the phone during the week . . . he referred to the passage in Deuteronomy (18:21–22) which teaches that the ultimate truth of a prophecy lies in its fulfilment. Thus we wait for Sunday [when people were to gather at a special service to pray for him] and what follows.

For my wife, this is not an easy time . . . While being excited and moved by the words of others she is fearful of my hopes being raised, in case they are dashed to the ground . . . She is the one who will be called upon to live with me through these times . . .

◆　◆　◆

The following is Robert Hillman's record of a service held on the morning of Sunday 18 March 1990, at which he received prayer for healing:

During this last week following intravenous chemotherapy I have had five days on Prednisolone. Yesterday the dosage was reduced and I felt myself beginning to go through withdrawal symptoms. Last night my deep sleep was very disturbed with great restlessness and dreams (I think I now have some small idea of how heroin addicts must feel!). At last I rose, at about 2.30 a.m., to lie in the lounge room listening to 2CBA-FM [a Christian radio station]. Toward morning I drifted into a light sleep and awoke to hear the words from the Sermon on the Mount being read:

> On that day many will say to me, 'Lord, Lord, did we not prophesy in your name, and cast out demons in your name, and do many mighty works in your name?' And then will I declare to them, 'I never knew you; depart from me, you evildoers.' Every one then who hears these words of mine and does them will be like a wise man who builds his house upon the rock . . . (Mt. 7:22–24 *RSV*)

This came as a prophetic word to me. If a spectacular miracle occurs today we *must* not focus on *it*. Our focus must be on Christ and on obedience to him. His word. His kingdom. His will.

The Sunday morning service was great. J.M. had been preparing it and himself all week. There was a strong emphasis on the glory of God. It was held in a small inner city church where an amazing cross section of people meet regularly for worship. There is a great deal of pain in the lives of a number of the members and the congregation has a strong sense of loving fellowship. There is an openness to what the Holy Spirit is doing in many areas, including healing, but there is also a healthy desire for balance. The service, a communion service which included opportunity for laying on of hands by the elders, was a beautiful blend of formal and informal worship. J.M. set the focus for the service by beginning with the first verse of the chorus:

> Father we love thee, we praise thee, we adore thee, Glorify thy Name
> in all the earth . . .

The service continued with some modern choruses and two older hymns, including *At the Name of Jesus*. No mention was made of healing in the magnificent sermon preached by J.M, which came from John 4. It was a Christ-centred sermon in which he pointed out that if any of us were to be blessed in this service it would be because of its focus on Christ.

Following the sermon, J.M. shared briefly concerning my request for the laying on of hands by the elders and two possible prophetic words about my healing were presented [see above]. He then led the elders of the local church and three other selected people in a special time of prayer; each one prayed in a very quiet way. Opportunity was given for others to avail themselves of this prayer and two others sought healing and healing of family relationships. The service proceeded, using the set liturgy for communion. I was given the opportunity to read out what I had written earlier in the day and to emphasise the prophetic word from the Sermon on the Mount which put the focus on Christ and obedience to him rather than any spectacular miracle . . .

Since the service I have been restfully looking for signs of healing. Before I took my usual medication that evening I checked my blood pressure. It was still high so I continued with the medication, seeking to monitor God's working in an objective way, resting in his sovereign love. Today (Monday) I can see that my neck is still swollen, although much less swollen than it was before I commenced chemotherapy. We wait on God daily determined to 'tell it as it is' as God does what he wants to do and as we pray for his name to be glorified, his kingdom to come and his will to be done on earth as in heaven.

♦   ♦   ♦

The following is an excerpt from a letter sent to Robert Hillman on

15 July 1990, used with permission. It seems that the experience was reported to him in the hope that it was truly prophetic, but without this presumption:

> I found myself moving into a very, very special time of prayer. I read again John 11:4 . . . As I prayed I felt we had come to the end of the road of man's effort to heal you and now it was time to claim [God's] direct intervention. I sat in silence for some time. I saw you finally in your lounge sitting on a chair. Christ was on the other side of the room talking to me . . . Now in your lounge Jesus was saying to me, 'You heal Bob!' So I acted on his invitation and laid hands on you and simply said, 'Bob be healed for the glory of God'. I felt exhausted and let out a deep sigh. The chorus *Glorify your name* kept ringing in my ears. I sang it. May Jesus be glorified in ways that we can't even imagine through this time, if it please him.

◆   ◆   ◆

Strictly speaking, we would have to say that the apparent 'words of knowledge' contained in these records were not prophetic; Robert Hillman was not healed of lymphoma. He was, however, spared for a further two years and given a remarkably rich and productive life despite his illness. Wisely and typically, he did not put all his hope in these 'prophecies' as clear promises of healing or cling desperately to them. But they did serve to strengthen him and spur him on to make tentative plans for the future, plans which will probably bear fruit even though he is not here to be part of their realisation. In addition, he continued working on this book during those years. Should we say then that all these 'words' were prophetic in a sense, or were they simply well-meant but erroneous human 'words' taken and used by the loving Heavenly Father to bring about his good purposes? Prophecy is indeed a subject full of mystery.

Appendix IV

Resources for Ministry

PART A:
HEALING THROUGH REMEMBERING

This is an approach to healing that may be helpful to certain people in assisting them to find emotional healing. Generally, however, it should not be attempted without the guidance and support of a mature Christian leader. In addition, an experienced psychologist or psychiatrist should be involved either in the role of group leader or as part of the ministry team. Prayer is the basis of this approach, in which people are invited to ask the Spirit of Christ help them find healing as, in his presence, they recall events from their past.

Practical considerations

The following principles should be kept in mind when planning and conducting healing through remembering sessions:

1. It is strongly recommended that this ministry be undertaken only by mature Christians with appropriate training in counselling.[1] If they do not have this experience themselves, they should set up a ministry team that includes someone with this level of expertise. It would be very unwise to embark on this ministry without ensuring that expert care is readily available to any participant in need of assistance in dealing with issues that arise.

2. Prayer is the backbone of any healing ministry and it is essential that the leader and other willing Christians spend time before, during and after these sessions in intercession for the participants. God has commanded us to pray and often works through our prayers to bring healing.

3. Individual therapy may be requested and can be helpful; however, this type of therapy seems to work best in groups, especially when members know one another and have established a degree of trust and closeness. The size of the group does not seem to be critical, but a smaller group may be helpful if it makes it easier for people to share their experiences at the end of the session.

4. I prefer that this ministry be requested by the person or persons seeking healing, rather than imposed or even strongly recommended by the leader. It is a cooperative effort between God, the ministry team and the group members and it needs to take place in God's 'ripe' time.

5. When dealing with a group, the leader in these sessions will set the tone of the whole proceeding by his or her own example of gentleness, self control and expectation of God's work. The session should be conducted quietly. While emotion is acceptable – people may need to cry or even call out – emotionalism (that is, artificially induced emotion and undue emphasis on emotion) is illegitimate. Members of the group must not be manipulated in any way. The emphasis must be on the work of the Holy Spirit alone in bringing to the attention of the participant any memory or other issue he would have them reflect on at that time. The session should be kept brief and to the point, usually no more than about half an hour for the introduction and meditation.

6. At the end of each session, a debriefing is held in which participants are invited to share their memories so that the leader and the group may help them begin the process of addressing any unresolved issues. As far as possible what the Spirit of God has initiated should not be left hanging in the air. On occasions this may involve expert ongoing counselling,[1] which should be recommended by the leader, rather than an immediate and public resolution. Insights gained during healing through remembering sessions can greatly facilitate the counselling process.

7. Participants should not feel pressured to disclose to the group. It is not always appropriate to do so. Naturally, all such disclosures should be regarded as confidential. It is the leader's responsibility to bring

the issue of confidentiality to the attention of the group, and all participants should be mature enough to be entrusted with the disclosures of others.

Example of healing through remembering session

The following is an example of a session for use with a group. This material can be adapted to the leader's own theology and style and ought to be used in a flexible way with openness to the Holy Spirit. I have given titles to the various sections only to assist the leader. They are not intended to be part of the presentation itself.

Bible reading

Begin the session with an appropriate Bible passage(s). I have found the following helpful: Isaiah 53:5 (the need for healing through Christ's death); Matthew 18:35 (the need to forgive from the heart); John 21:4ff esp. vv. 9,15 and cf. Luke 22:54–62 esp. v. 55 (the importance of having the memory quickened for radical healing from the legacies of the past); John 13:8 (the need to allow Jesus to cleanse us from past failure).

Introduction

Use this outline as a guide only and remain open to the Spirit. You may start by saying something like this:

> Our Lord seems to have reminded Peter of his sins by lighting the charcoal fire by the lake. It was beside a charcoal fire that Peter had once denied him. Then the Lord asked him three times 'Do you love me?' bringing back the agony of his denial. The Lord may need to bring us back to those times when we sinned, when we were sinned against, or when we were deeply hurt. Today we will be asking the risen Christ to bring such things before us – so they no longer stay buried, rotting out our souls and bodies. We will ask him to search our memories and help us face our sins and hurts so that we may be forgiven, so that if necessary we may be able to forgive; so that deep hurts may be healed.
>
> It is up to you to decide just how much you participate in this session. In it we will try to help you receive inner healing – especially healing in relation to past events. It may be that some of you who have extremely deep-seated painful hurts will feel that you do not want to get too involved. You may leave – or you may stay and simply observe.
>
> This is what I plan to do. I will help you to visualise Christ and then with his protection we will allow him to bring before us, individually, any

memory that he chooses. Christ will be in control all the way so you can relax in the knowledge that, whatever happens you will not be overwhelmed. You may feel emotion and need to express it but you will be able to cope . . .

Continue, briefly summarising the steps of the session set out below, including the debriefing. Then give people an opportunity to decide whether or not to participate.[2]

Prayer

Ask two or three people to pray fervently for guidance and protection so that people will not be overwhelmed.

Visualising Christ – his love and protection

From this point on leave pauses as you go to allow time for visualisation and reflection, but avoid drawing the session out unnecessarily.

Close your eyes and visualise the risen, crucified Christ coming to you as he promised. You may wish to visualise the nail prints in his hands, which he showed to Thomas as evidence that he is the risen, crucified Lord. Or you may visualise him present as light filling the room.

He comes as the crucified Christ. He died for you. We believe that he is present as the loving Saviour. Your Saviour. He died to forgive you your sins and to heal your hurts. Thank him for his infinite love, his cleansing blood and healing grace.

Just as we are surrounded by air – so we are surrounded by God's grace. We are safe.[3]

See Christ, coming to you as risen Lord. Your Lord. Because he is love and because he is Lord, you need not be afraid.[3] [At this point it is important to allow time for the participants to greet Christ personally.]

Now ask him by his Spirit to bring to the surface any memory, painful or pleasant, he wants you to consider now. Ask him not to allow anything to surface that will overwhelm you or distract you from his purposes but only those memories he would have you face up to at this time.

Recalling the memory

Think back down through the years, allowing the Spirit of God to bring to the surface any memory, old or new, that he wants you to become aware of now so that you can be healed.

Is there any painful memory that you have repressed and that the Spirit of God would bring to the surface and heal? Think especially of situations where you were overwhelmed by fear or where your anger was repressed.

Feeling the pain – with Jesus there

As the Spirit of God releases this memory you may begin to feel the original hurt – intense fear or anger or shame or guilt. You may need to cry.

Visualise the loving sovereign Christ walking with you now into that original setting – that house or particular place. If the Spirit of God is releasing your memory let it come.

It may be that some experience or some person harmed you in a deep way. You were not able to cope with the pain then and you have kept it buried ever since. Perhaps it has made you unconsciously ill, sad, aggressive, hyperactive, resentful, bitter, afraid.

If this is your experience, ask the Spirit of God to allow you to feel in the presence of Jesus as much of that original pain as is good in his sight.

Perhaps you stand face to face now in your memory with someone who has greatly wronged you. We believe that the loving Lord Christ is also there. You are safe. In his strength you are able to face up to that hurtful memory.

Hear Jesus Christ say to the person who wronged you: 'I love you. I died for you so that you can be forgiven.'

Responding with forgiveness

If you feel Christ is telling you it is time to forgive this person, in your own words you may say something like this to them: 'Dad/Mum (or name some other person) you wronged me greatly when you . . . I was deeply hurt. I cannot justify what you did/said. But I know that Christ who died to forgive me died for you too. As he has freely forgiven me I freely forgive you. I do not gloss over what you did. We cannot undo it. But in Christ's name I can forgive you and I do forgive you . . .' (add anything else you need to). . . [long pause]

Visualising Christ's love for all involved

You may like to imagine the risen Christ touching or hugging the one who has wronged you and touching or hugging you as well – bringing you together. . . [pause]

You may be finding it difficult to forgive. There is no need to pretend.

Whether forgiveness is the issue for you or not, perhaps you need to bring your buried hurts to the crucified Lord – to lay them at the foot of his cross and to leave them there – to sense his healing balm – to stay kneeling at the cross as his Spirit heals your deep-seated pain. Imagine yourself kneeling there as long as you need to. . . [long pause]

Christ carries the pain for us

It may be that you have returned to some point in the past so traumatic to
you that you sense that Christ may be protecting you from being overwhelmed and it is therefore not appropriate for you to enter that room – to
go to that place. Feel free to ask the crucified Lord to enter into that place
while you for the time being wait outside.[4]

Saying farewell

Now you have dealt with as much of your past as God wants you to deal
with today. Here you are – just you and the risen Christ together. Take
your time to say your farewells to each other at the end of this special time
together and when you are ready, open your eyes. We have plenty of time
and we will wait for you. . . [pause]

In the weeks to come

In your meditation now and in the weeks to come remain open to the possibility that the risen Christ will bring to consciousness some memory that
will involve the need for conscious action, repentance or surrender for
healing. You may well need to seek ongoing assistance in dealing with these
issues.

A closing prayer

. . . in the strong name of the One who shed his blood, that we might be forgiven and healed, and who was raised that we might be released from all
that binds us. Amen.

Debriefing

Here an opportunity is given to share reflections or memories with the
group and for further ministry to take place. If the material is of a very
personal nature, participants may decide not to share it and they should
feel free to make this choice. Those who do not share in the group should
be encouraged to talk to the appropriate person, e.g. the team psychologist or psychiatrist.

General comments

In any ministry, we have missed the mark if we do not provide for the
future well being of those to whom we minister. Follow-up visitation may
be required. We must also ensure that participants in these healing sessions have easy access to expert support after these sessions. They may
have many feelings to work through and a string of consequences to deal

with as a result of delving into their past at both the conscious and unconscious level.

I have seen God gently release people from inner pain through its use. Of course, some participants do not recall significant memories at all. Interestingly, I have also seen wonderful healing come through the recollection of pleasant memories, which may be the only memories that surface.

I believe that Christ will continue his work of healing in the individual as he ministers through his body, the church, and the exercise of the gifts he has given them. In a sense the whole congregation can support this ministry by the provision of loving fellowship and encouragement.

My hope is that this outline for healing through remembering sessions will be used prayerfully and responsibly and only by those who have the expertise to use it safely. Ultimately, however, it is God who must be in control and we are utterly dependent on him. To him be the glory for lives set free from the past and renewed by his power.

PART B:
A PRAYER FOR WHOLENESS

This is an approach to personal prayer and meditation that grew out of my own struggle with serious illness. With all kinds of variations, it has been a part of my prayer life each day for several years. It brings together three procedures commonly used in the secular world – meditation, relaxation and visualisation – but puts them in a Christian context. The whole process is Christ-centred and Bible-based.

It is designed mainly for those who, like myself, are dealing with serious illness, but this way of praying and meditating is recommended to everyone. Even when perfectly well, we have a continuing need to pray for more and more wholeness and holiness.

This prayer is not meant to stand alone. God's healing comes in many different ways: for example, through medical treatment and psychological counselling, when necessary, or through his Word, Christian fellowship, prayer for others and repentance and forgiveness (see Chapter 7).

Some sections of the outline provided in this appendix deal with physical healing, others with emotional or 'inner' healing. There is nothing special about the wording I have used. I would encourage you to use your imagination and make changes to suit your own situation.[5]

I do not want to claim too much for this procedure. It is certainly not a magic formula for prayer that will guarantee healing. All I am saying is that it has been helpful to me and to others. Its main value, no doubt, is that it approaches healing in a way that combines the influence of the mind and faith. It is possible that the positive attitude and sense of empowerment it encourages in the patient using it may tip the balance in favour of healing.

Preparation

Read a Bible passage. I often use the Lord's Prayer (Mt. 6:9–13), Psalms 103:1–5 or 34:1–3, or 2 Corinthians 12:9, but many other Bible passages are suitable.

Relaxation

Let the various parts of your body relax. You may like to use the technique I have described elsewhere (see Note 10 in Chapter 7). The idea is to wind down physically, mentally and emotionally.

Biblical meditation

Choose some aspect of the Bible passage you read before relaxing to focus on, then as you meditate on it allow it to lead you into prayer.

First of all praise God and surrender yourself to him. For example, if you read the Lord's Prayer, thinking about (or meditating on) the first line could lead you into prayer like this:

'Our Father who art in heaven, hallowed be thy name. Thy Kingdom come . . .'

I want the kingdom of the Father to come – everywhere – and in my own life (whether that means healing or heaven or, for now, ongoing illness) . . .

Above all things I want the grace of Christ to be upon me . . .

I give thanks for . . . [give details of any indication of healing].

Then continue to pray:

I want to be open to all the healing that the Father has for me.

Let me be open to your *spiritual healing.*

I open my inner being to the searchlight of the Spirit.

I confess: 'Against you only have I sinned.'

I admit my failure to allow the love of God to enter fully the hidden depths of my being . . . and my failure to love the Father freely as I ought.

Let the Spirit expose these specific sins that deny your love . . .
I open my whole life, including my inner being and confess and surrender
deep-seated selfishness, unbelief, pride, resentment . . . [be specific
here!]
I seek cleansing in the blood of Jesus and renewal by the Spirit.
I open my whole life to the Father's love . . .
Let me be open to *emotional healing*.[6]
May I be liberated so that I will be more whole:
acting confidently from the centre of my personality . . .
free to love and serve . . .
less touchy . . . more mature . . .
more spontaneous . . . unobstructed . . . creative . . . fun-loving . . .
free to give myself to the present . . .
living for God a fruitful and fulfilled life, full of purpose.
I open my life to all the physical healing that God has for me.
I want nothing to hinder this.
I want to be sensitive to the truth of what is happening
in my life . . . to face reality
I want to learn to trust the Father more and more each day . . .
to accept that he alone knows what is best for me . . .
and to rest in his love.

Visualisation

This is my version; alter it to suit your own needs.
I *see* the chemotherapy flowing like lava throughout my whole body
burning the cancer cells . . . and paralysing them . . . knocking them
out . . .
I *experience* thousands of white cells, like white sharks with big
teeth, devouring the alien cells . . . joining with other healing agents to
promote health.
I *visualise* the cancer cells . . .
alien . . . weakening . . . diminishing . . .
dying . . . disappearing permanently . . .
as, and if, God in his love and wisdom permits it.

Closing meditation

Finally, *focus on Jesus himself in worship and adoration*:
I see Jesus Christ reigning in His kingdom of love, peace
and wholeness . . . Amen
While urgently seeking healing and confidently believing in God's

power to cure us, there should be a restful recognition that it may not happen in this life. We can be at peace about this because we know that, if we belong to Christ, dying means the beginning of perfect health and wholeness for us.

Notes

1. The term 'counsellor' needs careful qualification because it tends to be used rather loosely. I use it to refer specifically to people in the following categories:
    A. Registered practitioners, such as clinical psychologists and psychiatrists
    Before they can practise they must be registered by the relevant professional body. This involves postgraduate training and several years practical experience under supervision to ensure competence. Note that (at least in Australia), while anyone can call themselves a 'counsellor', it is illegal for an unregistered person to use the title 'psychologist' or 'psychiatrist';
    B. Other professional 'counsellors', who have relevant training in human behaviour as well as considerable skill in listening and offering helpful feedback
    People in this category are generally trained to assist individuals in developing insights and coping strategies and should be able to do this effectively. They fulfil a useful role in helping people deal with relatively 'normal' issues, especially people experiencing difficulty coping. As they work with their client, more complex underlying issues or evidence of psychological disorder may emerge and a competent counsellor will be equipped to recognise this and refer the individual on to the appropriate professional, that is, to someone in the first category.

    Of course, Christians who are not counsellors may be called upon, and should be prepared, to offer compassionate support to others under the guidance of the Spirit. Their role is more that of a loving friend or a brother/sister in Christ. For some who are specifically gifted as encouragers or pastors, this may be a special ministry. Ongoing expression of the love of Christ in these ways should be a normal part of the life of the church and be evident in all its dealings with the wider community; see John Mallison, *Caring for People* (Sydney: Unichurch, 1979). It is good for us to support and encourage each other through difficult times. It is good to say, 'I'll stand beside you in this, I'll listen to you, pray with you and offer you any insights from Scripture I may have'. People may want to see us as their 'counsellor' but, if we lack the appropriate training, it will be necessary at times to say, 'I'm sorry, I cannot be your counsellor. You are going to need someone with special training to guide you on that journey. But I'll be here to pray for you and encourage you through it all.'

    It seems preferable to avoid using the term 'counsellor' when referring to people in supportive roles who are not in category A or B described above, and that includes most of us. If we lack specific training, we are not equipped to recognise issues that require referral for proper diagnosis and treatment. If we do not realise this, it is possible for us to add to people's problems instead of helping them. For example, by providing bandaid help to someone who is psychologically disturbed, we may delay them from seeking the expert assistance they really need, or we may give inappropriate, or even unhelpful, advice. In addition, we may have unrecognised emotional needs of our own that distort our perception of the situation.

    I offer these suggestions as general guidelines only, recognising that the Spirit of God may sometimes choose to work in ways that go beyond human wisdom and that we need to be open to this possibility at all times.

2.   It is helpful to provide this explanation before the day of the healing through remembering session as well. This gives people time to consider their decision and allows them to withdraw without embarrassment if they feel unready or unsure.

3.   I believe this reassurance is important; people are more likely to face up to disturbing feelings when they feel secure.

4.   Some people find it helpful to put the whole memory under God's light to soak for several days or weeks; see Flora Slesson Wuellner, *Prayer, Stress, and Our Inner Wounds* (Nashville: The Upper Room, 1985), p. 30.

5.   In this kind of prayer it is good to say the words aloud, if you have the privacy to do so and feel comfortable about it. Instead of trying to read from this outline as you meditate, you may prefer to record yourself reading some parts of it (or your own version of it), with lengthy pauses between sections, so that you can use the tape to guide your meditation. As time goes by you will find yourself needing to use a guide less and less.

6.   If this section threatens to bring to the surface memories too painful for you to deal with, leave it out and seek assistance from a suitably qualified counsellor (see Note 1).

Bibliography

Berkouwer, G. C.

1962 *Studies in Dogmatics. Man the Image of God* (Grand Rapids: Eerdmans)

1971 *Studies in Dogmatics. Sin* (Grand Rapids: Eerdmans)

1972 *Studies in Dogmatics. The Return of Christ* (Grand Rapids: Eerdmans)

Bright, John

1984 *The Kingdom of God: The Biblical Concept and its Meaning for the Church* (Nashville: Abingdon)

Brown, Colin

1976 *The New International Dictionary of New Testament Theology* (Grand Rapids: Zondervan)

1984 *Miracles and the Critical Mind* (Grand Rapids: Eerdmans; Exeter: Paternoster)

Bruce, F. F.

1963 *The Epistle of Paul to the Romans: An Introduction and Commentary* (London: Tyndale)

Burns, David D.

1980 *Feeling Good: The New Mood Therapy* (New York: Morrow)

Carson, Donald A.

1990 *How Long O Lord: Reflections on Suffering and Evil* (Grand Rapids: Baker Book House)

Cassidy, M.

1989 *The Passing Summer: A South African Pilgrimage in the Politics of Love* (London: Hodder and Stoughton)

Claxton, Robert

1987 *A Christian Doctor Speaks on Healing* (Sydney: Lancer)

Cloud, Henry

1992 *Changes that Heal: How to Understand Your Past to Ensure a Healthier Future* (Grand Rapids: Zondervan)

Clowney, E. P.

1980 *Christian Meditation* (Leicester: Inter-Varsity Press)

Coggins, J. R. and Hiebert P. G., eds
  1989 *Wonders and the Word: An Examination of Issues Raised by John Wimber and the Vineyard Movement* (Winnipeg: Kindred)
Collins, Gary R.
  1986–1991 *Resources for Christian Counselling* (Dallas: Word)
Croucher, Roland
  1986 *Recent Trends Among Evangelicals: Biblical Agendas, Justice and Spirituality* (Sydney, Albatross Books; Bromley: MARC Europe)
Eareckson, Joni and Estes, Steve
  1981 *A Step Further* (Melbourne: S John Bacon)
Edwards, Brian H.
  1990 *Revival! A People Saturated with God* (Darlington: Evangelical Press)
Frost, Henry W.
  1951 *Miraculous Healing: A Personal Testimony and Biblical Study* (London: Evangelical Press)
Gaté, Gabriel
  1987 *Family Food* (Melbourne: Anne O'Donovan)
Geisler, Norman L.
  1982 *Miracles and Modern Thought* (Grand Rapids:Zondervan; Dallas: Probe Ministries International)
Green, Michael
  1982 *To Corinth With Love: The Vital Relevance Today of Paul's Advice to the Corinthian Church* (London: Hodder and Stoughton)
  1985 *I Believe in the Holy Spirit* (London: Hodder and Stoughton)
Guelich, Robert A.
  1982 *The Sermon on the Mount: A Foundation for Understanding* (Waco: Word)
Haldane, R.
  1958 *Exposition of the Epistle to the Romans* (London: Banner of Truth Trust)
Hallesby, O.
  1961 *Prayer* (London: Hodder and Stoughton)
Hart, Archibald
  1984 *Coping with Depression in the Ministry and Other Helping Professions* (Dallas: Word)
  1986 *The Hidden Link Between Adrenalin and Stress* (Waco: Word)

Hillman, Robert J.
1981 *The Church: Growing Up and Growing Out* (Sydney: Unichurch)
1986 *27 Spiritual Gifts* (Melbourne: JBCE)
1992 *There is hope: For Those Who Are Ill and Those Who Care For Them* (Sydney: ANZEA)

Horton, M. S. ed.,
1992 *Power Religion: The Selling Out of the Evangelical Church?* (Sydney: ANZEA; Amersham-on-the-Hill: Scripture Press Foundation)

Hughes, P. E.
1962 *Paul's Second Epistle to the Corinthians* (London: Marshall, Morgan and Scott)

Janov, Arthur
1973 *The Primal Scream: Primal Therapy: The Cure for Neurosis* (London: Abacus)

Jansen, David and Newman, Margaret, with Carmichael, Claire
1989 *Really Relating: How to Build an Enduring Relationship* (Sydney: Random House)

Kelsey, M. T.
1976 *Healing and Christianity* (New York: Harper and Row)

Kidman, Antony
1988 *From Thought to Action. A Self-Help Manual* (Sydney: Biochemical and General Services)

Kildahl, J. P.
1972 *The Psychology of Speaking in Tongues* (London: Hodder and Stoughton)

Kimel, A. F., Jr, ed.
1992 *Speaking the Christian God: The Holy Trinity and the Challenge of Feminism* (Grand Rapids: Eerdmans; Leominster: Gracewing)

Kittel G.
1964 *Theological Dictionary of the New Testament* (Grand Rapids: Eerdmans 1964)

Koenig, John
1978 *Charismata: God's Gifts for God's People* (Philadelphia: Westminster)

Kraft, Charles H.
1989 *Christianity with Power: Your Worldview and Your Experience of the Supernatural* (Ann Arbor: Vine Books)

Kruse, C.
  1987 *Tyndale New Testament Commentaries: 2 Corinthians* (Leicester: Inter Varsity Press; Grand Rapids, Eerdmans)
Ladd, George Eldon
  1952 *Crucial Questions about the Kingdom of God* (Grand Rapids: Eerdmans)
  1974 *The Presence of the Future* (Grand Rapids: Eerdmans)
Lewis, David C.
  1989 *Healing: Fiction, Fantasy or Fact* (London: Hodder and Stoughton)
Link, Mark
  1976 *You, Prayer for Beginners and Those Who Have Forgotten How* (Niles: Argus Communications)
MacNutt, Francis
  1988 *Healing* (Altamonte Springs: Creation House)
Mallison, John
  1979 *Caring for People* (Sydney: Unichurch)
  1996 *The Small-Group Leader: A Manual to Develop Vital Small Groups* (Adelaide: Openbook)
Martin, Ralph
  1981 *Reconciliation: A Study of Paul's Theology* (Atlanta: John Knox)
Meares, Ainslie
  1968 *Relief Without Drugs* (London: Souvenir)
Mills, W. E., ed.
  1986 *Speaking in Tongues: A Guide to Research on Glossolalia* (Grand Rapids: Eerdmans)
Moffatt, J.
  1931 *Grace in the New Testament* (London: Hodder and Stoughton)
Morris, Thomas V.
  1992: *Making Sense of it All. Pascal and the Meaning of Life* (Grand Rapids: Eerdmans)
Moyers, Bill D.
  1987 *Healing and the Mind* (New York: Doubleday)
Mounce, R. H.
  1960 *The Essential Nature of New Testament Preaching* (Grand Rapids: Eerdmans)
Murray, Andrew
  1978 *Waiting on God* (Fort Washington: Christian Literature Crusade)

Myers, Peter and Catherine
  1980 *Gifts Differing* (Palo Alto: Consulting Psychologists Press)
Orr, J. Edwin
  1952 *The Second Evangelical Awakening in America* (London: Marshall, Morgan and Scott)
  1975 *Evangelical Awakenings in Southern Asia* (Minneapolis: Bethany Fellowship)
  1975 *The Eager Feet: Evangelical Awakenings 1790–1830* (Chicago: Moody)
  1976 *Evangelical Awakenings in the South Seas* (Minneapolis: Bethany Fellowship)
Packer, J. I.
  1984 *Keep in Step with the Spirit* (Leicester: Inter-Varsity Press)
  1992 *Rediscovering Holiness* (Ann Arbor: Servant) / *A Passion for Holiness* (Cambridge: Crossway)
Peretti, Frank J.
  1989 *This Present Darkness* (Westchester: Crossway)
  1990 *Piercing the Darkness* (Eastbourne: Monarch)
Peterson, Evelyn H.
  1980 *Who Cares? A Handbook of Christian Counselling* (Exeter: Paternoster)
Pfeifer, Samuel
  1988 *Healing at any Price?* (Milton Keynes: Word)
Pine-Coffin, R. S., tr.
  1961 *St Augustine's Confessions* (London: Penguin)
Ralphs, P. A. R.
  1992 *A New Testament Theology of Healing* (Sydney: Australian College of Theology)
Saxelby, Catherine
  1989 *Food What's in It: A to Z of Food and Nutrition* (Sydney: Reed Books)
Seamonds, D. A.
  n.d. Healing for Damaged Emotions (Amersham-on-the-Hill: Scripture Press)
Schaeffer, Francis
  1971 *True Spirituality* (Wheaton, Illinois: Tyndale House)
Sherlock, Charles
  1991 *God on the Inside: Trinitarian Spirituality* (Canberra: Acorn)

Simonton, Carl O., et. al.
  1980 *Getting Well Again* (New York: Bantam)
Smedes, Lewis B.,
  1984 *Forgive and Forget: Healing the Hurts We Don't Deserve* (New York: Pocket)
  1987 ed., *Ministry and the Miraculous: A Case Study at Fuller Theological Seminary* (Pasadena: Fuller)
Smoot, George and Davidson, Keay
  1993 *Wrinkles in Time* (London: Little, Brown and Co.)
Stanton, Rosemary
  1988 *Eating for Peak Performance* (Sydney: Allen and Unwin)
  1989 *Complete Book of Food and Nutrition* (Sydney: Simon and Schuster)
Stapleton, Ruth Carter
  1977 *The Gift of Inner Healing* (London: Hodder and Stoughton)
Stibbs, Alan M.
  1950 *Understanding God's Word* (London: Inter-Varsity Fellowship)
Stott, J. R. W.
  1966 *Men Made New* (London: Inter-Varsity Fellowship)
  1986 *The Cross of Christ* (Leicester: Inter-Varsity Press)
Tournier, Paul
  1966 *The Healing of Persons* (London: Collins)
Wagner, C. Peter
  1979 *Your Spiritual Gifts Can Help Your Church Grow* (Ventura: Regal)
  1981 *Church Growth and the Whole Gospel: A Biblical Mandate* (San Francisco: Harper and Row)
  1988 *How to Have a Healing Ministry Without Making Your Church Sick* (Eastbourne: Monarch)
Watson, David
  1983 *You are My God* (London: Hodder and Stoughton)
White, John
  1982 *Masks of Melancholy: A Christian Psychiatrist Looks at Depression and Suicide* (Leicester: Inter-Varsity Press)
Wilkinson, John
  1980 *Health and Healing: Studies in New Testament Principles and Practice* (Edinburgh: Handsel)
Wimber, John and Springer, Kevin
  1985 *Power Evangelism: Signs and Wonders Today* (London: Hodder and Stoughton)

1986 *Power Healing* (London: Hodder and Stoughton)

1990 *The Dynamics of Spiritual Growth* (London: Hodder and Stoughton)

Wuellner, Flora Slesson

1985 *Prayer, Stress and Our Inner Wounds* (Nashville: The Upper Room)

Index of Authors

THERE IS HOPE

FOR THOSE WHO ARE ILL AND THOSE WHO CARE FOR THEM

Robert Hillman with Coral Chamberlain

Based on the author's own experience of 'living with dying', this small book lifts the spirit. It offers strategies for promoting healing and maximising quality of life: physically, emotionally, spiritually and socially. In a balanced way, it also deals with the tension between God's promise of healing and the reality of suffering and death in the human experience.

This easy-to-read book is suitable for both Christians and non-Christians.

A beautiful book . . . love, tenderness and compassion shine through.

It held my attention, touched my heart, and filled me with praise for the God who loves and strengthens his children to overcome in apparently hopeless situations.

First published, ANZEA Publishers, 1992.
A new edition is in preparation.

Available soon from:

- Openbook, 205 Halifax Street, Adelaide SA 5000 Australia; tel. 61-8-8223-5468; www.openbook.com.au
- Regnum Books International, PO Box 70, Oxford OX2 6HB, UK; tel. 44-1865 556071; www.regnumbooks.com
- Regnum Books International, PO Box 1047, Waynesboro GA 30830-2047, USA; tel. 1-706-554-5827; www.regnumbooks.com
- Koorong, 28 West Parade, West Ryde NSW 2114, Australia; tel. 61-2-9857-4477; www.Koorong.com.au